16.1

21ST
PUBLICATION
DESIGN
ANNUAL

ACKNOWLEDGEMENTS

21ST PUBLICATION
DESIGN ANNUAL

DESIGNERS:
*Walter Bernard/
Milton Glaser
WBMG, Inc.
New York, NY*

ART DIRECTOR:
*Colleen McCudden
WBMG, Inc.*

PHOTOGRAPHER, COVER
AND TITLE PAGES:
*Matthew Klein
Matthew Klein Studio
New York, NY*

PRODUCTION CONSULTANT:
*Susan Roecker
Madison Square Press, Inc.
New York, NY*

PUBLISHING COORDINATOR:
*Arpi Ermoyan
Madison Square Press, Inc.
New York, NY*

TYPOGRAPHER:
*True to Type, Inc.
New York, NY*

———————

COMPETITION
CHAIRPERSONS:
*Michael Grossman
Amy Bogert*

COMPETITION COMMITTEE:
*John Belknap
Jean Chambers
Vera Steiner*

EXHIBITION COMMITTEE:
*David Armario
Patricia McGurn
Jessica Helfand*

CALL FOR ENTRIES
ILLUSTRATOR:
*Dave Calver
Rochester, NY*

SPECIAL THANKS TO:

*Madison Square Press, Inc.
New York, NY*

*The Westvaco Corporation
New York, NY*

*Master Eagle Gallery,
Master Eagle Family of
Companies
New York, NY*

*Jack Golden, Designers 3
New York, NY*

———————

SPECIAL THANKS FOR
THE CALL FOR ENTRIES:

*Federated
Lithographers, Inc.
Providence, RI*

*Lindenmyer Central Paper
Corporation
New York, NY*

*Gotham Graphics, Inc.
Lyndhurst, NJ*

*Scarlett Letters
New York, NY*

OFFICERS 1986-1987

PRESIDENT:
*Melissa Tardiff
Town & Country*

VICE PRESIDENT:
*Diana LaGuardia
The New York Times
Magazine*

VICE PRESIDENT:
*David Armario
Consumer Electronics*

SECRETARY:
*Amy Bogert
American Bookseller*

TREASURER:
*Lee Ann Jaffee
Lee Ann Jaffee Design*

———————

BOARD OF DIRECTORS:

*Robert Altemus
Art Director
Ira Friedman, Inc.*

*Carla Barr
Connoisseur*

*Mary K. Baumann
Time-Life Development*

*Alice Cooke
A to Z Design, Inc.*

*Nancy Cutler
View Magazine*

*Jerry Demoney
Mobil Oil Corporation*

*Michael Grossman
The Village Voice*

*Steven Heller
The New York Times
Book Review*

*Virginia Smith
Baruch College*

*Derek Ungless
Rolling Stone*

———————

DIRECTOR:
Bride M. Whelan

DISTRIBUTORS TO THE TRADE
IN THE UNITED STATES:
*Robert Silver Associates
307 East 37th Street
New York, NY 10036*

DISTRIBUTORS TO THE TRADE
IN CANADA:
*General Publishing Co. Ltd.
30 Lesmill Road
Don Mills, Ontario, Canada
M3B 2T6*

DISTRIBUTORS THROUGHOUT
THE REST OF THE WORLD:
*RotoVision SA
10 Rue de l'Arquebuse
Casa Postale 434
CH-1211 Geneve 11 Suisse*

PUBLISHER:
*Madison Square Press, Inc.
10 East 23rd Street
New York, NY 10010*

ISBN 0-942604-20-2

ISSN 0885-6370

PRINTED IN JAPAN

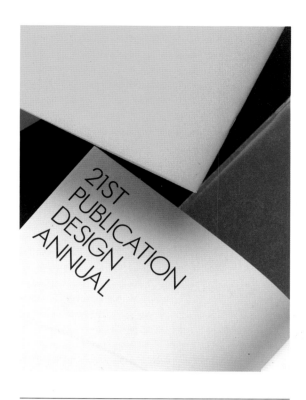

21ST
PUBLICATION
DESIGN
ANNUAL

161929185

JUDGES

ROBERT PRIEST
Art Director
US

NANCY BUTKUS
Art Director
Manhattan, inc.

ANTHONY RUSSELL
Principal
Anthony Russell, Inc.

TIBOR KALMAN
Principal
M & Co.

MARY ZISK
Art Director
PC

MARY K. BAUMANN
Art Director
Time-Life Development

THOMAS P. RUIS
Art Director
Daily News—Graphics

CHAIRPERSONS

AMY BOGERT
Art Director
American Bookseller

MICHAEL GROSSMAN
Art Director
The Village Voice

PRESIDENT'S LETTER

Jonathan Becker

*Melissa Tardiff, Art Director of Town & Country Magazine and
President of the Society of Publication Designers, 1986-87.*

It has been said that, "...being creative without talent is like being a perfectionist without ever getting it right." This beautifully designed annual honors those who have the talent, and who have certainly gotten it right.

Talent alone does not make a success story. Persistence, timing and luck are often most crucial. Those art directors, designers, illustrators and photographers whose work is included in this book are those whose talents stand out in a large crowd.

There are more than 11,000 publications in today's marketplace, which means thousands of art directors and many thousands of pages. When you begin to think that the market is saturated—where nearly every slice of every market has at least several publications—a talented art director comes along doing the right thing at the right time to prove you wrong.

The Society of Publication Designers honors work of this exceptional quality in its awards, annual publication and exhibition. This is work that sets standards and redefines what we have accomplished, while achieving new levels of confidence.

We all know that behind every successful magazine, newspaper, annual report or special publication, lurks a talented art director. Great work is being done by very creative and talented professionals whose work, in no small way, contributes enormously to the success of their publications.

—*Melissa Tardiff*

HERB LUBALIN AWARD

For Continuing Excellence
In the Field of Publication Design
BRADBURY THOMPSON

Melissa Tardiff, Art Director of Town & Country Magazine,
and President of the Society of Publication Designers, presenting the
Herb Lubalin Award for Continuing Excellence in
the field of Publication Design to Bradbury Thompson.

For his continuous commitment to excellence in the field of graphic design, the Society of Publication Designers was honored to present its most prestigious award to Bradbury Thompson at the Society's annual awards gala in Astor Hall of the New York Public Library, May 1, 1986.

Bradbury Thompson has been called the Dean of American Designers for his enormous and prolific contributions to the graphic arts. His work has spanned over half a century, and he continues to be a moving force in the community of innovative designers.

Highlights of Thompson's career, which included his work with West-vaco Corporation, Mademoiselle magazine, the U.S. Postal Service, and the Smithsonian magazine, were presented in a slide show to the more than 300 assembled art directors and designers in the industry.

Thompson's career has included, most particularly for this award, the design and/or redesign of over thirty-five publications, plus the role of art director of some of America's most notable magazines.

Brad Thompson's profound knowledge of his art and his special skills are universally recognized. Throughout his career he has taken on volumes of work, including that of teacher, being a member of the Yale University faculty for over thirty years.

The Society of Publication Designers is fortunate to have in Bradbury Thompson the epitome of the timeless artist whose contributions to the printed page have done so much to enhance the face of contemporary design.

SPD

The art of publication design is a specialized area in the graphic arts. Editorial designers and art directors are specialists whose unique skills blend the diverse elements of a publication into a unified visual concept that has recognizable continuity from issue to issue. Members of the Society of Publication Designers belong to a most prestigious group of artists. The publication designer's role is critical to the overall success of every consumer and trade magazine, newspaper, and annual report.

The Society was created to offer a professional meeting ground for designers and art directors, which provides a means of continuing communication and exchange of ideas with others in the field.

One way of continuing this dialogue is to assemble, judge, and show the best work done each year by designers and art directors in a national juried competition. This competition seeks to encourage experimentation and to serve as a source of new ideas in graphic design, as well as to recognize the consistently excellent work being done by new as well as proven designers in the publication field.

The Society was incorporated as a non-profit, educationally-oriented professional association in 1965. Its function and activities are governed by a chartered Constitution. The variety of activities offered by the Society includes a monthly Speaker's Evening that brings together individuals or panels of distinguished professionals to share with the membership unique contributions to publication design. The membership receives a bi-monthly newsletter called GRIDS which highlights activities and information of the Society and publication community.

The Society also sponsors Portfolio Shows, showcases for new editorial illustrators and photographers. The SPD Awards Gala, honoring the recipients of Gold, Silver, and Merit Awards of the annual Competition, is a highlight of the spring season, attended by the country's most illustrious designers. The Awards Exhibition of the Society, held yearly at the Master Eagle Gallery, gives the members an opportunity to meet and greet the designers and art directors, and to view and enjoy the individual winning pieces of publication work. The SPD Annual, a full-color book which catalogues the annual winning entries for reference and artistic and editorial concepts, is available free to the membership.

The Society of Publication Designers is a strong influence in maintaining the standards of excellence and quality in publication design. By recognizing and promoting current achievements and innovative graphic practices, the members are constantly associated with the best and most up-to-date works available.

Active involvement is encouraged in the Society of Publication Designers. Many new and innovative projects are in the planning stages for the coming years. The support and continued interest of the graphic design community is vital to the growth of the Society.

COVERS

1

PUBLICATION:	*LIRE*
ART DIRECTOR:	*Jean-Pierre Cliquet*
DESIGNER:	*Jean-Pierre Cliquet*
PHOTOGRAPHER:	*Harenberg Kommunikation*
PUBLISHER:	*Groupe Express*
CATEGORY:	*Cover—Design*
TITLE:	*"Le Sida/Aids"*
AWARD:	*Silver*

2

PUBLICATION:	*The Clarion*
ART DIRECTORS:	*Faye H. Eng, Anthony T. Yee*
DESIGNERS:	*Faye H. Eng, Anthony T. Yee*
TINTER:	*Paula Hible*
PHOTOGRAPHER:	*Solomon D. Butcher*
PUBLISHER:	*Museum of American Folk Art*
CATEGORY:	*Cover—Design*
TITLE:	*"Windmill Weights"*
AWARD:	*Silver*

3

PUBLICATION:	*Plain Dealer*
ART DIRECTOR:	*Gerard Sealy*
ILLUSTRATOR:	*Matt Mahurin*
PUBLISHER:	*Plain Dealer Magazine Co.*
CATEGORY:	*Cover—Design*
TITLE:	*"Confessions of a Madman"*
AWARD:	*Silver*

4

PUBLICATION:	*Architectural Record*
ART DIRECTOR:	*Alex Stillano*
DESIGNER:	*Alex Stillano*
PHOTOGRAPHER:	*Timothy Hursley*
PUBLISHER:	*McGraw-Hill*
CATEGORY:	*Cover—Design*
TITLE:	*"Seagram Museum"*
AWARD:	*Silver*

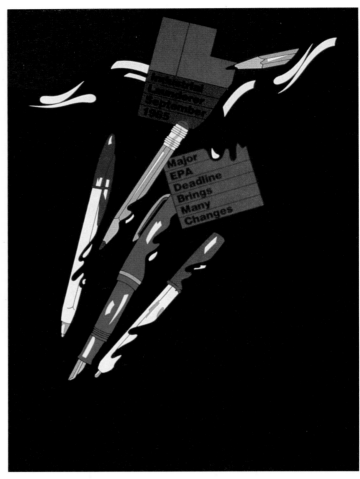

5

PUBLICATION:	*Artforum*
ART DIRECTOR:	*Roger Gorman*
DESIGNER:	*Frances Reinfeld*
PHOTOGRAPHER:	*Lucas Samaras*
PUBLISHER:	*Artforum, Inc.*
CATEGORY:	*Cover—Design*
TITLE:	*"Lucas Samaras"*
AWARD:	*Silver*

6

PUBLICATION:	*Industrial Launderer*
ART DIRECTOR:	*Jack Lefkowitz*
DESIGNER:	*Jack Lefkowitz*
ILLUSTRATOR:	*Virginia Strnad*
PUBLISHER:	*Institute of Industrial Launderers*
CATEGORY:	*Cover—Design*
TITLE:	*"Major EPA Deadlines"*
AWARD:	*Silver*

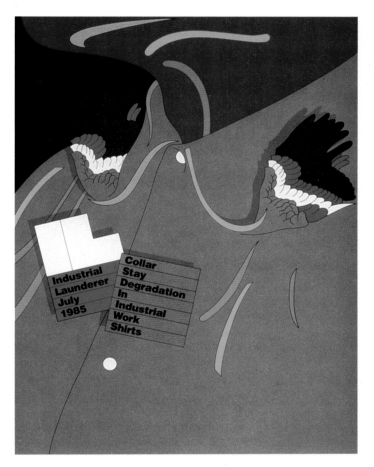

7

PUBLICATION: *Industrial Launderer*
ART DIRECTOR: *Jack Lefkowitz*
DESIGNER: *Jack Lefkowitz*
ILLUSTRATOR: *Virginia Strnad*
PUBLISHER: *Institute of Industrial*
                  Launderers
CATEGORY: *Cover—Design*
TITLE: *"Collar Stays"*
AWARD: *Silver*

8

PUBLICATION: *Industrial Launderer*
ART DIRECTOR: *Jack Lefkowitz*
DESIGNER: *Jack Lefkowitz*
ILLUSTRATOR: *Virginia Strnad*
PUBLISHER: *Institute of Industrial*
                  Launderers
CATEGORY: *Cover—Design*
TITLE: *"Kissinger on Gorbachev"*
AWARD: *Silver*

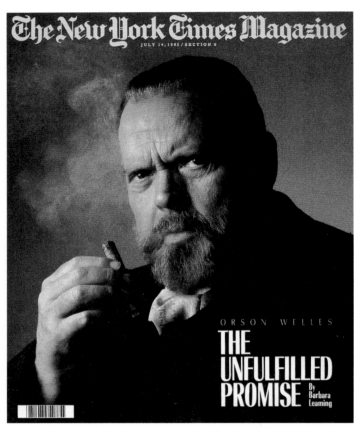

9

PUBLICATION:	*The New York Times Magazine*
ART DIRECTOR:	*Ken Kendrick*
DESIGNER:	*Diana LaGuardia*
ILLUSTRATOR:	*Matt Mahurin*
PUBLISHER:	*The New York Times*
CATEGORY:	*Cover—Illustration*
TITLE:	*"How We See Each Other"*
AWARD:	*Silver*

10

PUBLICATION:	*The New York Times Magazine*
ART DIRECTOR:	*Ken Kendrick*
DESIGNER:	*Diana LaGuardia*
PHOTOGRAPHER:	*Michael O'Neill*
PUBLISHER:	*The New York Times*
CATEGORY:	*Cover—Photography*
TITLE:	*"The Unfulfilled Promise"*
AWARD:	*Silver*

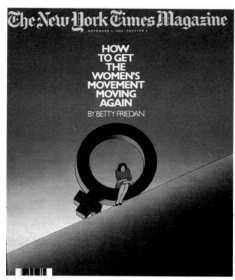

11

PUBLICATION:	*The New York Times Magazine*
ART DIRECTOR:	*Ken Kendrick*
DESIGNER:	*Ken Kendrick*
ILLUSTRATOR:	*Robert Goldstrom*
PUBLISHER:	*The New York Times*
CATEGORY:	*Cover—Design*
TITLE:	*"IBM"*
AWARD:	*Merit*

12

PUBLICATION:	*The New York Times Magazine*
ART DIRECTOR:	*Ken Kendrick*
DESIGNER:	*Ken Kendrick*
ILLUSTRATOR:	*Guy Billout*
PUBLISHER:	*The New York Times*
CATEGORY:	*Cover—Design*
TITLE:	*"Women's Movement"*
AWARD:	*Merit*

13

PUBLICATION:	*The New York Times Magazine*
ART DIRECTOR:	*Diana LaGuardia*
DESIGNER:	*Diana LaGuardia*
ILLUSTRATOR:	*Mark Steele*
PUBLISHER:	*The New York Times*
CATEGORY:	*Cover—Illustration*
TITLE:	*"At The Met"*
AWARD:	*Merit*

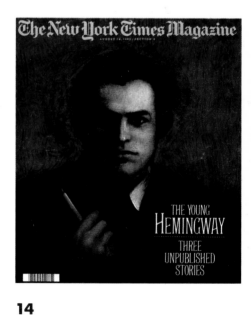

14

PUBLICATION:	*The New York Times Magazine*
ART DIRECTOR:	*Ken Kendrick*
DESIGNER:	*Richard Samperi*
ILLUSTRATOR:	*Greg Spalenka*
PUBLISHER:	*The New York Times*
CATEGORY:	*Cover—Illustration*
TITLE:	*"Hemingway"*
AWARD:	*Merit*

15

PUBLICATION:	*The New York Times Magazine*
ART DIRECTOR:	*Ken Kendrick*
DESIGNER:	*Ken Kendrick*
ILLUSTRATOR:	*Tim Lewis*
PUBLISHER:	*The New York Times*
CATEGORY:	*Cover—Illustration*
TITLE:	*"Christmas Issue"*
AWARD:	*Merit*

16

PUBLICATION:	*The New York Times Magazine*
ART DIRECTORS:	*Ken Kendrick, Diana LaGuardia*
DESIGNER:	*Diana LaGuardia*
PHOTOGRAPHER:	*Andy Levin*
PUBLISHER:	*The New York Times*
CATEGORY:	*Cover—Design*
TITLE:	*"Crime"*
AWARD:	*Merit*

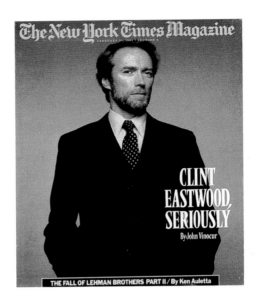

17

PUBLICATION:	*The New York Times Magazine*
ART DIRECTOR:	*Ken Kendrick*
DESIGNER:	*Ken Kendrick*
PHOTOGRAPHER:	*Michael O'Neill*
PUBLISHER:	*The New York Times*
CATEGORY:	*Cover—Photography*
TITLE:	*"Clint Eastwood"*
AWARD:	*Merit*

18

PUBLICATION:	*The New York Times Magazine*
ART DIRECTOR:	*Ken Kendrick*
DESIGNER:	*Ken Kendrick*
ILLUSTRATOR:	*Robert Goldstrom*
PUBLISHER:	*The New York Times*
CATEGORY:	*Cover—Illustration*
TITLE:	*"I.B.M."*
AWARD:	*Merit*

19

PUBLICATION:	*The New York Times Magazine*
ART DIRECTOR:	*Ken Kendrick*
DESIGNER:	*Diana LaGuardia*
PHOTOGRAPHER:	*Michael O'Neill*
PUBLISHER:	*The New York Times*
CATEGORY:	*Cover—Photography*
TITLE:	*"Disney"*
AWARD:	*Merit*

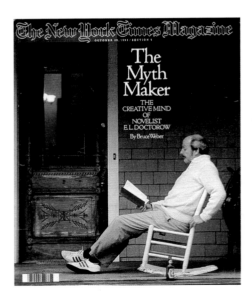

20

PUBLICATION:	*The New York Times Magazine*
ART DIRECTOR:	*Ken Kendrick*
DESIGNER:	*Ken Kendrick*
ILLUSTRATOR:	*Guy Billout*
PUBLISHER:	*The New York Times*
CATEGORY:	*Cover—Illustration*
TITLE:	*"Women's Movement"*
AWARD:	*Merit*

21

PUBLICATION:	*The New York Times Magazine*
ART DIRECTOR:	*Ken Kendrick*
DESIGNER:	*Richard Samperi*
PHOTOGRAPHER:	*Barbara Walz*
PUBLISHER:	*The New York Times*
CATEGORY:	*Cover—Photography*
TITLE:	*"The Myth Maker"*
AWARD:	*Merit*

MERIT

22

PUBLICATION:	*The New York Times Magazine*
ART DIRECTOR:	*Tom Bodkin*
DESIGNER:	*Tom Bodkin*
ILLUSTRATOR:	*Jeffery Smith*
PUBLISHER:	*The New York Times*
CATEGORY:	*Cover—Illustration*
TITLE:	*"Sophisticated Traveler/ First Encounters"*
AWARD:	*Merit*

23

PUBLICATION:	*The New York Times Magazine*
ART DIRECTOR:	*Tom Bodkin*
DESIGNER:	*Tom Bodkin*
ILLUSTRATOR:	*Barry Root*
PUBLISHER:	*The New York Times*
CATEGORY:	*Cover—Illustration*
TITLE:	*"Sophisticated Traveler/ High Roads"*
AWARD:	*Merit*

24

PUBLICATION:	*The New York Times Magazine*
ART DIRECTOR:	*Tom Bodkin*
DESIGNER:	*Tom Bodkin*
ILLUSTRATOR:	*Jeffery Smith*
PUBLISHER:	*The New York Times*
CATEGORY:	*Cover—Design*
TITLE:	*"Sophisticated Traveler/ First Encounters"*
AWARD:	*Merit*

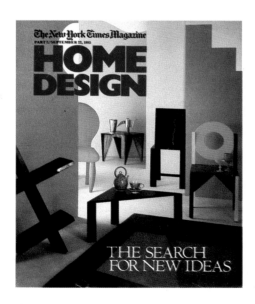

25

PUBLICATION:	*The New York Times Magazine*
ART DIRECTOR:	*Nancy Kent*
DESIGNER:	*Nancy Kent*
PHOTOGRAPHER:	*Raeanne Giovanni*
PUBLISHER:	*The New York Times*
CATEGORY:	*Cover—Design*
TITLE:	*"Home Design"*
AWARD:	*Merit*

26

PUBLICATION: *Architectural Record*
ART DIRECTOR: *Alex Stillano*
DESIGNER: *Anna Egger-Schlesinger*
PHOTOGRAPHER: *Timothy Hursley*
PUBLISHER: *McGraw-Hill*
CATEGORY: *Cover—Design*
TITLE: *"Hildenbrandth House"*
AWARD: *Merit*

27

PUBLICATION: *Architectural Record*
ART DIRECTOR: *Alex Stillano*
DESIGNER: *Anna Egger-Schlesinger*
PHOTOGRAPHER: *Paul Warchol*
PUBLISHER: *McGraw-Hill*
CATEGORY: *Cover—Design*
TITLE: *"Southport, New York"*
AWARD: *Merit*

28

PUBLICATION: *Architectural Record*
ART DIRECTOR: *Alex Stillano*
DESIGNER: *Alberto Bucchianeri*
PHOTOGRAPHER: *Cervin Robinson*
PUBLISHER: *McGraw-Hill*
CATEGORY: *Cover—Design*
TITLE: *"Ohio Theatre"*
AWARD: *Merit*

31

PUBLICATION: *Businessweek*
ART DIRECTORS: *Malcolm Frouman, Mitch Shostak*
DESIGNERS: *Malcolm Frouman, Mitch Shostak*
ILLUSTRATOR: *José Cruz*
PUBLISHER: *McGraw-Hill*
CATEGORY: *Cover—Design*
TITLE: *"The Baby Bells"*
AWARD: *Merit*

32

PUBLICATION: *Businessweek*
ART DIRECTORS: *Malcolm Frouman, Mitch Shostak*
DESIGNERS: *Malcolm Frouman, Mitch Shostak*
ILLUSTRATOR: *Ralph Wernli*
PHOTOGRAPHER: *Walter Chrywski*
PUBLISHER: *McGraw-Hill*
CATEGORY: *Cover—Design*
TITLE: *"New? Improved?"*
AWARD: *Merit*

33

PUBLICATION: *Businessweek*
ART DIRECTORS: *Malcolm Frouman, Mitch Shostak*
DESIGNERS: *Malcolm Frouman, Mitch Shostak*
ILLUSTRATOR: *Marvin Mattelson*
PUBLISHER: *McGraw-Hill*
CATEGORY: *Cover—Design*
TITLE: *"The Raiders"*
AWARD: *Merit*

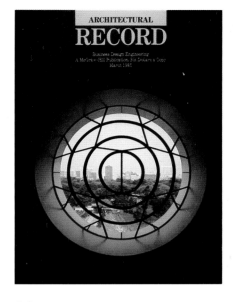

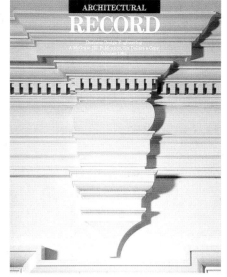

29

PUBLICATION:	*Architectural Record*
ART DIRECTOR:	*Alex Stillano*
DESIGNER:	*Alberto Bucchianeri*
PHOTOGRAPHER:	*Tomio Ohashi*
PUBLISHER:	*McGraw-Hill*
CATEGORY:	*Cover—Design*
TITLE:	*"Tokyo, Japan"*
AWARD:	*Merit*

30

PUBLICATION:	*Architectural Record*
ART DIRECTOR:	*Alex Stillano*
DESIGNER:	*Alex Stillano*
PHOTOGRAPHER:	*Robert Cheek*
PUBLISHER:	*McGraw-Hill*
CATEGORY:	*Cover—Design*
TITLE:	*"U.S. Department of State"*
AWARD:	*Merit*

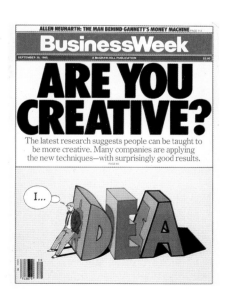

34

PUBLICATION:	*Businessweek*
ART DIRECTORS:	*Malcolm Frouman,*
	Mitch Shostak
DESIGNERS:	*Malcolm Frouman,*
	Mitch Shostak
ILLUSTRATOR:	*Jean Tuttle*
PUBLISHER:	*McGraw-Hill*
CATEGORY:	*Cover—Design*
TITLE:	*"Splitting Up"*
AWARD:	*Merit*

35

PUBLICATION:	*Businessweek*
ART DIRECTOR:	*Malcolm Frouman*
DESIGNERS:	*Malcolm Frouman,*
	Laura Baer
ILLUSTRATOR:	*Istvan Banyai*
PUBLISHER:	*McGraw-Hill*
CATEGORY:	*Cover—Design*
TITLE:	*"Are You Creative?"*
AWARD:	*Merit*

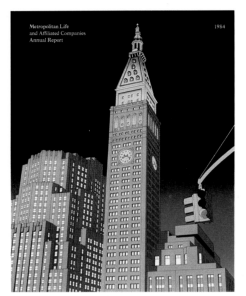

36

PUBLICATION:	*Metropolitan Life Annual Report*
ART DIRECTOR:	*Bennett Robinson*
DESIGNER:	*Bennett Robinson*
ILLUSTRATOR:	*Guy Billout*
PUBLISHER:	*Metropolitan Life Insurance Co.*
CATEGORY:	*Cover—Illustration*
AWARD:	*Merit*

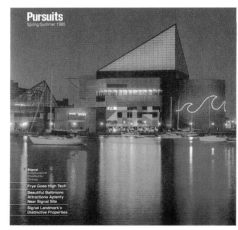

37

PUBLICATION:	*Pursuits*
ART DIRECTOR:	*Ann O'Brien*
DESIGNER:	*Ann O'Brien*
PUBLISHER:	*The Signal Companies*
CATEGORY:	*Cover—Design*
TITLE:	*Spring/Summer '85*
AWARD:	*Merit*

38

PUBLICATION:	*The Newsday Magazine*
ART DIRECTOR:	*Miriam Smith*
ILLUSTRATOR:	*Carol Wald*
PUBLISHER:	*Times-Mirror, Inc.*
CATEGORY:	*Cover—Illustration*
TITLE:	*"The Lies of Everyday People"*
AWARD:	*Merit*

39

PUBLICATION: *US*
ART DIRECTOR: *Robert Priest*
DESIGNER: *Janet Waegel*
PHOTOGRAPHERS: *Michael Comte, Acey Harper,*
                 Theo Westenberger
PUBLISHER: *Straight Arrow Publications*
CATEGORY: *Cover—Design*
TITLE: *"Fall '85 Preview"*
AWARD: *Merit*

40

PUBLICATION: *Texas Monthly*
ART DIRECTOR: *Fred Woodward*
DESIGNER: *Fred Woodward*
PHOTOGRAPHER: *Richard Avedon*
PUBLISHER: *Texas Monthly, Inc.*
CATEGORY: *Cover—Design*
TITLE: *"Faces of the West"*
AWARD: *Merit*

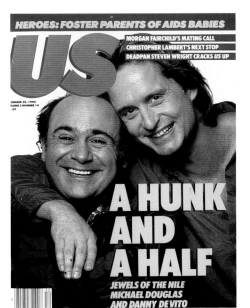

41

PUBLICATION: *US*
ART DIRECTOR: *Robert Priest*
DESIGNER: *Janet Waegel*
PHOTOGRAPHER: *David Baily*
PUBLISHER: *Straight Arrow Publications*
CATEGORY: *Cover—Design*
TITLE: *"A Hunk and a Half"*
AWARD: *Merit*

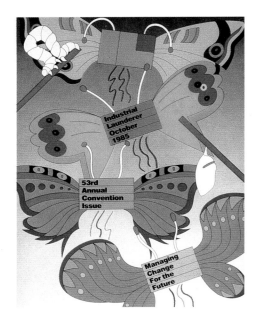

42

PUBLICATION:	*Industrial Launderer*
ART DIRECTOR:	*Jack Lefkowitz*
DESIGNER:	*Jack Lefkowitz*
ILLUSTRATOR:	*Virginia Strnad*
PUBLISHER:	*Institute of Industrial Launderers*
CATEGORY:	*Cover—Design*
TITLE:	*"Convention Issue"*
AWARD:	*Merit*

43

PUBLICATION:	*Industrial Launderer*
ART DIRECTOR:	*Jack Lefkowitz*
DESIGNER:	*Jack Lefkowitz*
ILLUSTRATOR:	*Virginia Strnad*
PUBLISHER:	*Institute of Industrial Launderers*
CATEGORY:	*Cover—Design*
TITLE:	*"Wellness"*
AWARD:	*Merit*

44

PUBLICATION:	*Industrial Launderer*
ART DIRECTOR:	*Jack Lefkowitz*
DESIGNER:	*Jack Lefkowitz*
ILLUSTRATOR:	*Virginia Strnad*
PUBLISHER:	*Institute of Industrial Launderers*
CATEGORY:	*Cover—Design*
TITLE:	*"Strategic Analysis"*
AWARD:	*Merit*

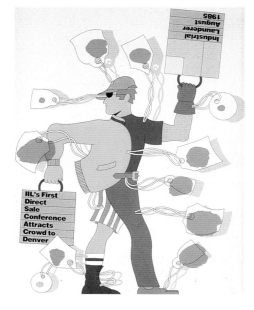

45

PUBLICATION:	*Industrial Launderer*
ART DIRECTOR:	*Jack Lefkowitz*
DESIGNER:	*Jack Lefkowitz*
ILLUSTRATOR:	*Virginia Strnad*
PUBLISHER:	*Institute of Industrial Launderers*
CATEGORY:	*Cover—Design*
TITLE:	*"San Antonio III"*
AWARD:	*Merit*

46

PUBLICATION:	*Industrial Launderer*
ART DIRECTOR:	*Jack Lefkowitz*
DESIGNER:	*Jack Lefkowitz*
ILLUSTRATOR:	*Virginia Strnad*
PUBLISHER:	*Institute of Industrial Launderers*
CATEGORY:	*Cover—Design*
TITLE:	*"Direct Sale"*
AWARD:	*Merit*

47

PUBLICATION:	*Industrial Launderer*
ART DIRECTOR:	*Jack Lefkowitz*
DESIGNER:	*Jack Lefkowitz*
ILLUSTRATOR:	*Virginia Strnad*
PUBLISHER:	*Institute of Industrial Launderers*
CATEGORY:	*Cover—Design*
TITLE:	*"Clean '85"*
AWARD:	*Merit*

48

PUBLICATION:	*Industrial Launderer*
ART DIRECTOR:	*Jack Lefkowitz*
DESIGNER:	*Jack Lefkowitz*
ILLUSTRATOR:	*Virginia Strnad*
PUBLISHER:	*Institute of Industrial Launderers*
CATEGORY:	*Cover—Design*
TITLE:	*"Best Ever"*
AWARD:	*Merit*

49

PUBLICATION:	*Industrial Launderer*
ART DIRECTOR:	*Jack Lefkowitz*
DESIGNER:	*Jack Lefkowitz*
ILLUSTRATOR:	*Virginia Strnad*
PUBLISHER:	*Institute of Industrial Launderers*
CATEGORY:	*Cover—Design*
TITLE:	*"Waste Water"*
AWARD:	*Merit*

50

PUBLICATION:	*Industrial Launderer*
ART DIRECTOR:	*Jack Lefkowitz*
DESIGNER:	*Jack Lefkowitz*
ILLUSTRATOR:	*Virginia Strnad*
PUBLISHER:	*Institute of Industrial Launderers*
CATEGORY:	*Cover—Design*
TITLE:	*"Charlotte Project"*
AWARD:	*Merit*

51

PUBLICATION: *SPD Management*
ART DIRECTORS: *Will Hopkins,*
Ira Friedlander
PHOTOGRAPHER: *Brownie Harris*
PUBLISHER: *IBM System Products*
CATEGORY: *Cover—Design*
TITLE: *"Face to Face Management"*
AWARD: *Merit*

52

PUBLICATION: *Financial Executive*
ART DIRECTOR: *Chris Sloan*
DESIGNER: *Chris Sloan*
ILLUSTRATOR: *Joe Ciardiello*
PUBLISHER: *Financial Executives*
CATEGORY: *Cover—Illustration*
AWARD: *Merit*

53

PUBLICATION: *TV Guide*
ART DIRECTOR: *Jerry Alten*
DESIGNER: *Jerry Alten*
ILLUSTRATOR: *Braldt Bralds*
PUBLISHER: *Triangle Publications*
CATEGORY: *Cover—Illustration*
TITLE: *"Christopher Columbus"*
AWARD: *Merit*

54

PUBLICATION: *Today's Office*
ART DIRECTOR: *Virginia Murphy-Hamill*
DESIGNER: *Virginia Murphy-Hamill*
ILLUSTRATOR: *John Rush*
PUBLISHER: *Hearst Business*
Communications
CATEGORY: *Cover—Illustration*
TITLE: *"Business Ethics"*
AWARD: *Merit*

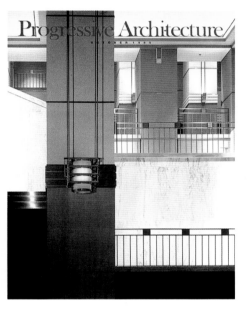

55

PUBLICATION:	*Progressive Architecture*
ART DIRECTOR:	*Richelle Huff*
DESIGNER:	*Richelle Huff*
PHOTOGRAPHER:	*Keld Helmer-Petersen*
PUBLISHER:	*Penton Publications*
CATEGORY:	*Cover—Design*
TITLE:	*March '85*
AWARD:	*Merit*

56

PUBLICATION:	*Progressive Architecture*
ART DIRECTOR:	*Richelle Huff*
DESIGNER:	*Richelle Huff*
PHOTOGRAPHER:	*Barbara Karant*
PUBLISHER:	*Penton Publications*
CATEGORY:	*Cover—Design*
TITLE:	*October '85*
AWARD:	*Merit*

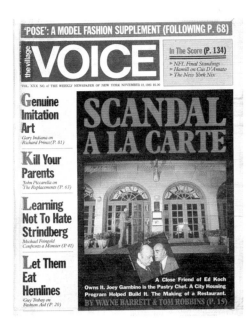

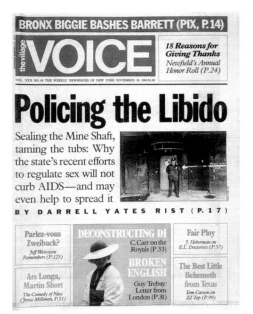

57

PUBLICATION:	*The Village Voice*
ART DIRECTOR:	*Michael Grossman*
PHOTOGRAPHERS:	*Susan Ferguson,*
	Donna Svennevir
PUBLISHER:	*VV Publishing Corp.*
CATEGORY:	*Cover—Design*
TITLE:	*"Scandal A La Carte"*
AWARD:	*Merit*

58

PUBLICATION:	*The Village Voice*
ART DIRECTOR:	*Michael Grossman*
PHOTOGRAPHER:	*James Hamilton*
PUBLISHER:	*VV Publishing Corp.*
CATEGORY:	*Cover—Design*
TITLE:	*"Policing the Libido"*
AWARD:	*Merit*

59

PUBLICATION:	*The Village Voice*
ART DIRECTOR:	*Michael Grossman*
ILLUSTRATORS:	*Gene Greif,*
	Mark Alan Stamaty
PUBLISHER:	*VV Publishing Corp.*
CATEGORY:	*Cover—Design*
TITLE:	*"Making Moviemakers"*
AWARD:	*Merit*

60

PUBLICATION:	*The Boston Globe*
ART DIRECTOR:	*James Pavlovich*
DESIGNER:	*James Pavlovich*
ILLUSTRATOR:	*Anthony Russo*
PUBLISHER:	*The Boston Globe*
CATEGORY:	*Cover—Design*
TITLE:	*"A Calendar"*
AWARD:	*Merit*

61

PUBLICATION:	*The Boston Globe*
ART DIRECTOR:	*James Pavlovich*
DESIGNER:	*James Pavlovich*
ILLUSTRATOR:	*Ken Maryanski*
PUBLISHER:	*The Boston Globe*
CATEGORY:	*Cover—Design*
TITLE:	*"A Calendar"*
AWARD:	*Merit*

62

PUBLICATION:	*The Boston Globe*
ART DIRECTOR:	*James Pavlovich*
DESIGNER:	*James Pavlovich*
ILLUSTRATOR:	*David Frampton*
PUBLISHER:	*The Boston Globe*
CATEGORY:	*Cover—Design*
TITLE:	*"A Calendar"*
AWARD:	*Merit*

63

PUBLICATION:	*The New York Times*
ART DIRECTOR:	*Linda Brewer*
DESIGNER:	*Linda Brewer*
PHOTOGRAPHER:	*Robin Laurence*
PUBLISHER:	*The New York Times*
CATEGORY:	*Cover—Design*
TITLE:	*"Travel—Discovering Rumpole's World"*
AWARD:	*Merit*

64

PUBLICATION:	*The New York Times*
ART DIRECTOR:	*Linda Brewer*
DESIGNER:	*Linda Brewer*
PHOTOGRAPHER:	*Bill Allen*
PUBLISHER:	*The New York Times*
CATEGORY:	*Cover—Design*
TITLE:	*"Looking West to the East"*
AWARD:	*Merit*

65

PUBLICATION:	*The New York Times*
ART DIRECTOR:	*Linda Brewer*
DESIGNER:	*Linda Brewer*
ILLUSTRATOR:	*Paul Meisel*
PUBLISHER:	*The New York Times*
CATEGORY:	*Cover—Design*
TITLE:	*"Travel: In Europe, It's Time to Buy"*
AWARD:	*Merit*

66

PUBLICATION:	*The New York Times*
ART DIRECTOR:	*Martine Winter*
DESIGNER:	*Martine Winter*
ILLUSTRATOR:	*Michael Hostovich*
PHOTOGRAPHER:	*Gene Maggio*
PUBLISHER:	*The New York Times*
CATEGORY:	*Cover—Design*
TITLE:	*"Home: New York's World of Design"*
AWARD:	*Merit*

67

PUBLICATION:	*Style*
ART DIRECTOR:	*Ed Barnett*
DESIGNER:	*Barbara Bose*
ILLUSTRATOR:	*Barbara Bose*
PHOTOGRAPHER:	*Ted Ancher*
PUBLISHER:	*The Boston Herald*
CATEGORY:	*Cover—Design*
TITLE:	*"Valentine's Day"*
AWARD:	*Merit*

68

PUBLICATION:	*Daily News Magazine*
ART DIRECTOR:	*Janet Froelich*
DESIGNER:	*Janet Froelich*
PHOTOGRAPHER:	*Tom Arma*
PUBLISHER:	*New York News, Inc.*
CATEGORY:	*Cover—Design*
TITLE:	*"Zabar's"*
AWARD:	*Merit*

69

PUBLICATION:	*Daily News Magazine*
ART DIRECTOR:	*Janet Froelich*
DESIGNER:	*Janet Froelich*
PHOTOGRAPHER:	*Deborah Feingold*
PUBLISHER:	*New York News, Inc.*
CATEGORY:	*Cover—Design*
TITLE:	*"Madonna"*
AWARD:	*Merit*

70

PUBLICATION:	*Daily News Magazine*
ART DIRECTOR:	*Arthur McGee*
DESIGNER:	*Arthur McGee*
ILLUSTRATOR:	*Marcos Oksenhendler*
PUBLISHER:	*New York News, Inc.*
CATEGORY:	*Cover—Design*
TITLE:	*"All That Glitters is Gold"*
AWARD:	*Merit*

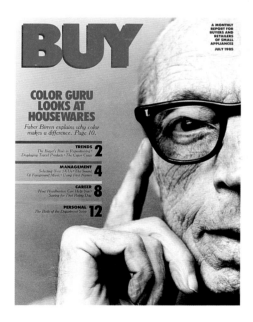

71

PUBLICATION:	*Buy*
ART DIRECTORS:	*Bett McLean,*
	Lawrence Arnett
DESIGNER:	*Lawrence Arnett*
PHOTOGRAPHER:	*Britain Hill*
PUBLISHER:	*13-30 Corporation*
CATEGORY:	*Cover—Design*
TITLE:	*"Faber Birren"*
AWARD:	*Merit*

72

PUBLICATION:	*Progressive Grocer*
ART DIRECTOR:	*Alice Cooke*
DESIGNER:	*Alice Cooke*
ILLUSTRATOR:	*Carter Goodrich*
PUBLISHER:	*MacLean Hunter Media, Inc.*
CATEGORY:	*Cover—Illustration*
TITLE:	*"Buyer's Best Friend"*
AWARD:	*Merit*

73

PUBLICATION:	*Artforum*
ART DIRECTOR:	*Roger Gorman*
PUBLISHER:	*Artforum, Inc.*
CATEGORY:	*Cover—Design*
TITLE:	*"Grande Gesto Vegetale"*
AWARD:	*Merit*

74

PUBLICATION:	*Artforum*
ART DIRECTOR:	*Roger Gorman*
ILLUSTRATOR:	*Solonevich*
PUBLISHER:	*Artforum, Inc.*
CATEGORY:	*Cover—Design*
TITLE:	*"Cities in Flight"*
AWARD:	*Merit*

75

PUBLICATION:	*American Health*
ART DIRECTORS:	*Will Hopkins,*
	Ira Friedlander
PHOTOGRAPHER:	*Bill Haywood*
PUBLISHER:	*American Health Partners*
CATEGORY:	*Cover—Design*
TITLE:	*"Your Emotional Skin"*
AWARD:	*Merit*

76

PUBLICATION:	*American Photographer*
ART DIRECTOR:	*Howard Klein*
DESIGNER:	*Howard Klein*
PHOTOGRAPHER:	*Renato Grignaschi*
PUBLISHER:	*CBS Magazines*
CATEGORY:	*Cover—Design*
TITLE:	*"Cosmetics"*
AWARD:	*Merit*

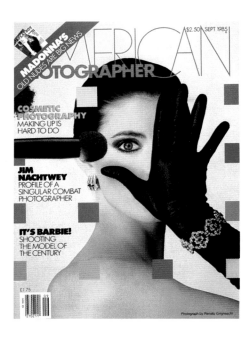

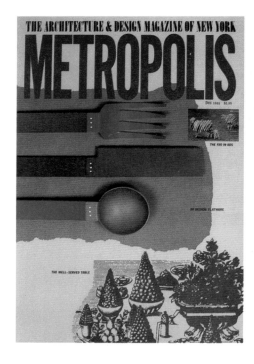

77

PUBLICATION:	*Metropolis*
ART DIRECTOR:	*Helene Silverman*
DESIGNER:	*Helene Silverman*
PUBLISHER:	*Metropolis Magazine*
CATEGORY:	*Cover—Design*
TITLE:	*"Cover—December 1985"*
AWARD:	*Merit*

78

PUBLICATION:	*LIRE*
ART DIRECTOR:	*Jean-Pierre Cliquet*
DESIGNER:	*Jean-Pierre Cliquet*
ILLUSTRATOR:	*Jean-Pierre Cliquet*
PUBLISHER:	*Groupe Express*
CATEGORY:	*Cover—Design*
TITLE:	*"Youth Culture"*
AWARD:	*Merit*

79

PUBLICATION:	*IDC New York 16*
ART DIRECTOR:	*Massimo Vignelli*
DESIGNERS:	*Michael Bierut,*
	Lucy Cossentino
PUBLISHER:	*International Design*
	Center/New York
CATEGORY:	*Cover—Design*
AWARD:	*Merit*

80

PUBLICATION:	*IDC New York 15*
ART DIRECTOR:	*Massimo Vignelli*
DESIGNERS:	*Michael Bierut,*
	Lucy Cossentino
PUBLISHER:	*International Design*
	Center/New York
CATEGORY:	*Cover—Design*
AWARD:	*Merit*

81

PUBLICATION:	*Adweek*
ART DIRECTOR:	*Giona Maiarelli*
DESIGNER:	*Giona Maiarelli*
ILLUSTRATOR:	*Andrzej Dudzinski*
PUBLISHER:	*ASM Communications*
CATEGORY:	*Cover—Illustration*
TITLE:	*"Direct Marketing"*
AWARD:	*Merit*

82

PUBLICATION:	*Adweek*
ART DIRECTOR:	*Giona Maiarelli*
DESIGNER:	*Mark Winterford*
ILLUSTRATOR:	*Kinuko Craft*
PUBLISHER:	*ASM Communications*
CATEGORY:	*Cover—Illustration*
TITLE:	*"Japanese Design"*
AWARD:	*Merit*

83

PUBLICATION:	*The Boston Globe Magazine*
ART DIRECTOR:	*Lynn Staley*
DESIGNER:	*Lynn Staley*
ILLUSTRATOR:	*Steven Guarnaccia*
PUBLISHER:	*The Boston Globe*
CATEGORY:	*Cover—Design*
TITLE:	*"Snap Decisions"*
AWARD:	*Merit*

84

PUBLICATION:	*The Boston Globe Magazine*
ART DIRECTOR:	*Ronn Campisi*
DESIGNER:	*Ronn Campisi*
ILLUSTRATOR:	*Patrick Blackwell*
PUBLISHER:	*The Boston Globe*
CATEGORY:	*Cover—Design*
TITLE:	*"Road Warrior"*
AWARD:	*Merit*

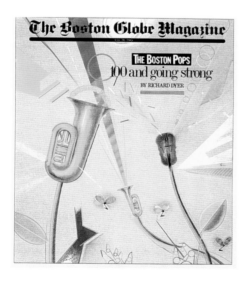

85

PUBLICATION:	*The Boston Globe Magazine*
ART DIRECTOR:	*Ronn Campisi*
DESIGNER:	*Ronn Campisi*
ILLUSTRATOR:	*Andrzej Dudzinski*
PUBLISHER:	*The Boston Globe*
CATEGORY:	*Cover—Design*
TITLE:	*"The Boston Pops"*
AWARD:	*Merit*

86

PUBLICATION:	*The Boston Globe Magazine*
ART DIRECTOR:	*Ronn Campisi*
DESIGNER:	*Ronn Campisi*
ILLUSTRATOR:	*Gene Greif*
PUBLISHER:	*The Boston Globe*
CATEGORY:	*Cover—Design*
TITLE:	*"A Class Portrait"*
AWARD:	*Merit*

87

PUBLICATION:	*Newsweek on Health*
ART DIRECTOR:	*Steven Hoffman*
DESIGNER:	*Steven Hoffman*
ILLUSTRATOR:	*Sandro Botticelli*
PUBLISHER:	*Washington Post Co.*
CATEGORY:	*Cover—Design*
TITLE:	*"Cosmetic Surgery"*
AWARD:	*Merit*

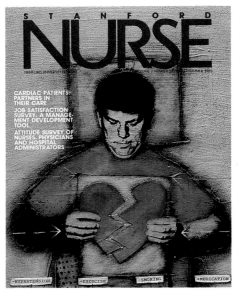

88

PUBLICATION:	*Stanford Nurse*
ART DIRECTOR:	*Alexander Atkins*
DESIGNER:	*Alexander Atkins*
ILLUSTRATOR:	*Dave Lesh*
PUBLISHER:	*Stanford University Hospital*
CATEGORY:	*Cover—Design*
TITLE:	*"Cardiac Patients"*
AWARD:	*Merit*

89

PUBLICATION:	*Science '85*
ART DIRECTOR:	*Wayne Fitzpatrick*
DESIGNER:	*Wayne Fitzpatrick*
ILLUSTRATOR:	*Brad Holland*
PUBLISHER:	*Science '85/American Association for the Advancement of Science*
CATEGORY:	*Cover—Illustration*
TITLE:	*"Technology for Peace"*
AWARD:	*Merit*

90

PUBLICATION:	*Columbia*
ART DIRECTOR:	*Florence Keller*
DESIGNER:	*Tom Lunde*
ILLUSTRATOR:	*Tom Lunde*
PUBLISHER:	*Columbia University*
CATEGORY:	*Cover—Design*
AWARD:	*Merit*

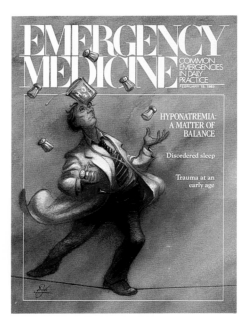

91

PUBLICATION:	*Emergency Medicine*
ART DIRECTOR:	*Lois Erlacher*
DESIGNER:	*Lois Erlacher*
ILLUSTRATOR:	*Peter DeSeve*
PUBLISHER:	*Cahners Publishing*
CATEGORY:	*Cover—Design*
TITLE:	*"Hyponatremia: A Matter of Balance"*
AWARD:	*Merit*

92

PUBLICATION:	*Postgraduate Medicine*
ART DIRECTOR:	*Tina Adamek*
ILLUSTRATOR:	*Matt Mahurin*
PUBLISHER:	*McGraw-Hill*
CATEGORY:	*Cover—Illustration*
TITLE:	*"Transfer of the Severely Injured"*
AWARD:	*Merit*

93

PUBLICATION:	*The Plain Dealer Magazine*
ART DIRECTOR:	*Gerard Sealy*
DESIGNER:	*Gerard Sealy*
ILLUSTRATOR:	*Matt Mahurin*
PUBLISHER:	*Plain Dealer Publishing Co.*
CATEGORY:	*Cover—Design*
TITLE:	*"The Victim"*
AWARD:	*Merit*

94

PUBLICATION:	*The Plain Dealer Magazine*
ART DIRECTOR:	*Gerard Sealy*
DESIGNER:	*Gerard Sealy*
ILLUSTRATOR:	*Mark Penberthy*
PUBLISHER:	*Plain Dealer Publishing Co.*
CATEGORY:	*Cover—Design*
TITLE:	*"Crisis of Confidence"*
AWARD:	*Merit*

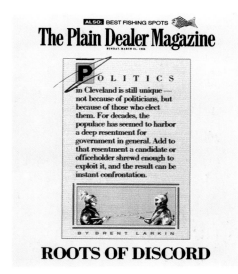

95

PUBLICATION:	*The Plain Dealer Magazine*
ART DIRECTOR:	*Gerard Sealy*
DESIGNER:	*Gerard Sealy*
ILLUSTRATOR:	*Kevin Pope*
PUBLISHER:	*Plain Dealer Publishing Co.*
CATEGORY:	*Cover—Design*
TITLE:	*"Politics in Cleveland"*
AWARD:	*Merit*

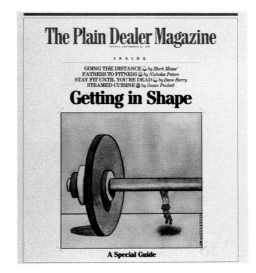

96

PUBLICATION:	*The Plain Dealer Magazine*
ART DIRECTOR:	*Gerard Sealy*
DESIGNER:	*Gerard Sealy*
ILLUSTRATOR:	*Steven Guarnaccia*
PUBLISHER:	*Plain Dealer Publishing Co.*
CATEGORY:	*Cover—Design*
TITLE:	*"Getting into Shape"*
AWARD:	*Merit*

97

PUBLICATION:	*The Plain Dealer Magazine*
ART DIRECTOR:	*Gerard Sealy*
DESIGNER:	*Gerard Sealy*
ILLUSTRATOR:	*Greg Spalenka*
PUBLISHER:	*Plain Dealer Publishing Co.*
CATEGORY:	*Cover—Design*
TITLE:	*"A Visit to Hiroshima"*
AWARD:	*Merit*

98

PUBLICATION:	*Time*
ART DIRECTOR:	*Nigel Holmes*
ILLUSTRATOR:	*Braldt Bralds*
PUBLISHER:	*Time Inc.*
CATEGORY:	*Cover—Illustration*
TITLE:	*"Did Comets Kill the Dinosaurs?"*
AWARD:	*Merit*

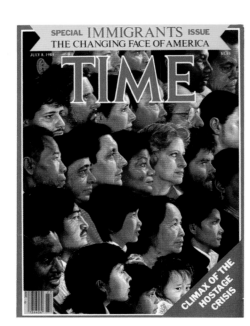

99

PUBLICATION:	*Time*
ART DIRECTOR:	*Rudy Hoglund*
ILLUSTRATOR:	*Richard Hess*
PUBLISHER:	*Time Inc.*
CATEGORY:	*Cover—Illustration*
TITLE:	*"Immigrants"*
AWARD:	*Merit*

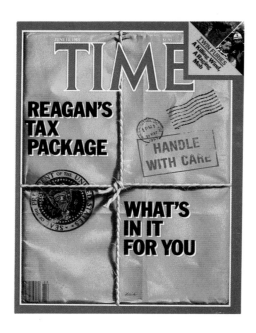

100

PUBLICATION:	*Time*
ART DIRECTOR:	*Nigel Holmes*
ILLUSTRATOR:	*Birney Lettick*
PUBLISHER:	*Time Inc.*
CATEGORY:	*Cover—Design*
TITLE:	*"Reagan's Tax Package"*
AWARD:	*Merit*

101

PUBLICATION:	*U.S. News & World Report*
ART DIRECTORS:	*Walter Bernard,*
	Milton Glaser
DESIGNERS:	*Walter Bernard,*
	Milton Glaser
ILLUSTRATOR:	*Marvin Mattelson*
PUBLISHER:	*U.S. News & World Report, Inc.*
CATEGORY:	*Cover—Illustration*
TITLE:	*"Lure of Capitalism"*
AWARD:	*Merit*

102

PUBLICATION:	*Fortune*
ART DIRECTOR:	*Margery Peters*
DESIGNER:	*Margery Peters*
ILLUSTRATOR:	*Guy Billout*
PUBLISHER:	*Time Inc.*
CATEGORY:	*Cover—Design*
TITLE:	*"What's Next for the*
	Raiders?"
AWARD:	*Merit*

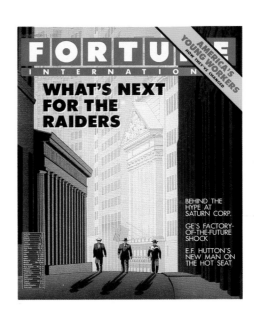

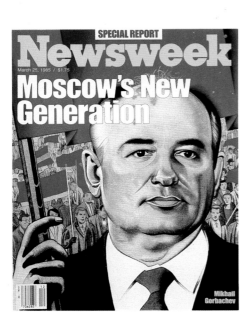

103

PUBLICATION:	*Newsweek*
ART DIRECTOR:	*Robert Priest*
DESIGNER:	*Margaret Joskow*
ILLUSTRATOR:	*Jeffery Smith*
PUBLISHER:	*Washington Post Co.*
CATEGORY:	*Cover—Design*
TITLE:	*"Moscow's New Generation"*
AWARD:	*Merit*

104

PUBLICATION:	*Enterprise*
ART DIRECTOR:	*Douglas Wolfe*
DESIGNER:	*John Howze*
ILLUSTRATOR:	*Michael McGurl*
AGENCY:	*Hawthorne/Wolfe Design*
CLIENT:	*Southwestern Bell Corporation*
CATEGORY:	*Cover—Design*
TITLE:	*"The Hottest Issue in D.C."*
AWARD:	*Merit*

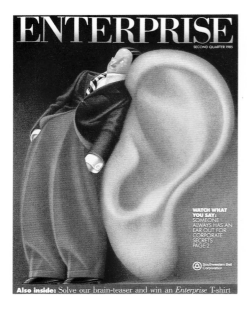

105

PUBLICATION:	*Enterprise*
ART DIRECTOR:	*Douglas Wolfe*
DESIGNER:	*Douglas Wolfe*
ILLUSTRATOR:	*Michel Guire Vaka*
AGENCY:	*Hawthorne/Wolfe Design*
CLIENT:	*Southwestern Bell Corporation*
CATEGORY:	*Cover—Design*
TITLE:	*"Watch What You Say"*
AWARD:	*Merit*

106

PUBLICATION:	*Enterprise*
ART DIRECTOR:	*Douglas Wolfe*
DESIGNER:	*Douglas Wolfe*
ILLUSTRATOR:	*Barry Root*
AGENCY:	*Hawthorne/Wolfe Design*
CLIENT:	*Southwestern Bell Corporation*
CATEGORY:	*Cover—Design*
TITLE:	*"Creativity"*
AWARD:	*Merit*

107

PUBLICATION:	*Enterprise*
ART DIRECTOR:	*Douglas Wolfe*
DESIGNER:	*Douglas Wolfe*
ILLUSTRATOR:	*Gary Overacre*
AGENCY:	*Hawthorne/Wolfe Design*
CLIENT:	*Southwestern Bell Corporation*
CATEGORY:	*Cover—Design*
TITLE:	*"Armed for the Battle"*
AWARD:	*Merit*

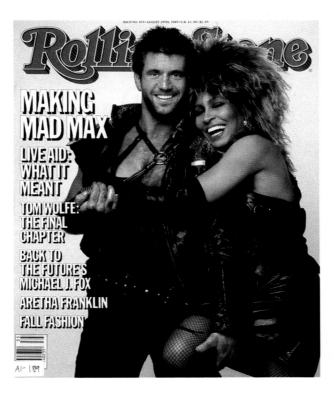

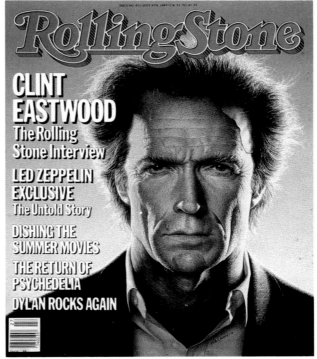

108

PUBLICATION:	*Rolling Stone*
ART DIRECTOR:	*Derek W. Ungless*
DESIGNER:	*Derek W. Ungless*
PHOTOGRAPHER:	*Herb Ritts*
PHOTO EDITOR:	*Laurie Kratchovil*
PUBLISHER:	*Straight Arrow Publications*
CATEGORY:	*Cover—Design*
TITLE:	*"Making Mad Max"*
AWARD:	*Merit*

109

PUBLICATION:	*Rolling Stone*
ART DIRECTOR:	*Derek W. Ungless*
DESIGNER:	*Derek W. Ungless*
ILLUSTRATOR:	*Gottfried Helnwein*
PHOTO EDITOR:	*Laurie Kratchovil*
PUBLISHER:	*Straight Arrow Publications*
CATEGORY:	*Cover—Design*
TITLE:	*"Clint Eastwood—The Rolling Stone Interview"*
AWARD:	*Merit*

110

PUBLICATION:	*House & Garden*
ART DIRECTOR:	*Lloyd Ziff*
DESIGNER:	*Lloyd Ziff*
PHOTOGRAPHER:	*Marina Schinz*
PUBLISHER:	*Condé Nast, Inc.*
CATEGORY:	*Cover—Design*
TITLE:	*"Roses"*
AWARD:	*Merit*

111

PUBLICATION:	*American Bookseller*
ART DIRECTOR:	*Amy Bogert*
DESIGNER:	*Amy Bogert*
ILLUSTRATOR:	*Mark Penberthy*
PUBLISHER:	*Booksellers Publishing, Inc.*
CATEGORY:	*Cover—Illustration*
TITLE:	*"1985 Fall Announcements"*
AWARD:	*Merit*

112

PUBLICATION:	*American Bookseller*
ART DIRECTOR:	*Amy Bogert*
DESIGNER:	*Amy Bogert*
ILLUSTRATOR:	*Wendy Burden*
PUBLISHER:	*Booksellers Publishing, Inc.*
CATEGORY:	*Cover—Illustration*
TITLE:	*"The Summer Merchandising Campaign"*
AWARD:	*Merit*

113

PUBLICATION:	*American Bookseller*
ART DIRECTOR:	*Amy Bogert*
DESIGNER:	*Amy Bogert*
ILLUSTRATOR:	*Henrik Drescher*
PUBLISHER:	*Booksellers Publishing, Inc.*
CATEGORY:	*Cover—Illustration*
TITLE:	*"Spring 1985 Children's Books"*
AWARD:	*Merit*

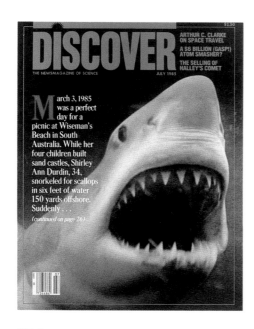

114

PUBLICATION:	*Discover*
ART DIRECTOR:	*Eric Seidman*
DESIGNER:	*Eric Seidman*
PHOTOGRAPHER:	*Time Inc.*
CATEGORY:	*Cover—Design*
TITLE:	*"On the Track of the Real Shark"*
AWARD:	*Merit*

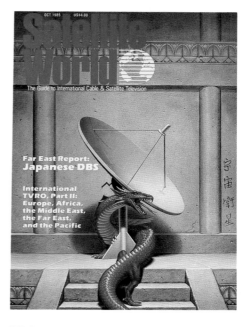

115

PUBLICATION:	*PC Tech Journal*
ART DIRECTOR:	*Ina Saltz*
DESIGNER:	*Ina Saltz*
PHOTOGRAPHER:	*John Lei*
PUBLISHER:	*Ziff-Davis Publishing Co.*
CATEGORY:	*Cover—Design*
TITLE:	*"Enhanced Graphics"*
AWARD:	*Merit*

116

PUBLICATION:	*Satellite World*
ART DIRECTOR:	*Michael Quinney*
DESIGNER:	*Michael Quinney*
ILLUSTRATOR:	*Todd Lockwood*
PUBLISHER:	*Commtek Publishing*
CATEGORY:	*Cover—Illustration*
TITLE:	*"Far East Report"*
AWARD:	*Merit*

117

PUBLICATION:	*Audubon*
ART DIRECTOR:	*Daniel J. McClain*
DESIGNER:	*Daniel J. McClain*
ILLUSTRATOR:	*J.J. Audubon*
PUBLISHER:	*National Audubon Society*
CATEGORY:	*Cover—Design*
AWARD:	*Merit*

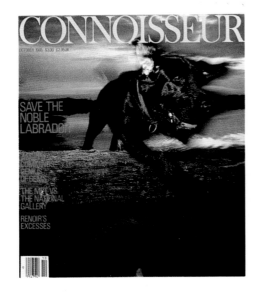

118

PUBLICATION:	*Connoisseur*
ART DIRECTOR:	*Carla Barr*
DESIGNER:	*Carla Barr*
PHOTOGRAPHER:	*José Azel*
PUBLISHER:	*Hearst Corporation*
CATEGORY:	*Cover—Design*
TITLE:	*"Save the Noble Labrador"*
AWARD:	*Merit*

119

PUBLICATION:	*Connoisseur*
ART DIRECTOR:	*Carla Barr*
DESIGNER:	*Carla Barr*
CALLIGRAPHER:	*Takako Takahashi*
PUBLISHER:	*Hearst Corporation*
CATEGORY:	*Cover—Design*
TITLE:	*"The Spirit of Tokyo"*
AWARD:	*Merit*

120

PUBLICATION:	*Connoisseur*
ART DIRECTOR:	*Carla Barr*
DESIGNER:	*Carla Barr*
PHOTOGRAPHER:	*Sandi Fellman*
PUBLISHER:	*Hearst Corporation*
CATEGORY:	*Cover—Design*
TITLE:	*"Sensuous American Ceramics"*
AWARD:	*Merit*

121

PUBLICATION:	*Connoisseur*
ART DIRECTOR:	*Carla Barr*
DESIGNER:	*Carla Barr*
PHOTOGRAPHER:	*Jan Michael*
PUBLISHER:	*Hearst Corporation*
CATEGORY:	*Cover—Design*
TITLE:	*"Paris' New Fashion Museum"*
AWARD:	*Merit*

122

PUBLICATION:	*Connoisseur*
ART DIRECTOR:	*Carla Barr*
DESIGNER:	*Carla Barr*
PHOTOGRAPHER:	*Brian Hagiwara*
PUBLISHER:	*Hearst Corporation*
CATEGORY:	*Cover—Design*
TITLE:	*"Edible Avant-Garde"*
AWARD:	*Merit*

123

PUBLICATION:	*Manhattan, inc.*
ART DIRECTOR:	*Nancy Butkus*
DESIGNER:	*Nancy Butkus*
ILLUSTRATOR:	*Andy Warhol*
PHOTOGRAPHER:	*Debrah Feingold*
PUBLISHER:	*Metrocorp*
CATEGORY:	*Cover—Illustration*
TITLE:	*"The Passions of Mario Cuomo"*
AWARD:	*Merit*

124

PUBLICATION:	*Manhattan, inc.*
ART DIRECTOR:	*Nancy Butkus*
DESIGNER:	*Nancy Butkus*
PHOTOGRAPHER:	*William Coupon*
PUBLISHER:	*Metrocorp*
CATEGORY:	*Cover—Photography*
TITLE:	*"Donald Trump's Ultimate Deal"*
AWARD:	*Merit*

MERIT

125

PUBLICATION:	*New York*
ART DIRECTOR:	*Robert Best*
DESIGNER:	*Robert Best*
PUBLISHER:	*Murdoch Magazines*
CATEGORY:	*Cover—Design*
TITLE:	*"Best of New York"*
AWARD:	*Merit*

126

PUBLICATION:	*New York*
ART DIRECTOR:	*Robert Best*
DESIGNER:	*Robert Best*
ILLUSTRATOR:	*Laurie Rosenwald*
PUBLISHER:	*Murdoch Magazines*
CATEGORY:	*Cover—Design*
TITLE:	*"Fall Preview"*
AWARD:	*Merit*

127

PUBLICATION:	*New York*
ART DIRECTOR:	*Robert Best*
DESIGNER:	*Robert Best*
PHOTOGRAPHER:	*Farrell Grehan*
PUBLISHER:	*Murdoch Magazines*
CATEGORY:	*Cover—Design*
TITLE:	*"On the Waterfront"*
AWARD:	*Merit*

128

PUBLICATION:	*New York*
ART DIRECTOR:	*Robert Best*
DESIGNER:	*Robert Best*
PHOTOGRAPHER:	*Steve McCurry*
PUBLISHER:	*Murdoch Magazines*
CATEGORY:	*Cover—Design*
TITLE:	*"Yupper West Side"*
AWARD:	*Merit*

129

PUBLICATION:	*New York*
ART DIRECTOR:	*Robert Best*
DESIGNER:	*Robert Best*
ILLUSTRATOR:	*Gary Hallgren*
PUBLISHER:	*Murdoch Magazines*
CATEGORY:	*Cover—Design*
TITLE:	*"Co-ops & Condos"*
AWARD:	*Merit*

130

PUBLICATION:	*New York*
ART DIRECTOR:	*Robert Best*
DESIGNER:	*Robert Best*
ILLUSTRATOR:	*Andrea Barubbi*
PUBLISHER:	*Murdoch Magazines*
CATEGORY:	*Cover—Design*
TITLE:	*"What's Really Going On?"*
AWARD:	*Merit*

SINGLE PAGE/SPREADS

131

PUBLICATION: *Rolling Stone*
ART DIRECTOR: *Derek W. Ungless*
DESIGNER: *Derek W. Ungless*
PHOTOGRAPHER: *Albert Watson*
PHOTO EDITOR: *Laurie Kratchovil*
PUBLISHER: *Straight Arrow Publications*
CATEGORY: *Single Page/Spread—*
                  Photography
TITLE: *"Clint Eastwood"*
AWARD: *Gold*

For Penn and Teller,
these are the days of
wine and roaches.
That became
apparent one recent
afternoon, as the bad
boys of magic — and
the sensations of the
current off-Broadway
season — rehearsed in
their seedy New York
studio for an

DO YOU BELIEVE IN MAGIC?

appearance on the
David Letterman
show. "We're going to
show you a work in
progress," said Penn
Jillette, the peculiarly
pompadoured one, to
an assistant standing
in as Letterman.
"We'd like your
opinion." Then, while
the Lovin' Spoonful's
"Do You Believe in
Magic?" blared in the
background, Teller,
who uses [Cont. on 72]

42

**Penn and Teller do. How else
can you explain the overnight
success of two guys who've
been doing the same things
since they were fourteen-
year-old social outcasts.**

By Charles Leerhsen

Photograph by Chris Callis

Penn Jillette and
Teller pull each.

132

PUBLICATION:	*Rolling Stone*
ART DIRECTOR:	*Derek W. Ungless*
DESIGNER:	*Angelo Savaides*
PHOTOGRAPHER:	*Chris Callis*
PUBLISHER:	*Straight Arrow Publications*
CATEGORY:	*Single Page/Spread— Photography*
TITLE:	*"Do You Believe in Magic?"*
AWARD:	*Gold*

133

PUBLICATION:	*Elle*
ART DIRECTOR:	*Ron Albrecht*
PUB. DIRECTOR:	*Régis Pagniez*
PHOTOGRAPHER:	*Toscani*
PUBLISHER:	*Elle Publishing, Inc.*
CATEGORY:	*Single Page/Spread—Design*
TITLE:	*"Fake Fur Folly"*
AWARD:	*Silver*

134

PUBLICATION:	*Rolling Stone*
ART DIRECTOR:	*Derek W. Ungless*
DESIGNER:	*Derek W. Ungless*
PHOTOGRAPHER:	*Richard Avedon*
PUBLISHER:	*Straight Arrow Publications*
CATEGORY:	*Single Page/Spread— Photography*
TITLE:	*"Here Comes the Son"*
AWARD:	*Silver*

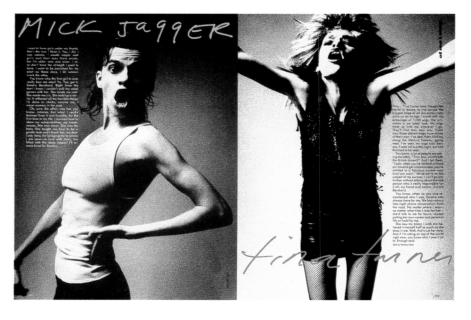

135

PUBLICATION:	*Mademoiselle*
ART DIRECTOR:	*Kati Korpijaakko*
DESIGNER:	*Wynn Dan*
PHOTOGRAPHER:	*Vadukul*
PUBLISHER:	*Condé Nast*
CATEGORY:	*Single Page/Spread— Photography*
TITLE:	*"Sandra Bernhard"*
AWARD:	*Silver*

UNMASKING A MURDERER

by Fred Moody

The Green River killer, like all serial murderers, will stop only when caught—a day that might never come without the use of a new investigative tool.

HE ENTERS CAUTIOUSLY, THROUGH AN IMPER-ceptible scissure in the seamless fabric of the night. Cunningly, he selects and stalks a victim, then quietly carries her off and kills her in a ritual frenzy. He carefully disposes of her body and retreats as invisibly as he had advanced. So unremarkable have been his entrance and exit that nothing is known of him until well after he has gone. He is as featureless as his crimes are gruesome. He has been dubbed by default the "Green River killer," after the area in which the bodies of most of his victims have been found. To investigators his killings are devoid of readily discernible motivation. The odds against catching criminals like him are astronomical.

He is, by police count, known to have killed 28 young women and is suspected of killing 14 more—all linked to prostitution and all in the span of less than two years. Following Ted Bundy and Kenneth Bianchi, he is the third "serial killer" (a multiple murderer who kills at intervals, one victim at a time, for as long as it takes police to apprehend him) to emerge in the Northwest in recent years. He is one of more than 30 such criminals said by the FBI to be currently roaming the country, and who are believed to be responsible for at least two-thirds of the nation's 5,000 unsolved murders per year.

Twenty years ago, according to FBI statistics, more than 80 percent of America's murder victims had some kind of previous relationship with their killers. A police officer was safe in assuming that the murderer could be found among acquaintances of the deceased. In recent years, though, there has been a dramatic drop in such readily solvable crimes. By 1981, 45 percent of the nation's 22,516 murders were classified as "stranger murders," and more

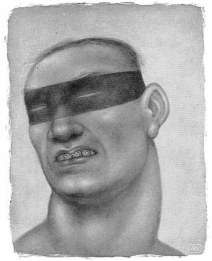

136

PUBLICATION: *Pacific Northwest*
ART DIRECTOR: *Steven Bialer*
ILLUSTRATOR: *Anita Kunz*
PUBLISHER: *Pacific Northwest*
CATEGORY: *Single Page/Spread—Illustration*
TITLE: *"Unmasking a Murderer"*
AWARD: *Silver*

PHOBIAS

Recent research in behavior modification and common sense approaches provide new cures for one of man's darkest traits.

by Spyros Andreopoulos

137

PUBLICATION: *Stanford Medicine*
ART DIRECTOR: *Mike Shenon*
DESIGNER: *Mike Shenon*
ILLUSTRATOR: *James Endicott*
PUBLISHER: *Stanford University Medical Center*
CATEGORY: *Single Page/Spread—Illustration*
TITLE: *"Phobias"*
AWARD: *Silver*

First of three symposium articles in this issue

Steven L. Berk, MD
Salvador Alvarez, MD

Bacterial infections in the elderly

Special considerations for a special patient population

Preview questions

What disease has been described as the "special enemy of old age"?

What accounts for the disproportionate increase in new cases of Mycobacterium tuberculosis infection among the elderly?

What is the most common cause of bacteremia in the elderly?

By the end of this century, 30 million people living in the United States will be over the age of 65. The conquest of infectious disease in early life has been a major factor in increasing longevity in this and other developed countries; tuberculosis, rheumatic fever, typhus, and pneumococcal pneumonia are no longer common causes of death in young people.

This conquest, however, has created a new problem and thereby a new challenge. The elderly patient with underlying degenerative disease and perhaps with a senescent immune system faces morbidity and death due to infection. The pathogens and clinical presentations are different from those in young people, but the consequences are the same.

Pneumonia and influenza are leading causes of death in elderly patients. Gram-negative bacteremia has emerged as a common and lethal disease. Decubitus ulcers and herpes zoster are more frequent because of underlying disease and decreased immunity.

The infectious diseases that threaten elderly patients may have unusual clinical presentations, may be caused by unusual pathogens, and may require special considerations when therapy is chosen. These infections have become of special interest to all who care for the aged.

Factors that predispose the elderly to infection

While it is a mistake to think of all elderly persons as debilitated by underlying disease, many conditions that predispose to infection—in particular, diabetes mellitus, emphysema, and cancer—are most common in an older population. In addition, increasing evidence suggests that as the immune system ages, it may become less effective in preventing infection.

In vitro data support the concept of cell-mediated immunologic senescence. In the elderly, the T cells have a diminished capacity for mitogen-responsive

continued

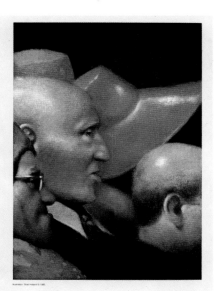

138

PUBLICATION: *Postgraduate Medicine*
ART DIRECTOR: *Tina Adamek*
ILLUSTRATOR: *Brad Holland*
PUBLISHER: *McGraw-Hill*
CATEGORY: *Single Page/Spread—Illustration*
TITLE: *"Infections In The Elderly"*
AWARD: *Silver*

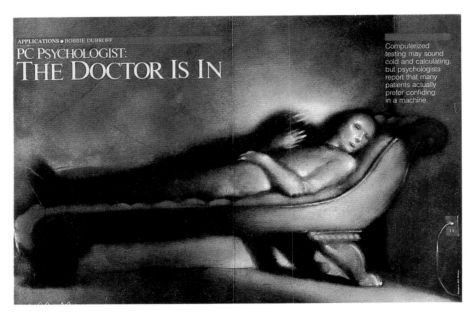

139

PUBLICATION: *PC*
ART DIRECTOR: *Mary Zisk*
DESIGNER: *Louise White*
ILLUSTRATOR: *Matt Mahurin*
PUBLISHER: *Ziff Davis*
CATEGORY: *Single Page/Spread—*
Illustration
TITLE: *"PC Psychologist:*
The Doctor Is In"
AWARD: *Silver*

140

PUBLICATION: *Tables Magazine*
ART DIRECTOR: *Shelley Williams*
DESIGNER: *Sara Christensen*
ILLUSTRATOR: *Andrzej Dudzinski*
PUBLISHER: *13-30 Corporation*
CATEGORY: *Single Page/Spread—*
Illustration
TITLE: *"Dissecting the Waiter"*
AWARD: *Silver*

141

PUBLICATION: *Home Satellite Marketing*
ART DIRECTOR: *Marjorie Crane*
DESIGNER: *Marjorie Crane*
ILLUSTRATOR: *Doug Fraser*
PUBLISHER: *CES Publishing*
CATEGORY: *Single Page/Spread—*
Illustration
TITLE: *"Quotes of the Year"*
AWARD: *Silver*

142

PUBLICATION: *Campus Voice Biweekly*
ART DIRECTOR: *Sally Ham*
DESIGNER: *Sally Ham*
ILLUSTRATOR: *Henrik Drescher*
PUBLISHER: *13-30 Corporation*
CATEGORY: *Single Page/Spread—*
Illustration
TITLE: *"Combatting Mid-Term Stress"*
AWARD: *Silver*

143

PUBLICATION: *Science '85*
ART DIRECTOR: *Wayne Fitzpatrick*
DESIGNER: *Wayne Fitzpatrick*
ILLUSTRATOR: *Andrzej Dudzinski*
PUBLISHER: *Science '85/American*
Association for the
Advancement of Science
CATEGORY: *Single Page/Spread—*
Illustration
TITLE: *"Pacemaker's Going*
to the Dogs"
AWARD: *Silver*

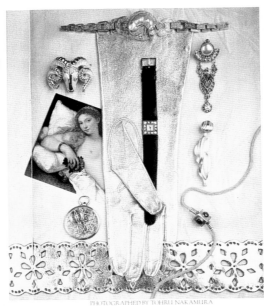

144

PUBLICATION: *New York*
ART DIRECTOR: *Robert Best*
DESIGNER: *Robert Best*
PHOTOGRAPHER: *Tohru Nakamura*
PUBLISHER: *Murdoch Magazines*
CATEGORY: *Single Page/Spread—*
Photography
TITLE: *"Going for the Gold"*
AWARD: *Silver*

145

PUBLICATION:	*Monthly Detroit*
ART DIRECTOR:	*Wendy Thomas*
DESIGNER:	*Dugald Stermer*
ILLUSTRATOR:	*Dugald Stermer*
PUBLISHER:	*Detroit News*
CATEGORY:	*Single Page/Spread—Illustration*
TITLE:	*"Joe Louis"*
AWARD:	*Silver*

AMERICA
THE POWERFUL

We wave, we cheer, we protest, we succeed. A single gesture instantly expresses our personal, professional, and political selves. Our vital link to the surroundings, hands are the most used—and most overworked—part of us. Good news: hand care is moving in a more sophisticated, more scientific direction.

BOLD GESTURES

146

PUBLICATION:	*Elle*
ART DIRECTOR:	*Ron Albrecht*
PUB. DIRECTOR:	*Régis Pagniez*
PHOTOGRAPHER:	*Toscani*
PUBLISHER:	*Elle Publishing, Inc.*
CATEGORY:	*Single Page/Spread—Design*
TITLE:	*"America the Powerful"*
AWARD:	*Merit*

THE BLACK OUT

In a season with such a rich variety of shapes, textures, moods, so clearly, so simply, as black—with an exclamation of white. On these eight pages, glimpses of the most graphic color couple now...

BODY DRESSING NOW...

147

PUBLICATION:	*Elle*
ART DIRECTOR:	*Ron Albrecht*
PUB. DIRECTOR:	*Régis Pagniez*
PHOTOGRAPHER:	*Gilles Bensimon*
PUBLISHER:	*Elle Publishing, Inc.*
CATEGORY:	*Single Page/Spread—Design*
TITLE:	*"The Black Out"*
AWARD:	*Merit*

Makeup for makeup's sake? Why not! Electric color, glamour-glitter, costume jewels—all come together in America's new party attitude. All-night partying, exotic dinners, gallery-openings ... any-night-out—is cause to celebrate and decorate.

THE NEW HUE

AMERICA
THE PLAYFUL

148

PUBLICATION:	*Elle*
ART DIRECTOR:	*Ron Albrecht*
PUB. DIRECTOR:	*Régis Pagniez*
PHOTOGRAPHER:	*Toscani*
PUBLISHER:	*Elle Publishing, Inc.*
CATEGORY:	*Single Page/Spread—Design*
TITLE:	*"America the Playful"*
AWARD:	*Merit*

149

PUBLICATION: *Elle*
ART DIRECTOR: *Ron Albrecht*
PUB. DIRECTOR: *Régis Pagniez*
PHOTOGRAPHER: *Toscani*
PUBLISHER: *Elle Publishing, Inc.*
CATEGORY: *Single Page/Spread—Design*
TITLE: *"Fake Fur Folly"*
AWARD: *Merit*

150

PUBLICATION: *Elle*
ART DIRECTOR: *Ron Albrecht*
PUB. DIRECTOR: *Régis Pagniez*
PHOTOGRAPHER: *Gilles Bensimon*
PUBLISHER: *Elle Publishing, Inc.*
CATEGORY: *Single Page/Spread—Design*
TITLE: *"Flash/Style is Character"*
AWARD: *Merit*

151

PUBLICATION: *Elle*
ART DIRECTOR: *Ron Albrecht*
PUB. DIRECTOR: *Régis Pagniez*
PHOTOGRAPHER: *Toscani*
PUBLISHER: *Elle Publishing, Inc.*
CATEGORY: *Single Page/Spread—Design*
TITLE: *"America the Colorful"*
AWARD: *Merit*

MERIT

152

PUBLICATION: *Elle*
ART DIRECTOR: *Ron Albrecht*
PUB. DIRECTOR: *Régis Pagniez*
PHOTOGRAPHER: *Gilles Bensimon*
PUBLISHER: *Elle Publishing, Inc.*
CATEGORY: *Single Page/Spread—Design*
TITLE: *"The Black Out"*
AWARD: *Merit*

153

PUBLICATION: *Elle*
ART DIRECTOR: *Ron Albrecht*
PUB. DIRECTOR: *Régis Pagniez*
PHOTOGRAPHER: *Albert Watson*
PUBLISHER: *Elle Publishing, Inc.*
CATEGORY: *Single Page/Spread—Design*
TITLE: *"Baroque Con Brio!"*
AWARD: *Merit*

154

PUBLICATION: *Elle*
ART DIRECTOR: *Ron Albrecht*
PUB. DIRECTOR: *Régis Pagniez*
PHOTOGRAPHER: *Albert Watson*
PUBLISHER: *Elle Publishing, Inc.*
CATEGORY: *Single Page/Spread—Design*
TITLE: *"Holiday Loot"*
AWARD: *Merit*

MERIT

forget-me-not FRIENDS

by Judy Bachrach

cocaine
a pretty poison

by Alan Weitz

155

PUBLICATION: *Elle*
ART DIRECTOR: *Ron Albrecht*
PUB. DIRECTOR: *Régis Pagniez*
PHOTOGRAPHER: *Gilles Bensimon*
PUBLISHER: *Elle Publishing, Inc.*
CATEGORY: *Single Page/Spread—Design*
TITLE: *"The Black Out"*
AWARD: *Merit*

156

PUBLICATION: *Mademoiselle*
ART DIRECTOR: *Kati Korpijaakko*
DESIGNER: *Marilu Lopez*
ILLUSTRATOR: *Anthony Russo*
PUBLISHER: *Condé Nast*
CATEGORY: *Single Page/Spread—Illustration*
TITLE: *"Forget Me Not Friends"*
AWARD: *Merit*

157

PUBLICATION: *Mademoiselle*
ART DIRECTOR: *Kati Korpijaakko*
DESIGNER: *Trey Speegle*
ILLUSTRATOR: *Anthony Russo*
PUBLISHER: *Condé Nast*
CATEGORY: *Single Page/Spread—Illustration*
TITLE: *"Cocaine—A Pretty Poison"*
AWARD: *Merit*

MERIT

BY BRUCE WEBER

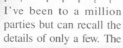

I've been to a million parties but can recall the details of only a few. The

rest of them just sort of blend into one festive tableau – food, music, some kind of crowd. Which is not to say I don't
(continued)

BRIGHT LIGHTS, BIG PARTY
SEXY STUFF FOR THE NEW NIGHTLIFE

158

PUBLICATION: *Mademoiselle*
ART DIRECTOR: *Kati Korpijaakko*
DESIGNER: *Marilu Lopez*
PHOTOGRAPHER: *Steven Meisel*
PUBLISHER: *Condé Nast*
CATEGORY: *Single Page/Spread—Photography*
TITLE: *"Bright Lights"*
AWARD: *Merit*

TIGHT ON TOP...BILLOWY ON THE BOTTOM!

159

PUBLICATION: *Mademoiselle*
ART DIRECTOR: *Kati Korpijaakko*
DESIGNER: *Marilu Lopez*
PHOTOGRAPHER: *Steven Meisel*
PUBLISHER: *Condé Nast*
CATEGORY: *Single Page/Spread—Photography*
TITLE: *"Bright Lights"*
AWARD: *Merit*

BEAUTY BULLETIN: WHAT'S NEW **TO DO**

THE NO-RULE RULE:

THE MAXIMUM mouth

160

PUBLICATION: *Mademoiselle*
ART DIRECTOR: *Kati Korpijaakko*
DESIGNER: *Marilu Lopez*
PHOTOGRAPHER: *Michel Comte*
PUBLISHER: *Condé Nast*
CATEGORY: *Single Page/Spread—Photography*
TITLE: *"Beauty Bulletin"*
AWARD: *Merit*

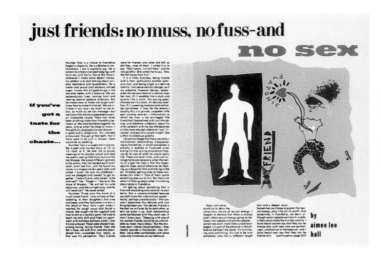

just friends: no muss, no fuss-and no sex

161

PUBLICATION:	*Mademoiselle*
ART DIRECTOR:	*Kati Korpijaakko*
DESIGNER:	*Marilu Lopez*
ILLUSTRATOR:	*Susan Curtis*
PUBLISHER:	*Condé Nast*
CATEGORY:	*Single Page/Spread—Illustration*
TITLE:	*"Just Friends"*
AWARD:	*Merit*

162

PUBLICATION:	*Mademoiselle*
ART DIRECTOR:	*Kati Korpijaakko*
DESIGNER:	*Wynn Dan*
PHOTOGRAPHER:	*Max Vadukul*
PUBLISHER:	*Condé Nast*
CATEGORY:	*Single Page/Spread—Design*
TITLE:	*"Sandra Bernhard"*
AWARD:	*Merit*

163

PUBLICATION:	*Mademoiselle*
ART DIRECTOR:	*Kati Korpijaakko*
DESIGNER:	*Marilu Lopez*
PHOTOGRAPHER:	*Steven Meisel*
PUBLISHER:	*Condé Nast Publications*
CATEGORY:	*Single Page/Spread—Design*
TITLE:	*"Bright Lights"*
AWARD:	*Merit*

164

PUBLICATION:	*Mademoiselle*
ART DIRECTOR:	*Kati Korpijaakko*
DESIGNER:	*Susan Cropper*
ILLUSTRATOR:	*Lynda Barry*
PUBLISHER:	*Condé Nast*
CATEGORY:	*Single Page/Spread—Illustration*
TITLE:	*"Can't Love It—Can't Leave It"*
AWARD:	*Merit*

165

PUBLICATION:	*Health*
ART DIRECTOR:	*Reilly Sierra*
DESIGNER:	*Reilly Sierra*
PHOTOGRAPHER:	*Michael Momy*
PUBLISHER:	*Family Media*
CATEGORY:	*Single Page/Spread—Design*
TITLE:	*"The Shadow of a Doubt"*
AWARD:	*Merit*

166

PUBLICATION:	*Mademoiselle*
ART DIRECTOR:	*Kati Korpijaakko*
DESIGNER:	*Marilu Lopez*
ILLUSTRATOR:	*Sheba Ross*
PUBLISHER:	*Condé Nast*
CATEGORY:	*Single Page/Spread— Illustration*
TITLE:	*"Some Day Your Prince Will Come"*
AWARD:	*Merit*

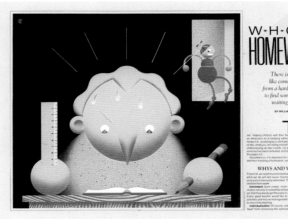

167

PUBLICATION:	*Working Mother*
ART DIRECTOR:	*Nina Scerbo*
DESIGNER:	*Jenny Adams*
ILLUSTRATOR:	*José Cruz*
PUBLISHER:	*McCalls*
CATEGORY:	*Single Page/Spread— Illustration*
TITLE:	*"Whose Homework?"*
AWARD:	*Merit*

168

PUBLICATION:	*Ms.*
ART DIRECTOR:	*Phyllis Schefer*
DESIGNER:	*Gary Mele*
ILLUSTRATOR:	*Greg Spalenka*
PUBLISHER:	*Ms. Foundation for Education and Communication, Inc.*
CATEGORY:	*Single Page/Spread—Design*
TITLE:	*"Olive Oil"*
AWARD:	*Merit*

169

PUBLICATION:	*Ms.*
ART DIRECTOR:	*Phyllis Schefer*
DESIGNER:	*Phyllis Schefer*
PHOTOGRAPHER:	*Chris Callas*
PUBLISHER:	*Ms. Foundation for Education and Communication, Inc.*
CATEGORY:	*Single Page/Spread—Design*
TITLE:	*"Setting the Pace"*
AWARD:	*Merit*

170

PUBLICATION:	*Esquire*
ART DIRECTOR:	*April Silver*
DESIGNER:	*Nancy Harris*
ILLUSTRATOR:	*Alison Seiffer*
PUBLISHER:	*Esquire Magazine Group, Inc.*
CATEGORY:	*Single Page/Spread— Illustration*
TITLE:	*"Underground Tests"*
AWARD:	*Merit*

MERIT

USING THE BODY TO MEND THE MIND

Exercise could be a psychiatric wonder drug. In specific doses, combined with psychotherapy, workouts can help with most common ailments. By Dianne Hales and Robert Hales, M.D.

Imagine a drug so powerful it can alter brain chemistry, so versatile it can help prevent or treat many common psychological problems, so safe that moderate doses cause few, if any, side effects and so inexpensive anyone can afford it. For the last few years, doctors and psychotherapists have been experimenting with just such a potential wonder drug—exercise.

Studies are showing that aerobic exercise—the kind that strengthens the heart and lungs—is a practical way to treat the emotional problems of daily living. From depressed men and women in Madison, WI, to driven Type A's in California and anxious students at Harvard, exercise is proving its healing power. It's "the single most effective way to lift a patient's spirits and to restore feelings of potency about all aspects of life," says Harvard

171

PUBLICATION:	*American Health*
ART DIRECTORS:	*Will Hopkins/ Ira Friedlander*
PHOTOGRAPHER:	*Carl Fischer*
PUBLISHER:	*American Health Partners*
CATEGORY:	*Single Page/Spread—Design*
TITLE:	*"Using the Body to Mend the Mind"*
AWARD:	*Merit*

"CLEAN" CALIFORNIA CUISINE

It's an elegant, delicious and simple style of cooking. But is it as healthy as it tastes? By Patricia Lynden

172

PUBLICATION:	*American Health*
ART DIRECTORS:	*Will Hopkins/ Ira Friedlander*
PHOTOGRAPHER:	*Philippe Louis Houze*
PUBLISHER:	*American Health Partners*
CATEGORY:	*Single Page/Spread—Design*
TITLE:	*"Clean California Cuisine"*
AWARD:	*Merit*

GIRLS IN SUITS AT LUNCH

BY DEANNE STILLMAN

Over the first of many strawberry daiquiris they discuss G spots. Then the talk turns to sex

Two women in their early thirties are having lunch at an elegant tearoom. They have known each other since they were roommates at Barnard and consider themselves each other's best friend. Just as the men in their lives suspect, they tell each other everything. Both are now "coming into their own," experiencing the kind of success that was always just around the corner. They handle this in the style characteristic of their friendship: with a sense of humor that has gotten them through many painful moments.

Trish Bryant, once a dedicated tomboy, now a perfect specimen of physical fitness and traditional prettiness, has just been made a junior partner in a prestigious law firm. She sits across the pink-clothed table from the urbanely attractive Jane Lazarus. Jane is taking Trish out to celebrate the publication of Jane's second novel, which has appeared to wild critical acclaim. What Jeff Did is a roman à clef about Dave, her off-and-on-and-off-again boyfriend of the past six years. Jane's calm exterior masks the fact that she is actually an excitable girl.

TRISH: *[Raising drink in toast]* Here's to what Jeff did. I mean Dave.

[They click glasses in toast.]

TRISH: *[Continuing]* What did he do anyway? I mean, we haven't talked in twenty-four hours. You must have left out something.

JANE: Read my book, like everyone else.

TRISH: Okay, sorry. Why do you call him Jeff, anyway?

JANE: Because Dave sounds less final than Jeff. Something about that "F" sound. Also, I wanted to avoid a lawsuit.

TRISH: You mean it's okay as long as you say that Jeff did what Dave really did?

JANE: Well, I haven't heard from Dave yet. Maybe he thinks Jeff is someone else. Anyway, I thought we weren't going to talk about men today. Remember?

TRISH: You're right, we have to operate on the assumption that there are other things in life. Like—

JANE: Men.

[They laugh and make another toast.]

JANE: *[Continuing]* Speaking of which, I'll be right back. I have to make a call.

TRISH: Couldn't you wait?

JANE: Should I?

TRISH: Even if you should, could you?

JANE: I don't know. Would you?

TRISH: *[Exasperated]* Would I what?

JANE: Wait until later to call him.

TRISH: Yes.

[A beat]

JANE: Okay. It's later.

[She rushes off to make the call and returns several minutes later.]

JANE: *[Continuing, as if everything is fine]* Busy. Anyway, we're here to toast your new job. *[Offering toast]* Here's to Schwartz Field Weiss Malign Traduce and Bill. Isn't that the firm that hired you?

TRISH: *[With equal sarcasm]* Thanks a lot. I mean just because we're doing pro bono work for Exxon doesn't mean you have to make remarks like that.

JANE: Sorry. I couldn't resist.

TRISH: It is my job, you know.

JANE: And they did have the good taste to hire you.

[They click glasses in another toast and order another round of strawberry daiquiris.]

TRISH: So what did Jeff, I mean Dave, do? Come on, Jane, spill the beans.

JANE: Well, he did a lot of things, most of which I found extremely irritating.

TRISH: So why were you with him for five years?

JANE: Sex. Because he found my G spot.

TRISH: *[Incredulous]* There's no such thing!

JANE: Oh, yes there is.

TRISH: Where is it?

JANE: Down there somewhere. I can't explain it. Doesn't Robert know what he's doing? Get him to investigate.

TRISH: We're doing just fine, thanks. Anyway, that whole G spot thing worried me. I mean, I don't know if it's such a great idea for women to think that there's another kind of orgasm they're not having.

JANE: Or for men to have to find something new. You know those bras that hook in front? John Kloss for Lily of France?

TRISH: Yeah. I don't like them. They're not very romantic. European women would never wear them.

JANE: Well, I'm American and I'm wearing one right now. Nice *(continued on page 318)*

173

PUBLICATION:	*GQ*
ART DIRECTOR:	*Mary Shanahan*
DESIGNER:	*Margot Frankel*
ILLUSTRATOR:	*Catherine Denvir*
PUBLISHER:	*Condé Nast*
CATEGORY:	*Single Page/Spread—Design*
TITLE:	*"Girls in Suits at Lunch"*
AWARD:	*Merit*

MERIT

174

PUBLICATION: *US*
ART DIRECTOR: *Robert Priest*
DESIGNER: *Janet Waegel*
PHOTOGRAPHER: *Steve Lyne*
PUBLISHER: *Straight Arrow Publications*
CATEGORY: *Single Page/Spread—Design*
TITLE: *"Smooth Operator"*
AWARD: *Merit*

175

PUBLICATION: *US*
ART DIRECTOR: *Robert Priest*
DESIGNER: *Janet Waegel*
PHOTOGRAPHER: *Herb Ritts*
PUBLISHER: *Straight Arrow Publications*
CATEGORY: *Single Page/Spread—Design*
TITLE: *"Private Tina"*
AWARD: *Merit*

176

PUBLICATION: *US*
ART DIRECTOR: *Robert Priest*
DESIGNER: *Janet Waegel*
PHOTOGRAPHER: *Mark Hanauer*
PUBLISHER: *Straight Arrow Publications*
CATEGORY: *Single Page/Spread—Design*
TITLE: *"Toy Boy"*
AWARD: *Merit*

By James McBride

THE MISSION OF ROBERT BLAKE

THE TOUGHEST GUY ON TV PUTS ON A PRIEST'S ROBES—AND TAKES ON 'DYNASTY'

177

PUBLICATION: *US*
ART DIRECTOR: *Robert Priest*
DESIGNER: *Janet Waegel*
PHOTOGRAPHER: *E.J. Camp*
PUBLISHER: *Straight Arrow Publications*
CATEGORY: *Single Page/Spread—Design*
TITLE: *"The Mission of Robert Blake"*
AWARD: *Merit*

A Pair of Aces

MICHAEL & DANNY

THE NINETEEN-YEAR FRIENDSHIP BEHIND 'JEWEL OF THE NILE'

By Fred Schruers

178

PUBLICATION: *US*
ART DIRECTOR: *Robert Priest*
DESIGNER: *Janet Waegel*
PHOTOGRAPHER: *David Montgomery*
PUBLISHER: *Straight Arrow Publications*
CATEGORY: *Single Page/Spread—Design*
TITLE: *"Michael and Danny"*
AWARD: *Merit*

Faces & Places

JULIO'S KIDS • DRAWLING JERRY HALL • PRINCESS CARO-
LINE'S GONDOLA RIDE • SEAN LENNON'S DEEJAY DEBUT
TOM JONES PASSES THE SOAP • SULTRY SYDNEY WALSH

TOP GUNS

179

PUBLICATION: *US*
ART DIRECTOR: *Robert Priest*
DESIGNER: *Janet Waegel*
PHOTOGRAPHERS: *D. Kirkland/Bruce McBroom*
PUBLISHER: *Straight Arrow Publications*
CATEGORY: *Single Page/Spread—Design*
TITLE: *"Top Guns"*
AWARD: *Merit*

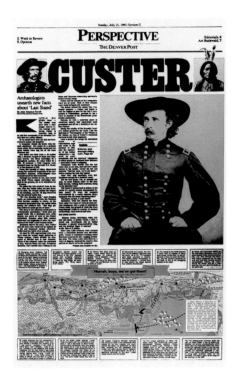

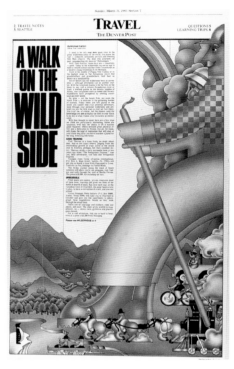

180

PUBLICATION:	*Denver Post*
ART DIRECTOR:	*David Miller*
DESIGNER:	*David Miller*
ILLUSTRATOR:	*David Miller*
PUBLISHER:	*Denver Post*
CATEGORY:	*Single Page/Spread—Design*
TITLE:	*"Custer"*
AWARD:	*Merit*

181

PUBLICATION:	*Denver Post*
ART DIRECTOR:	*David Miller*
DESIGNER:	*David Miller*
ILLUSTRATOR:	*David Miller*
PUBLISHER:	*Denver Post*
CATEGORY:	*Single Page/Spread—Design*
TITLE:	*"Walk on the Wild Side"*
AWARD:	*Merit*

182

PUBLICATION:	*USA Today*
ART DIRECTOR:	*Richard Curtis*
DESIGNER:	*Web Bryant*
ILLUSTRATOR:	*Web Bryant*
PUBLISHER:	*USA Today, Inc.*
CATEGORY:	*Single Page/Spread—Design*
TITLE:	*"Wall Street"*
AWARD:	*Merit*

183

PUBLICATION:	*The Boston Globe Magazine*
ART DIRECTOR:	*Aldona Charlton*
DESIGNER:	*Aldona Charlton*
ILLUSTRATOR:	*Patrick Blackwell*
PUBLISHER:	*The Boston Globe*
CATEGORY:	*Single Page/Spread—Design*
TITLE:	*"A Simple Sensibility"*
AWARD:	*Merit*

184

PUBLICATION:	*The Boston Globe Magazine*
ART DIRECTOR:	*Richard Baker*
DESIGNER:	*Richard Baker*
ILLUSTRATOR:	*Mark Penberthy*
PUBLISHER:	*The Boston Globe*
CATEGORY:	*Single Page/Spread—Design*
TITLE:	*"Thanksgiving"*
AWARD:	*Merit*

185

PUBLICATION:	*The New York Times*
ART DIRECTOR:	*Jerelle Kraus*
DESIGNER:	*Jerelle Kraus*
ILLUSTRATOR:	*Brad Holland*
PUBLISHER:	*The New York Times*
CATEGORY:	*Single Page/Spread— Illustration*
TITLE:	*"Op Ed Page—Moscow"*
AWARD:	*Merit*

MERIT

186

PUBLICATION:	*The Boston Globe Magazine*
ART DIRECTOR:	*Lynn Staley*
DESIGNER:	*Lynn Staley*
ILLUSTRATOR:	*Dagmar Frinta*
PUBLISHER:	*The Boston Globe*
CATEGORY:	*Single Page/Spread—Design*
TITLE:	*"The Fat of the Land"*
AWARD:	*Merit*

187

PUBLICATION:	*The Boston Globe Magazine*
ART DIRECTOR:	*Ronn Campisi*
DESIGNER:	*Ronn Campisi*
ILLUSTRATOR:	*Anthony Russo*
PUBLISHER:	*The Boston Globe*
CATEGORY:	*Single Page/Spread—Design*
TITLE:	*"Against All Odds"*
AWARD:	*Merit*

188

PUBLICATION:	*The Boston Globe Magazine*
ART DIRECTOR:	*Lynn Staley*
DESIGNER:	*Lynn Staley*
ILLUSTRATOR:	*Various*
PUBLISHER:	*The Boston Globe*
CATEGORY:	*Single Page/Spread—Design*
TITLE:	*"Good Heavens"*
AWARD:	*Merit*

189

PUBLICATION:	*The Boston Globe Magazine*
ART DIRECTOR:	*Ronn Campisi*
DESIGNER:	*Ronn Campisi*
ILLUSTRATOR:	*Anthony Russo*
PUBLISHER:	*The Boston Globe*
CATEGORY:	*Single Page/Spread—Design*
TITLE:	*"Dinner at Aunt Fred's"*
AWARD:	*Merit*

MERIT

190

PUBLICATION:	*The Boston Globe Magazine*
ART DIRECTOR:	*Ronn Campisi*
DESIGNER:	*Ronn Campisi*
ILLUSTRATOR:	*Anita Kunz*
PUBLISHER:	*The Boston Globe*
CATEGORY:	*Single Page/Spread—Design*
TITLE:	*"The Cast-Iron Lady"*
AWARD:	*Merit*

191

PUBLICATION:	*The Boston Globe Magazine*
ART DIRECTOR:	*Lynn Staley*
DESIGNER:	*Lynn Staley*
ILLUSTRATOR:	*Vivienne Flescher*
PUBLISHER:	*The Boston Globe*
CATEGORY:	*Single Page/Spread—Design*
TITLE:	*"The American Wife"*
AWARD:	*Merit*

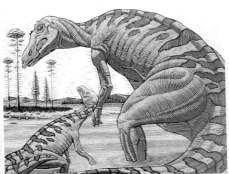

192

PUBLICATION:	*The Boston Globe Magazine*
ART DIRECTOR:	*Lynn Staley*
DESIGNER:	*Lynn Staley*
ILLUSTRATOR:	*Doug Smith*
PUBLISHER:	*The Boston Globe*
CATEGORY:	*Single Page/Spread—Design*
TITLE:	*"The Social Life of Dinosaurs"*
AWARD:	*Merit*

193

PUBLICATION:	*The Boston Globe Magazine*
ART DIRECTOR:	*Ronn Campisi*
DESIGNER:	*Ronn Campisi*
ILLUSTRATOR:	*Alexa Grace*
PUBLISHER:	*The Boston Globe*
CATEGORY:	*Single Page/Spread—Design*
TITLE:	*"Garage Artist"*
AWARD:	*Merit*

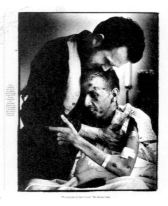

194

PUBLICATION:	*The Boston Globe Magazine*
ART DIRECTOR:	*Lynn Staley*
DESIGNER:	*Lynn Staley*
PHOTOGRAPHER:	*Keith Jenkins*
PUBLISHER:	*The Boston Globe*
CATEGORY:	*Single Page/Spread—Design*
TITLE:	*"The Poor Get Poorer"*
AWARD:	*Merit*

195

PUBLICATION:	*The Boston Globe Magazine*
ART DIRECTOR:	*Ronn Campisi*
DESIGNER:	*Ronn Campisi*
PHOTOGRAPHER:	*Janet Knott*
PUBLISHER:	*The Boston Globe*
CATEGORY:	*Single Page/Spread—Design*
TITLE:	*"AIDS"*
AWARD:	*Merit*

196

PUBLICATION:	*The Boston Globe Magazine*
ART DIRECTOR:	*Lynn Staley*
DESIGNER:	*Lynn Staley*
ILLUSTRATOR:	*Lou Beach*
PUBLISHER:	*The Boston Globe*
CATEGORY:	*Single Page/Spread—Design*
TITLE:	*"Silence"*
AWARD:	*Merit*

197

PUBLICATION:	*The Boston Globe Magazine*
ART DIRECTOR:	*Lynn Staley*
DESIGNER:	*Lynn Staley*
ILLUSTRATOR:	*Anthony Russo*
PUBLISHER:	*The Boston Globe*
CATEGORY:	*Single Page/Spread—Design*
TITLE:	*"The Boston Globe Photo Awards, 1985"*
AWARD:	*Merit*

198

PUBLICATION:	*Daily News Magazine*
ART DIRECTORS:	*Janet Froelich/ Randy Dunbar*
DESIGNER:	*Randy Dunbar*
ILLUSTRATOR:	*Dave Shannon*
PUBLISHER:	*New York News*
CATEGORY:	*Single Page/Spread— Illustration*
TITLE:	*"Topless Girl"*
AWARD:	*Merit*

199

PUBLICATION:	*Daily News Magazine*
ART DIRECTORS:	*Janet Froelich/Tom Ruis*
DESIGNER:	*Tom Ruis*
ILLUSTRATOR:	*Matt Mahurin*
PUBLISHER:	*New York News*
CATEGORY:	*Single Page/Spread— Illustration*
TITLE:	*"Generation Gap"*
AWARD:	*Merit*

200

PUBLICATION:	*Daily News Magazine*
ART DIRECTOR:	*Janet Froelich*
DESIGNER:	*Zoe Brotman*
PHOTOGRAPHER:	*Ken Korotkin*
PUBLISHER:	*New York News*
CATEGORY:	*Single Page/Spread—Design*
TITLE:	*"The Hoax of Higbee Beach"*
AWARD:	*Merit*

201

PUBLICATION:	*Daily News Magazine*
ART DIRECTOR:	*Janet Froelich*
DESIGNER:	*Janet Froelich*
ILLUSTRATOR:	*Robert Risko*
PUBLISHER:	*New York News*
CATEGORY:	*Single Page/Spread—Design*
TITLE:	*"Soup for Supper"*
AWARD:	*Merit*

PEE WEE HERMAN

SMALLER THAN LIFE

GUESS WHAT, BOYS AND girls, did I have a day and a half yesterday! Know what I did? I went to the Catcht Himself! It was on order! Boy was that ever haute! All these rich people huffing and puffing and casting their luggage, their own luggage! Know what else? Art Carney came down in the elevator and then I thought of Ed Norton — and boy, did I last her harder ha! ha! He mailed a letter at the lobby box! That was kind of funny, too! Then I went upstairs, to a suite on the 12th floor! Then I interviewed Pee Wee Herman! What a joke.

Pee Wee Herman is sort of a moron. Well, not sort of, he is. He appeals to other morons, masses of them, apparently, as well in some crude and cranky people like David Letterman, who has him on his show every now and then, just so Pee Wee can make a fool of himself, which he does with distressing regularity.

Pee Wee Herman specializes in flagrant juvenilia: plastic doo-doos, rubber frogs, silly wings, giant underpants and bags of surprises, most of which can predictably be found in the 5-and-10. He wears a funny suit, two sizes too small, sometimes glen plaid, sometimes plain gray, a white shirt and a little red bow tie. He has a crewcut and looks like Peter Lorre in his pre-pudgy period; he also looks like Garry Moore on angel dust. He also looks like Fisky Lee. Vroom vroom. He says he is a comic, but I don't know. He sometimes sports a fake voice like Gilda Radner's Lisa Loprist, and when I hear Pee Wee, I think of Lisa's more celebrated line: that's so funny I forgot to laugh.

With Pee Wee, as with a great many rising young stars, drive replaces talent, calculation replaces inspiration. Pee Wee Herman is just one more signpost on the long stretch of banality that winds through

ment of pop culture these days. His greatest talent is for being in the right place at the right time: MTV on New Year's Eve, the "Tonight" show, HBO, and now, alas, a movie "Pee Wee Goes to Hollywood." It is probably a good thing that Pee Wee Herman is moving in his own movie, for show-biz physics has it that the faster things run, the quicker they fall. Let us pray that this is so.

When I was in college, everyone went nuts over Snoopy fades; after class, undergrads would race back to the dorm to catch Snoopy's show, which wasn't just for kids. Little tykes liked the puppets and the characters and the silly things that Snoopy did, but the teenagers got off on Snoopy's sly wisecracks and smartsy innuendo. Now Pee Wee Herman is doing much the same thing, only this time around the sly innuendo is prime and the modless music energy simply baffles. Is this what they call a barrel of laugh? Watching Pee Wee's HBO special is an insufferable act of masochism that only the most drugged-out, burnt-out, washed-out low-level sociological spectators could withstand. This is Pee Wee's craft: parlaying a smaller-than-life persona into the ranks of high-level publicity, anything you read about Pee Wee Herman is testimony only to the efforts of his publicist, Bobby Zarem, whose press releases are quoted verbatim in gossip columns around town. Now that's talent.

Still, Pee Wee Herman is a human being (that information is based on reliable sources), and even though he never does interviews out of character, journalists get briefed before they walk through the door as though Pee Wee were the effing Prez of the U.S. I suppose we must give the man his due, out of compassion, if nothing else—and believe me there is nothing else.

Pee Wee in person looks poignant and pathetic. He has beautiful finger-

long, knobby, delicate. He wants to talk widely about his forthcoming movie; he is here expressly for that purpose and refuses to discuss any details of what might be a private life. We already know his real name is Paul Reubens, that he is 31 years old give or take, grew up in Florida and against New York before moving to California, where his brand of ersatz humor, devoid of wit, charm or intelligence, flourishes. He likes the La Brea tarpits. But mostly he likes to talk about how exciting it is to do a movie, as if no one in the history of fame has ever said that before. And he told me to tell you he hopes you will support that movie, so he can go on to do bigger and better things. Truly noted.

The verbal souvenirs he left on any tape recorder, during those few times I was able to steer him away from using the words "exciting" and "movie" in the same breath, included the news that his mother and father went to radio but Pee Wee performed, and it wasn't long before he made his first memorable appearance:

"The first show I was on was 'The Dating Game.' I was on three times. The first two times I lost a trip to Acapulco and somewhere else exotic. Then the third time I won a date right near my house. The girl I went out with got engaged about a week later. I guess I drove her into the arms of someone else."

Pee Wee still loves TV, old TV on the Christian Breakfast Network:

"It plays all the old comedy shows: 'I Married Joan,' 'My Little Margie,' 'Bachelor Father,' 'The Phil Silvers Show,' 'The Jack Benny Show.' That stuff was better, funnier and cruder than anything happening today. I don't like a lot of what's on now, I prefer to live in the past, so far in that stuff goes. I think that comedy is moving back to things from the heart. That may sound sorry, but a lot of what I do is continued on page 16

BY SUSIN SHAPIRO

202

PUBLICATION: *Daily News Magazine*
ART DIRECTOR: *Janet Froelich*
DESIGNERS: *Janet Froelich/*
Zoe Brotman
PHOTOGRAPHER: *Janette Beckman*
PUBLISHER: *New York News*
CATEGORY: *Single Page/Spread—Design*
TITLE: *"PeeWee Herman:*
Smaller Than Life"
AWARD: *Merit*

ACT III

Say what you will about his mayoralty, Koch is still the best show in town.

BY PETE HAMILL

> "It is the mask only
> that we dread and hate;
> the man may have
> something human
> about him."
> —WILLIAM HAZLITT

When at last the great performances is over and Edward I. Koch has left the New York stage, history will judge his genius. In my imperfect opinion, he is the most extraordinary mayor of the 20th century, eclipsing even Fiorello La Guardia in his impact on our daily lives. That is not to say that he has been the greatest mayor; the New Yorkers to come will differ, and I'll say that's accolade will always belong to Fiorello.

But nobody, nor his enemies, nor even historians laboring in dusty rooms, can deny that Koch has been the supreme New York political actor of the era, brilliant, infuriating, hilarious, morose, brutal, petty, generous, vicious, vulgar, contagious, devious, insurrectpalile.

He doesn't perform this dazzling act behind closed doors, privately battering his subordinates while calling up the angels in public (although those who pledged their lives from their closest unto the wayside since he took office almost eight years ago). Koch does his act in public. And he does it basically for television. One reason for his powerful impact on New York is obviously The Tube. Fiorello might have been a spectacular star on television; Jimmy Walker could have dazzled his audience; Bill O'Dwyer perhaps could have charmed voter multitudes. But they didn't have television and Koch does.

The Tube demands performance and that suggests the core of the man's genius. Historians might eventually agree that Koch made a basic decision early in his first term (and possibly before taking office) that New York truly was ungovernable. It was simply too huge, too addled, too structural and marginal and diverse, too broken into warring factions, too dramatical control of the city had been taken from the mayor's office by Big Mac and other institutions as a result of the fiscal

crisis. The mayor had no control of the Board of Education. He could do nothing about the subways because the MTA was run by Albany. He couldn't even force civil servants to live in the city that paid them and which they were supposed to serve; that power, too, resided in Albany.

But if Koch couldn't govern New York City, he could entertain it. And entertain New York he most certainly has.

Here is Koch, yelling "I am not Billy Budd! Billy Budd was a schmuck!" Here is Koch walking out on 1,000 middle-class Catholics in Queens because he wanted to make a two-minute opening speech at a debate and the presiding clergyman would give him only one. "They've got a Langston court in there and I don't happen to be a hangover!" Here is Koch saying at a synagogue that Ariour Sadat was the only statesman left on earth, getting booed, and telling the congregation, "Awww, shut up . . ." Koch appears during a snowstorm: "I believe that God is testing me. But what are we going to do when they need lozenge?" He asking people at a rally to raise their hands if they supported John Lindsay (when Koch supported when he was a Greenwich Village district leader) and then bellowing at them "DUMMIES!"

He stops on stage and draws the sword of rhetoric, and when he is through, someone is lying wounded and thousands of others are either angry or consoled. He has offended, continued on next page

---

203

PUBLICATION: *Daily News Magazine*
ART DIRECTOR: *Janet Froelich*
DESIGNER: *Janet Froelich*
PHOTOGRAPHER: *David Burnett*
PUBLISHER: *New York News*
CATEGORY: *Single Page/Spread—Design*
TITLE: *"Act III"*
AWARD: *Merit*

It's a crewel, crewel world, but bravery is rewarded. Eighties humble: a cheerful number of brass. Hebru jacket, $43, from New Republic, 13 Greene St. Pins from: New Republic, Larry Vrba, Bumblebish, Paulette Brooks, Detail, Sweet Romance, Joe Michaels, and Philip Fletcher. Rings from Suzanne Berkley; earrings, Detail; hat, Idiom.

The new baroque splash, right, in Coral Horn's crewel blazer, $250, and gold-lame shirt, $85, Macy's. Pin, Erart, Iowko pearls, Charles Marchand, pearls with stones, Domini Hammy; earrings, Richard Minoden. Far right, shirt, $45, shirt, $76, all by Falling Around, at Bonnie Saba in Woodmere. Earrings, David Raney; pin-necklace, Richard Minoden.

204

PUBLICATION: *Daily News Magazine*
ART DIRECTOR: *Janet Froelich*
DESIGNERS: *Janet Froelich/Zoe Brotman*
PHOTOGRAPHER: *Bob Murray*
PUBLISHER: *New York News*
CATEGORY: *Single Page/Spread—*
Photography
TITLE: *"New Wave Yuppie—Crewel"*
AWARD: *Merit*

DIARY OF A CANCER PATIENT

By Nathan Perlmutter

Nathan Perlmutter in his office at the Anti-Defamation League of B'nai B'rith. Just before entering a hospital for treatment, he wrote, "I feel that I'm on a ship, waiting to wade ashore and engage in battle."

205

PUBLICATION: *The New York Times Magazine*
ART DIRECTOR: *Ken Kendrick*
DESIGNER: *Kevin McPhee*
PHOTOGRAPHER: *Jeanne Strongin*
PUBLISHER: *The New York Times*
CATEGORY: *Single Page/Spread—Photography*
TITLE: *"Diary of a Cancer Patient"*
AWARD: *Merit*

The scene in East New Orleans, La. Two recent Vietnamese immigrants go home at dusk after working in their gardens.

206

PUBLICATION: *The New York Times Magazine*
ART DIRECTOR: *Ken Kendrick*
DESIGNER: *Ken Kendrick*
PHOTOGRAPHER: *Sara Krylwich*
PUBLISHER: *The New York Times*
CATEGORY: *Single Page/Spread—Photography*
TITLE: *"Vietnam"*
AWARD: *Merit*

Greene in his apartment in Antibes. He is not working now and says "I'm afraid of living too long away from writing."

THE SOUL-SEARCHING CONTINUES FOR GRAHAM GREENE

By John Vinocur

The celebrated writer, whose new book is a long-forgotten novella, still dwells on doubt and failure.

The English novelist as a toddler. He was born in 1904, the son of a headmaster.

207

PUBLICATION: *The New York Times Magazine*
ART DIRECTOR: *Ken Kendrick*
DESIGNER: *Diana LaGuardia*
PHOTOGRAPHER: *David Montgomery*
PUBLISHER: *The New York Times*
CATEGORY: *Single Page/Spread—Photography*
TITLE: *"Graham Greene"*
AWARD: *Merit*

EATING WITH THEIR MOUTHS OPEN

LISTENING IN ON THE IRREVERENT TABLE TALK OF THE GOURMET CLUB

208

PUBLICATION:	*The New York Times Magazine*
ART DIRECTOR:	*Tom Bodkin*
DESIGNER:	*Tom Bodkin*
ILLUSTRATOR:	*Victor Juhasz*
PUBLISHER:	*The New York Times*
CATEGORY:	*Single Page/Spread—Illustration*
TITLE:	*"World of New York—Gourmet Club"*
AWARD:	*Merit*

On BOXING

By Joyce Carol Oates

If boxing is a sport, it is the most tragic of sports.

209

PUBLICATION:	*The New York Times Magazine*
ART DIRECTOR:	*Ken Kendrick*
DESIGNER:	*Audrone Razgaitis*
ILLUSTRATOR:	*Harvey Dinnerstein*
PHOTOGRAPHER:	*Jules Allen*
PUBLISHER:	*The New York Times*
CATEGORY:	*Single Page/Spread—Illustration*
TITLE:	*"Boxing"*
AWARD:	*Merit*

RISING ISLANDERS OF BED-STUY

THE WEST INDIAN ZEST TO "BUY HOUSE" REJUVENATES A COMMUNITY

BY PAULE MARSHALL

THE ENTIRE CARIBBEAN ARCHIPELAGO IS FLOWERING ALONG FULTON AND NOSTRAND

210

PUBLICATION:	*The New York Times Magazine*
ART DIRECTOR:	*Tom Bodkin*
DESIGNER:	*Tom Bodkin*
ILLUSTRATOR:	*Toussaint Auguste*
PUBLISHER:	*The New York Times*
CATEGORY:	*Single Page/Spread—Illustration*
TITLE:	*"World of New York—West Indian"*
AWARD:	*Merit*

211

PUBLICATION:	*The New York Times Magazine*
ART DIRECTOR:	*Ken Kendrick*
DESIGNER:	*Audrone Razgaitis*
ILLUSTRATOR:	*Robert Goldstrom*
PUBLISHER:	*The New York Times*
CATEGORY:	*Single Page/Spread—Illustration*
TITLE:	*"About Men—Nicknames"*
AWARD:	*Merit*

212

PUBLICATION:	*The New York Times Magazine*
ART DIRECTOR:	*Ken Kendrick*
DESIGNER:	*Richard Samperi*
PHOTOGRAPHER:	*Michael Geiger*
PUBLISHER:	*The New York Times*
CATEGORY:	*Single Page/Spread—Design*
TITLE:	*"Cranberries"*
AWARD:	*Merit*

213

PUBLICATION:	*The New York Times Magazine*
ART DIRECTOR:	*Tom Bodkin*
DESIGNER:	*Tom Bodkin*
ILLUSTRATOR:	*Edward Gorey*
PUBLISHER:	*The New York Times*
CATEGORY:	*Single Page/Spread—Illustration*
TITLE:	*"Sophisticated Traveler/Back Home"*
AWARD:	*Merit*

214

PUBLICATION:	*The New York Times Magazine*
ART DIRECTOR:	*Ken Kendrick*
DESIGNER:	*Audrone Razgaitis*
PHOTOGRAPHER:	*Benno Friedman*
PUBLISHER:	*The New York Times*
CATEGORY:	*Single Page/Spread—Photography*
TITLE:	*"David Byrne"*
AWARD:	*Merit*

MERIT

TRUE VIRTUE

The author
says he's had
his fill of the
'virtucrat,' that
prig with cold
contempt for all
who disagree
with him.

215

PUBLICATION: *The New York Times Magazine*
ART DIRECTOR: *Ken Kendrick*
DESIGNER: *Kevin McPhee*
ILLUSTRATOR: *Peter de Seve*
PUBLISHER: *The New York Times*
CATEGORY: *Single Page/Spread—*
                 Illustration
TITLE: *"True Virtue"*
AWARD: *Merit*

WHO RUNS NEW YORK NOW?

216

PUBLICATION: *The New York Times Magazine*
ART DIRECTOR: *Tom Bodkin*
DESIGNER: *Tom Bodkin*
ILLUSTRATOR: *Mark Penberthy*
PUBLISHER: *The New York Times*
CATEGORY: *Single Page/Spread—*
                 Illustration
TITLE: *"Sophisticated Traveler—*
                 New York Now"
AWARD: *Merit*

First of a series

FEDERAL JUDGE PRENTICE H. MARSHALL
...speaks out on crowded courts, crooked lawyers, and justice delayed.

217

PUBLICATION: *Chicago*
ART DIRECTOR: *Bob Post*
DESIGNER: *Bob Post*
PHOTOGRAPHER: *Dennis Manarchy*
PUBLISHER: *WFMT, Inc.*
CATEGORY: *Single Page/Spread—*
                 Photography
TITLE: *"Federal Judge Prentice*
                 H. Marshall"
AWARD: *Merit*

218

PUBLICATION:	*New York*
ART DIRECTOR:	*Robert Best*
DESIGNER:	*Robert Best*
PHOTOGRAPHER:	*Oberto Gili*
PUBLISHER:	*Murdoch Magazines*
CATEGORY:	*Single Page/Spread—Photography*
TITLE:	*"Intimate Details"*
AWARD:	*Merit*

219

PUBLICATION:	*Florida Trend*
ART DIRECTOR:	*Steve Duckett*
DESIGNER:	*Gary Bernloehr*
ILLUSTRATOR:	*Peter de Seve*
PUBLISHER:	*Florida Trend*
CATEGORY:	*Single Page/Spread—Illustration*
TITLE:	*"Private Banking"*
AWARD:	*Merit*

220

PUBLICATION:	*Florida Trend*
ART DIRECTOR:	*Steve Duckett*
DESIGNER:	*Michael Bilicki*
ILLUSTRATOR:	*Rob Day*
PUBLISHER:	*Florida Trend*
CATEGORY:	*Single Page/Spread—Illustration*
TITLE:	*"Falling Dollar"*
AWARD:	*Merit*

221

PUBLICATION:	*Money*
ART DIRECTOR:	*Ellen Blissman*
DESIGNER:	*Dan Taylor*
ILLUSTRATOR:	*John Craig*
PUBLISHER:	*Time Inc.*
CATEGORY:	*Single Page/Spread—Illustration*
TITLE:	*"AT&T after the Big Bang"*
AWARD:	*Merit*

Spending

A Little Disk Music

This 4¾-inch prodigy plays 74 minutes on a single side and is relatively kidproof. But the price is far from pint-size.

by Steven J. Forbis

222

PUBLICATION:	*Money*
ART DIRECTOR:	*Ellen Blissman*
DESIGNER:	*Ellen Blissman*
PHOTOGRAPHER:	*Hal Davis*
PUBLISHER:	*Time Inc.*
CATEGORY:	*Single Page/Spread—Photography*
TITLE:	*"A Little Disk Music"*
AWARD:	*Merit*

Clevelander Reuben Sturman rode the wild fantasies of
a new morality to conquer his global X-rated empire,
but it is the real world of international finance and taxes
that threatens to bring him down.

PRINCE of PORN

BY EDWARD P. WHELAN

223

PUBLICATION:	*Cleveland Magazine*
ART DIRECTOR:	*Gary Sluzewski*
DESIGNER:	*Gary Sluzewski*
ILLUSTRATOR:	*Matt Mahurin*
CATEGORY:	*Single Page/Spread—Design*
TITLE:	*"Prince of Porn"*
AWARD:	*Merit*

MERIT

THE FLAK CATCHERS

Hill & Knowlton's Dick
Cheney has pulled many a PR stunt
on behalf of his clients. Can he
do the same for his firm?

BY JOHN TAYLOR

It was simple, indisputable: the worst scandal in the Bank of Boston's 200-year history. In early February, the bank pleaded guilty to failing to report $1.2 billion in cash transfers to Swiss banks and was fined $500,000. Two weeks later, bank officials conceded that the bank may have inadvertently allowed members of an alleged organized-crime family to launder as much as $2 million through a branch in Boston's North End. The bank argued that the transgressions had occurred because of "judgment errors by personnel." Nothing serious, the bankers seemed to think. No big deal.

But the press had gone berserk with the story. The New England papers always had their knives out for the bank, and their wretchedly excessive reporting was to be expected. But The New York Times and The Wall Street Journal were also playing the story on page one. Even television, where business pieces usually just pad the dead seconds before commercials, was hyping it to the hilt. The whole situation had a nightmarish quality. It was enough to make the bankers think of taking The Big Leap.

One of their problems, the bank officials came to agree, was a failure to communicate. It was a public relations problem. By mid-February the bank had

called Dick Cheney and asked him to fly in and help put out the fire.

Richard L. Cheney is vice chairman of Hill & Knowlton, which until recently was the largest public relations agency in existence. Cheney is also head of H&K's financial relations department, and for a long time he was widely considered the preeminent public relations specialist in corporate crises. Cheney practically invented the field of public relations during hostile takeovers. He had been involved in one of the first big corporate battles of the postwar era, the Mutchison brothers' proxy fight with Allegheny Corp.); in the largest (T. Boone Pickens's assault on Gulf Oil); and in the messiest (Bendix Corp.'s disastrous effort to acquire Martin Marietta).

But it had been a while since Cheney—and Hill & Knowlton—had racked up a major victory. In fact, in some respects, the past year had been almost embarrassing. Cheney was hired by Walt Disney Productions last summer when Saul Steinberg made his now-notorious bid for the studio. But the takeover, between Cheney and the Disney executives was poor. Cheney was frozen out of the important strategy discussions. Shortly thereafter, Pickens, for whom the firm had worked during previous battles, abruptly shucked Hill & Knowlton

for Kekst & Co. Cheney and Gershon Kekst are not merely the two most prominent PR agents specializing in hostile takeovers. They are virtually the only men. Bitter rivals, they have appeared on opposite sides in almost all recent corporate contests. But Pickens's unexpected departure left Hill & Knowlton sitting on the sidelines for the most exciting takeover plus last fall: Pickens's run at Phillips Petroleum Company.

As if that were not bad enough, last year Burson-Marsteller decisively seized Hill & Knowlton's crown as the world's largest public relations company. Officially, Hill & Knowlton executives argued that comparisons between the two companies were meaningless because of their radically different business mix. But privately, the firm reeled from the blow. "It was a shock," says one H&K executive. "It was taken to heart. In many of us, and in a very personal way, by Dick Cheney."

People began to wonder. Was Hill & Knowlton's luster fading? And was Cheney, at the age of 63, beginning to lose his touch? "They've been getting mixed reviews from us," says an executive at a large investment bank. Even Cheney

For chairman Cheney unwinds at home by practicing yoga

Photograph by George Lange

224

PUBLICATION: *Manhattan, inc.*
ART DIRECTOR: *Nancy Butkus*
DESIGNER: *Nancy Butkus*
PHOTOGRAPHER: *George Lange*
PUBLISHER: *Metrocorp*
CATEGORY: *Single Page/Spread—*
Photography
TITLE: *"The Flak Catchers"*
AWARD: *Merit*

THE BIG PICTURE   Con Ed Considered

On September 5, 1882, the "Miscellaneous City News" section of the *Times* reported that Thomas Edison's electric company successfully lit up one square mile of Manhattan. In 1936 "Consolidated" joined with "Edison" to reflect the acquisition, dissolution, and merger of some 170 companies.

In 1984 Con Ed produced 36 billion kilowatt hours of electricity, 28 billion pounds of steam, and 98.3 billion cubic feet of gas. Con Ed is paid to be powerful, and those numbers are large too. $5.7 billion in 1984 revenues, with a net income of $620 million. Earnings per share were $4.48 in 1984. The 200,000 common stockholders—some 30 percent are Con Ed customers—earned $2.12 a share in dividends. At recent prices, that would be worth about $7,000.

—Nina Liu

ILLUSTRATION BY STANISLAW ZAGARSKI

225

PUBLICATION: *Manhattan, inc.*
ART DIRECTOR: *Nancy Butkus*
DESIGNER: *Gina Davis*
ILLUSTRATOR: *Stanislawz Zagarski*
PUBLISHER: *Metrocorp*
CATEGORY: *Single Page/Spread—*
Illustration
TITLE: *"Con Ed Considered"*
AWARD: *Merit*

Southern District of New York: Rudolph Giuliani. "It isn't a justification it was you need to create a cloth fund so you can pay bribes. That would be like saying that, in order to run an office, I'm going to pay off congressmen, senators, and other public officials. The justification is you need: 'If we don't pay people off, and we don't cheat, we won't be able to do business.' Ritch is that the case. If you don't pay people off and don't cheat the government out of taxes, you're not unable to run a business. You're just not able to make a gigantic profit so that you can live in three or four homes, have four or five cars, and have millions of dollars to put in the bank. You're not talking about people that are paying low survival. They're paying murders the millionaires."

While news of the case flashed through the street, Markel the day moved from a prison hospital in the Midwest to the federal prison at Danbury, Conn., where Max was being held. Since he'd gone behind bars, Max had kept to himself, living in a shuttered cell and helping to turn out T-shirts in the prison's textile factory. He became more and more withdrawn.

Max wrote to the judge asking to help get out. "My whole life has fallen apart because of my stupidity. I feel like someone about to have a nervous breakdown. My appetite has diminished greatly, and I'm continuously walking and unable to

sleep, and am haunted by my mistake.

After all the millions they had held in their hands, the government wanted everything—from the Walburtons' clothing and Wyann bohus on the telephones of Max's children owned. Appraisers put price tags on most of their possessions and dumped them in a warehouse while Hodes and the IRS decided how to set up the pile.

"Max may have left his life in escrow," says Max. "Five years in jail is a long, long time.

It was until October, the leaves were beginning to turn in western Connecticut. About 5:30 a.m. on October 14, while his father was still sleeping, Max got up from his cot and took a walk around the exercise yard. He had several prison gowns belts with him, and he carefully tied them together and slipped them around a low branch of a tall oak tree.

He was 35.

In New York the following day, the judge called Alexander Walburne, his lawyer, before him. "I am granting your request for a shortened sentence," the judge told the attorneys. "It was freed the next day.

It, turned his son after that afternoon.

Peter Wilkinson is an associate reporter at Fairfield Publications.

226

PUBLICATION: *Manhattan, inc.*
ART DIRECTOR: *Nancy Butkus*
DESIGNER: *Janet Waegel*
ILLUSTRATOR: *Marc Tauss*
PUBLISHER: *Metrocorp*
CATEGORY: *Single Page/Spread—*
Illustration
TITLE: *"The Thin Man"*
AWARD: *Merit*

MERIT

227

PUBLICATION:	*Town & Country*
ART DIRECTOR:	*Melissa Tardiff*
DESIGNER:	*Mary Rosen*
PHOTOGRAPHER:	*Ronnie Kaufmann*
PUBLISHER:	*Hearst Corporation*
CATEGORY:	*Single Page/Spread—Design*
TITLE:	*"The Royal Blues"*
AWARD:	*Merit*

228

PUBLICATION:	*Town & Country*
ART DIRECTOR:	*Melissa Tardiff*
DESIGNER:	*Richard Turtletaub*
PHOTOGRAPHER:	*Matthew Klein*
PUBLISHER:	*Hearst Corporation*
CATEGORY:	*Single Page/Spread—Design*
TITLE:	*"Gold"*
AWARD:	*Merit*

229

PUBLICATION:	*Mother Jones*
ART DIRECTOR:	*Louise Kollenbaum*
DESIGNER:	*Dian-Aziza Ooka*
PHOTOGRAPHER:	*William Albert Allard*
PUBLISHER:	*Foundation for National Progress*
CATEGORY:	*Single Page/Spread—Design*
TITLE:	*"Cowboy Poets"*
AWARD:	*Merit*

EAVESDROPPING ON

WASHINGTON

BY BOB DEVINE

Ozzie Janson almost made it back to school this term. After walking out on Econ 201 last semester and subsequently drifting through San Francisco, he suddenly showed up again on campus. Unfortunately, he never made it past registration. He got the shakes at the door to the gym and fled, muttering something about Washington, D.C., being the only place for a political-science major like himself to learn the inner workings of government.

I felt like a zombie. Me, Ozzie the Terribly Dressed, scourge of the fashion world, and there I was all decked out in a borrowed pin-stripe suit that cost more than my car. What was really weird, I loved it. Wearing the get-up made me feel confident, powerful even.

Standing in a subway car on the Washington Metro system and straightening my cuff links, I looked around at the masses and sneered: *Mess with me, turkeys, and my lawyers will cut your hearts out.* The Metro, Washington's fast, cheap mass-transit system, was the perfect place to strut my stuff because everybody was there: lawyers.

230

PUBLICATION: *America*
ART DIRECTOR: *Linda Evans*
DESIGNER: *Evelyn Ellis*
PHOTOGRAPHERS: *R. Hamilton Smith/
David Luttrell*
PUBLISHER: *13-30 Corporation*
CATEGORY: *Single Page/Spread—Design*
TITLE: *"Eavesdropping on
Washington"*
AWARD: *Merit*

SERVERS
on the
ROCKS

Faced with increasing public pressure to get drunks off the roads, servers are being forced to decide how much is too much.

Article by
Vince Rause
Illustration by
Matt Mahurin

ooking back, Steve Morris believes that he and his staff did all they could to try to stop "Baz" Bastein, general manager of the Pittsburgh Penguins hockey club, from driving home that night. Bastein had attended a hockey writers' banquet held at Froggy's, Morris's popular saloon located in Pittsburgh's Market Square, and when bar manager Keith Hammet saw him knock over drinks at his table, he intervened and Bastein was shut off.

Morris himself repeatedly offered to call a cab for Bastein, but the offers were refused. When Bastein left the

231

PUBLICATION: *Tables*
ART DIRECTOR: *Shelley Williams*
DESIGNER: *Blair Caplinger*
ILLUSTRATOR: *Matt Mahurin*
PUBLISHER: *13-30 Corporation*
CATEGORY: *Single Page/Spread—
Illustration*
TITLE: *"Servers on the Rocks"*
AWARD: *Merit*

Customer Essay

The Joy of
SERVING
ME

A real jokester reveals why servers think he's the ideal customer.

232

PUBLICATION: *Tables*
ART DIRECTOR: *Shelley Williams*
DESIGNER: *Sara Christensen*
ILLUSTRATOR: *Richard McNeel*
PUBLISHER: *13-30 Corporation*
CATEGORY: *Single Page/Spread—
Illustration*
TITLE: *"The Joy of Serving Me"*
AWARD: *Merit*

MERIT

A LONG TIME GONE

He's been called rock's favorite
threat to society. But David Crosby
is a bigger threat to himself.

*He hates being an addict. He fights it
as much as he can, and I know that
he knows he's losing. He has a self-
hatred deeper than any man I've ever
known. He looks in the mirror and
sees a guy who is fat, ugly and forty-
five. He only sees the self he chooses
to see. This is not anything he's enjoying. This is not a joke. He's sick.*
*Freebasing is the worst addiction.
It's not too late for him to come back
from a bad problem, to be very strong.*
— GRAHAM NASH

BY MARK CHRISTENSEN

PHOTOGRAPH BY NORMAN SEEFF

236

PUBLICATION: *Rolling Stone*
ART DIRECTOR: *Derek W. Ungless*
DESIGNER: *Raul Martinez*
PHOTOGRAPHER: *Norman Seeff*
PUBLISHER: *Straight Arrow Publications*
CATEGORY: *Single Page/Spread—*
Photography
TITLE: *"A Long Time Gone"*
AWARD: *Merit*

Behind Schwarzenegger's brawn, there's brainpower you can bank on

PUMPING ARNOLD

By Nancy Collins

237

PUBLICATION: *Rolling Stone*
ART DIRECTOR: *Derek W. Ungless*
DESIGNER: *Derek W. Ungless*
PHOTOGRAPHER: *Moshe Brakea*
PUBLISHER: *Straight Arrow Publications*
CATEGORY: *Single Page/Spread—*
Photography
TITLE: *"Pumping Arnold"*
AWARD: *Merit*

THE PLAGUE YEARS

BY DAVID BLACK

*He belonged to that race…whose ideal is manly precisely because their
temperament is feminine, and who in ordinary life resemble other men in
appearance only…a race upon which a curse is laid….Their love…springs
not from an ideal of beauty…but from an incurable disease….*

MARCEL PROUST
Cities of the Plain

PROLOGUE: MAGNA MORTALITAS

ILLUSTRATION *by* MATT MAHURIN

238

PUBLICATION: *Rolling Stone*
ART DIRECTOR: *Derek W. Ungless*
DESIGNER: *Derek W. Ungless*
ILLUSTRATOR: *Matt Mahurin*
PUBLISHER: *Straight Arrow Publications*
CATEGORY: *Single Page/Spread—Design*
TITLE: *"The Plague Years"*
AWARD: *Merit*

239

PUBLICATION:	*Rolling Stone*
ART DIRECTOR:	*Derek W. Ungless*
DESIGNER:	*Derek W. Ungless*
ILLUSTRATOR:	*Janet Woolley*
PUBLISHER:	*Straight Arrow Publications*
CATEGORY:	*Single Page/Spread—Illustration*
TITLE:	*"Sting Gets into Swing"*
AWARD:	*Merit*

240

PUBLICATION:	*Rolling Stone*
ART DIRECTOR:	*Derek W. Ungless*
DESIGNER:	*Derek W. Ungless*
ILLUSTRATOR:	*Mark Marek*
PUBLISHER:	*Straight Arrow Publications*
CATEGORY:	*Single Page/Spread—Illustration*
TITLE:	*"Heavy Metal Mania"*
AWARD:	*Merit*

241

PUBLICATION:	*Rolling Stone*
ART DIRECTOR:	*Derek W. Ungless*
DESIGNER:	*Derek W. Ungless*
ILLUSTRATOR:	*Peter De Seve*
PUBLISHER:	*Straight Arrow Publications*
CATEGORY:	*Single Page/Spread—Illustration*
TITLE:	*"Joy Riding with Lady Soul"*
AWARD:	*Merit*

242

PUBLICATION:	*Rolling Stone*
ART DIRECTOR:	*Derek W. Ungless*
DESIGNER:	*Derek W. Ungless*
ILLUSTRATOR:	*Ian Pollock*
PUBLISHER:	*Straight Arrow Publications*
CATEGORY:	*Single Page/Spread—Illustration*
TITLE:	*"Solo Stone"*
AWARD:	*Merit*

243

PUBLICATION:	*Rolling Stone*
ART DIRECTOR:	*Derek W. Ungless*
DESIGNER:	*Derek W. Ungless*
ILLUSTRATOR:	*Ian Pollock*
PUBLISHER:	*Straight Arrow Publications*
CATEGORY:	*Single Page/Spread—Illustration*
TITLE:	*"Bob Dylan Rocks Again"*
AWARD:	*Merit*

244

PUBLICATION:	*Rolling Stone*
ART DIRECTOR:	*Derek W. Ungless*
DESIGNER:	*Derek W. Ungless*
ILLUSTRATOR:	*Ian Pollock*
PUBLISHER:	*Straight Arrow Publications*
CATEGORY:	*Single Page/Spread—Illustration*
TITLE:	*"Around The World in a Daze"*
AWARD:	*Merit*

245

PUBLICATION:	*Rolling Stone*
ART DIRECTOR:	*Derek W. Ungless*
DESIGNER:	*Derek W. Ungless*
PHOTOGRAPHER:	*Max Vandukul*
PUBLISHER:	*Straight Arrow Publications*
CATEGORY:	*Single Page/Spread—Photography*
TITLE:	*"Sting Feels the Burn"*
AWARD:	*Merit*

246

PUBLICATION:	*Rolling Stone*
ART DIRECTOR:	*Derek W. Ungless*
DESIGNER:	*Derek W. Ungless*
PHOTOGRAPHER:	*Davies Starr*
PUBLISHER:	*Straight Arrow Publications*
CATEGORY:	*Single Page/Spread—Design*
TITLE:	*"Bob Geldorf"*
AWARD:	*Merit*

SUMMER DISH

Some forty-five movies are coming out this summer. Listen in on what's hot and what's not.

BY LYNN HIRSCHBERG

247

PUBLICATION: *Rolling Stone*
ART DIRECTOR: *Derek W. Ungless*
DESIGNER: *Derek W. Ungless*
ILLUSTRATOR: *Blair Drawson*
PUBLISHER: *Straight Arrow Publications*
CATEGORY: *Single Page/Spread—Illustration*
TITLE: *"Summer Dish"*
AWARD: *Merit*

For Penn and Teller, these are the days of wine and roaches. That became apparent one recent afternoon, as the bad boys of magic – and the sensations of the current off-Broadway season – rehearsed in their seedy New York studio for an

DO YOU BELIEVE IN MAGIC?

appearance on the David Letterman show. "We're going to show you a work in progress," said Penn Jillette, the peculiarly pompadoured one, to an assistant standing in as Letterman. "We'd like your opinion." Then, while the Lovin' Spoonful's "Do You Believe in Magic?" blared in the background, Teller, who uses [Cont. on 72]

Penn and Teller do. How else can you explain the overnight success of two guys who've been doing the same things since they were fourteen-year-old social outcasts.

By Charles Leerhsen

248

PUBLICATION: *Rolling Stone*
ART DIRECTOR: *Derek W. Ungless*
DESIGNER: *Derek W. Ungless*
PHOTOGRAPHER: *Chris Callis*
PUBLISHER: *Straight Arrow Publications*
CATEGORY: *Single Page/Spread—Design*
TITLE: *"Do You Believe in Magic?"*
AWARD: *Merit*

DEATH OF A CHEERLEADER

The murder of fifteen-year-old Kirsten Costas wasn't supposed to happen in a town like this

BY RANDALL SULLIVAN

Cheerleader's fatal stabbing rocks Orinda

IT WAS TWENTY TO TEN at the end of one of the year's longest days, and the Berkeley Hills were still fading to black when the doorbell rang at the Arnold house on Idlewood Court.

A dinner guest named Pat Flaherty answered the door and called to Mary Jane Arnold, "Do you want to let this girl into your house?" Mrs. Arnold walked from her kitchen to the open door and saw a teenage girl under the porch light. The girl was strikingly pretty, a petite, big-eyed brunette dressed in a blue-plaid skirt, white tights and brand-new shoes.

Behind her, at the edge of a wall of shrubbery that divided their property from the driveway of Moraga Valley Presbyterian Church, Mrs. Arnold saw another teenager, in sweat pants, she said, "lurking

249

PUBLICATION: *Rolling Stone*
ART DIRECTOR: *Derek W. Ungless*
DESIGNER: *Derek W. Ungless*
PHOTOGRAPHER: *Matt Mahurin*
PUBLISHER: *Straight Arrow Publications*
CATEGORY: *Single Page/Spread—Design*
TITLE: *"Death of a Cheerleader"*
AWARD: *Merit*

250

PUBLICATION:	*Rolling Stone*
ART DIRECTOR:	*Derek W. Ungless*
DESIGNER:	*Derek W. Ungless*
PHOTOGRAPHER:	*Herb Ritts*
PUBLISHER:	*Straight Arrow Publications*
CATEGORY:	*Single Page/Spread—Design*
TITLE:	*"The Heroes of the Thunderdome"*
AWARD:	*Merit*

251

PUBLICATION:	*Rolling Stone*
ART DIRECTOR:	*Derek W. Ungless*
DESIGNER:	*Derek W. Ungless*
ILLUSTRATOR:	*Matt Mahurin*
PUBLISHER:	*Straight Arrow Publications*
CATEGORY:	*Single Page/Spread—Illustration*
TITLE:	*"The Plague Years"*
AWARD:	*Merit*

252

PUBLICATION:	*Connecticut's Finest*
ART DIRECTORS:	*Deb Hardison/Bett McLean*
DESIGNER:	*Deb Hardison*
PHOTOGRAPHER:	*John Kane*
PUBLISHER:	*13-30 Corporation*
CATEGORY:	*Single Page/Spread—Design*
TITLE:	*"Dante's Nutmeg Ballet"*
AWARD:	*Merit*

MERIT

253

PUBLICATION:	*Connecticut's Finest*
ART DIRECTORS:	*Deb Hardison/Bett McLean*
DESIGNER:	*Deb Hardison*
ILLUSTRATOR:	*Richard McNeel*
PUBLISHER:	*13-30 Corporation*
CATEGORY:	*Single Page/Spread—Design*
TITLE:	*"Hammonasset Beach"*
AWARD:	*Merit*

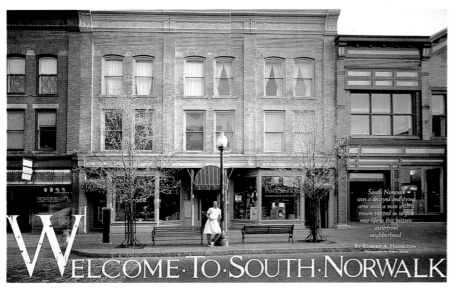

254

PUBLICATION:	*Connecticut's Finest*
ART DIRECTORS:	*Deb Hardison/Bett McLean*
DESIGNER:	*Deb Hardison*
PHOTOGRAPHER:	*Robert Benson*
PUBLISHER:	*13-30 Corporation*
CATEGORY:	*Single Page/Spread—Design*
TITLE:	*"South Norwalk"*
AWARD:	*Merit*

255

PUBLICATION:	*Connecticut's Finest*
ART DIRECTORS:	*Deb Hardison/Bett McLean*
DESIGNER:	*Deb Hardison*
ILLUSTRATOR:	*Richard McNeel*
PUBLISHER:	*13-30 Corporation*
CATEGORY:	*Single Page/Spread—Illustration*
TITLE:	*"Hammonassett Beach"*
AWARD:	*Merit*

MORE THAN THE SUM OF HIS PARTS

after the accident they pieced him back together—but something happened in the process

fiction
By JOE HALDEMAN

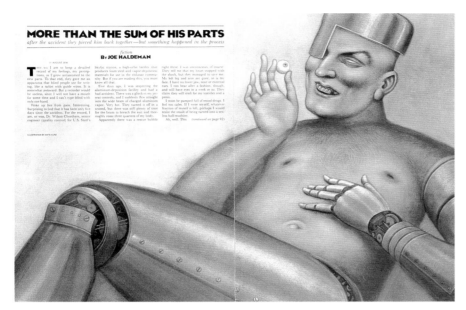

REDEFINING SMART

with information engulfing us, where do we draw the line between things we'd like to know and things we must know?

article By WILLIAM F. BUCKLEY, JR.

SEXUAL PASSAGES

why women in love give great head, and other short-lived phenomena

essay By D. KEITH MANO

256

PUBLICATION: *Playboy*
ART DIRECTOR: *Tom Staebler*
DESIGNER: *Kerig Pope*
ILLUSTRATOR: *Anita Kunz*
PUBLISHER: *Playboy Enterprises, Inc.*
CATEGORY: *Single Page/Spread—Design*
TITLE: *"More Than the Sum of His Parts"*
AWARD: *Merit*

257

PUBLICATION: *Playboy*
ART DIRECTOR: *Tom Staebler*
DESIGNER: *Theo Kouvatsos*
PHOTOGRAPHER: *Robert Giusti*
PUBLISHER: *Playboy Enterprises, Inc.*
CATEGORY: *Single Page/Spread—Design*
TITLE: *"Redefining Smart"*
AWARD: *Merit*

258

PUBLICATION: *Playboy*
ART DIRECTOR: *Tom Staebler*
DESIGNER: *Karen Gaebe*
PHOTOGRAPHER: *Lynda Barry*
PUBLISHER: *Playboy Enterprises, Inc.*
CATEGORY: *Single Page/Spread—Design*
TITLE: *"Sexual Passages"*
AWARD: *Merit*

259

PUBLICATION:	*European Travel & Life*
ART DIRECTOR:	*Terry Koppel*
DESIGNERS:	*Terry Koppel/*
	April Garston
PHOTOGRAPHER:	*Enrico Ferorelli*
PUBLISHER:	*Inabnit Communications*
CATEGORY:	*Single Page/Spread—Design*
TITLE:	*"The Triumph of Style"*
AWARD:	*Merit*

260

PUBLICATION:	*European Travel & Life*
ART DIRECTOR:	*Terry Koppel*
DESIGNER:	*Terry Koppel*
PUBLISHER:	*Inabnit Publications*
CATEGORY:	*Single Page/Spread—Design*
TITLE:	*"Shelter on the Lake"*
AWARD:	*Merit*

261

PUBLICATION:	*European Travel & Life*
ART DIRECTOR:	*Terry Koppel*
DESIGNERS:	*Terry Koppel/*
	April Garston
PHOTOGRAPHER:	*Guy Bouchet*
PUBLISHER:	*Inabnit Publications*
CATEGORY:	*Single Page/Spread—Design*
TITLE:	*"Italian Style"*
AWARD:	*Merit*

262

PUBLICATION:	*European Travel & Life*
ART DIRECTOR:	*Terry Koppel*
DESIGNER:	*Terry Koppel*
PHOTOGRAPHER:	*Harry Gruyaert*
PUBLISHER:	*Inabnit Publications*
CATEGORY:	*Single Page/Spread—Design*
TITLE:	*"Friends of French Art"*
AWARD:	*Merit*

THE NEW INGENUE

Making a statement that women are sure to copy, a new generation of French beauties step forward with intelligence, independence, and personality.

STYLE

FRENCH DESIGN STAR ANDRÉE PUTMAN HAS AN EYE FOR WHAT MATTERS TO THE SOPHISTICATED TRAVELER

A SENSE OF PLACE

BY JANET CARLSON

She would definitely stand out in a crowd, but she's not often in one. This tall, lanky woman with reddish hair, a smart expressive mouth, and a deep, gravelly voice doesn't keep still long enough, really, to be a marker. As she flits from continent to continent, Andrée Putman, the empress of the design field in France, carries herself not rigidly, so much as precisely. While her bearing is coolly erect, her eyes sparkle with warmth, her movements are graceful, and always accompanied by those strong French cigarettes.

263

PUBLICATION: *European Travel & Life*
ART DIRECTOR: *Terry Koppel*
DESIGNER: *Terry Koppel*
PUBLISHER: *Inabnit Communications*
CATEGORY: *Single Page/Spread—Design*
TITLE: *"The New Ingenue"*
AWARD: *Merit*

264

PUBLICATION: *European Travel & Life*
ART DIRECTOR: *Terry Koppel*
DESIGNER: *Terry Koppel*
PHOTOGRAPHERS: *Michael O'Neil/Guy Bouchet*
PUBLISHER: *Inabnit Communications*
CATEGORY: *Single Page/Spread—Design*
TITLE: *"A Sense of Place"*
AWARD: *Merit*

265

PUBLICATION: *Arizona Highways*
ART DIRECTOR: *Lorna Holmes*
DESIGNER: *Lorna Holmes*
PHOTOGRAPHER: *Rick Fisher*
PUBLISHER: *State of Arizona*
CATEGORY: *Single Page/Spread—Photography*
TITLE: *"Darkness to Light"*
AWARD: *Merit*

266

PUBLICATION: *The Journal*
ART DIRECTOR: *Samual Savage*
DESIGNER: *Elizabeth Greely*
PHOTOGRAPHER: *John Earle*
AGENCY: *McCormack And Dodge*
CATEGORY: *Single Page/Spread—Design*
TITLE: *"P.J. Carroll"*
AWARD: *Merit*

267

PUBLICATION:	*Chase Directions*
ART DIRECTORS:	*Robert Meyer/Julia Wyant*
DESIGNERS:	*Robert Meyer/Julia Wyant*
PHOTOGRAPHERS:	*Michael Pogany/Frank White*
AGENCY:	*Robert Meyer Design, Inc.*
CLIENT:	*Chase Manhattan Bank*
CATEGORY:	*Single Page/Spread—Design*
TITLE:	*"Planting the Chase Flag in Ohio"*
AWARD:	*Merit*

268

PUBLICATION:	*Chase Directions*
ART DIRECTORS:	*Robert Meyer/Julia Wyant*
DESIGNERS:	*Robert Meyer/Julia Wyant*
PHOTOGRAPHERS:	*Will McIntyre/Olita Day*
AGENCY:	*Robert Meyer Design*
CLIENT:	*Chase Manhattan Bank*
CATEGORY:	*Single Page/Spread—Design*
TITLE:	*"Recruiting Tomorrow's Banker"*
AWARD:	*Merit*

269

PUBLICATION:	*Consumer Electronics Monthly*
ART DIRECTOR:	*David Amario*
DESIGNER:	*David Amario*
ILLUSTRATOR:	*Mark Penberthy*
PUBLISHER:	*CES Publishing*
CATEGORY:	*Single Page/Spread— Illustration*
TITLE:	*"Battery Special/Market on the Move"*
AWARD:	*Merit*

270

PUBLICATION:	*Consumer Electronics Monthly*
ART DIRECTOR:	*David Amario*
DESIGNER:	*David Amario*
ILLUSTRATOR:	*Douglas Fraser*
PUBLISHER:	*CES Publishing*
CATEGORY:	*Single Page/Spread— Illustration*
TITLE:	*"A Family Affair"*
AWARD:	*Merit*

271

PUBLICATION:	*Home Satellite Marketing*
ART DIRECTOR:	*Marjorie Crane*
DESIGNERS:	*Marjorie Crane/Susan Walker*
ILLUSTRATOR:	*Mark Penberthy*
PUBLISHER:	*CES Publishing*
CATEGORY:	*Single Page/Spread—Design*
TITLE:	*"Commercial Market"*
AWARD:	*Merit*

272

PUBLICATION:	*Home Satellite Marketing*
ART DIRECTOR:	*Marjorie Crane*
DESIGNER:	*Marjorie Crane*
ILLUSTRATOR:	*Carl Wesley*
PUBLISHER:	*CES Publishing*
CATEGORY:	*Single Page/Spread—Design*
TITLE:	*"Bears and Bulls"*
AWARD:	*Merit*

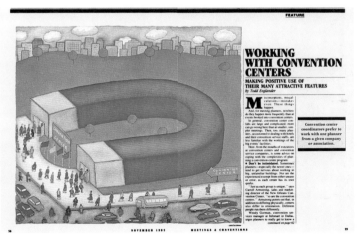

273

PUBLICATION:	*Home Satellite Marketing*
ART DIRECTOR:	*Marjorie Crane*
DESIGNER:	*Marjorie Crane*
ILLUSTRATOR:	*Mark Penberthy*
PUBLISHER:	*CES Publishing*
CATEGORY:	*Single Page/Spread— Illustration*
TITLE:	*"Commercial Market"*
AWARD:	*Merit*

274

PUBLICATION:	*Meetings and Conventions*
ART DIRECTOR:	*Barbara Groenteman*
DESIGNER:	*Doris Kogan*
ILLUSTRATOR:	*Lonni Sue Johnson*
PUBLISHER:	*Murdoch Business Magazines*
CATEGORY:	*Single Page/Spread— Illustration*
TITLE:	*"Convention Centers"*
AWARD:	*Merit*

275

PUBLICATION: *The Village Voice*
ART DIRECTOR: *Michael Grossman*
PUBLISHER: *VV Publishing Corp.*
CATEGORY: *Single Page/Spread—Design*
TITLE: *"Señor Big"*
AWARD: *Merit*

276

PUBLICATION: *The Village Voice*
ART DIRECTOR: *Michael Grossman*
ILLUSTRATOR: *Philippe Weisbecker*
PUBLISHER: *VV Publishing Corp.*
CATEGORY: *Single Page/Spread—Illustration*
TITLE: *"Paint Your Own"*
AWARD: *Merit*

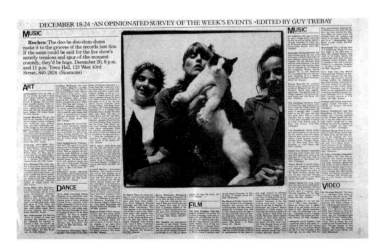

277

PUBLICATION: *The Village Voice*
ART DIRECTOR: *Michael Grossman*
DESIGNER: *Stephanie Hill*
PHOTOGRAPHER: *Sylvia Plachy*
PUBLISHER: *VV Publishing*
CATEGORY: *Single Page/Spread—Photography*
TITLE: *"The Roches"*
AWARD: *Merit*

278

PUBLICATION: *The Village Voice*
ART DIRECTOR: *Michael Grossman*
DESIGNERS: *Melanie Pitts, Stephanie Hill*
ILLUSTRATOR: *Martin Koslowski*
PUBLISHER: *VV Publishing Corp.*
CATEGORY: *Single Page/Spread—Illustration*
TITLE: *"The Discreet Charm of the Analees"*
AWARD: *Merit*

279

PUBLICATION: *California*
ART DIRECTOR: *John White*
DESIGNER: *Dugald Stermer*
ILLUSTRATOR: *Dugald Stermer*
PUBLISHER: *California Magazine*
CATEGORY: *Single Page/Spread—*
Illustration
TITLE: *"Meg Tilly"*
AWARD: *Merit*

280

PUBLICATION: *Cars '85*
ART DIRECTOR: *Steven Phillips*
DESIGNER: *Steven Phillips*
ILLUSTRATOR: *Lonni Sue Johnson*
AGENCY: *Steven Phillips Design, Inc.*
CATEGORY: *Single Page/Spread—*
Illustration
TITLE: *"To Your Car's Health"*
AWARD: *Merit*

281

PUBLICATION:	*House & Garden*
ART DIRECTOR:	*Karen Lee Grant*
DESIGNER:	*Lloyd Ziff*
PHOTOGRAPHER:	*Peter Margonelli*
PUBLISHER:	*Condé Nast*
CATEGORY:	*Single Page/Spread—Photography*
TITLE:	*"Garden of Gladness"*
AWARD:	*Merit*

282

PUBLICATION:	*House & Garden*
ART DIRECTOR:	*Karen Lee Grant*
DESIGNER:	*Lloyd Ziff*
PHOTOGRAPHER:	*Len Jenshel*
PUBLISHER:	*Condé Nast*
CATEGORY:	*Single Page/Spread—Photography*
TITLE:	*"Greentree"*
AWARD:	*Merit*

283

PUBLICATION:	*House & Garden*
ART DIRECTOR:	*Karen Lee Grant*
DESIGNER:	*Lloyd Ziff*
PHOTOGRAPHER:	*Len Jenshel*
PUBLISHER:	*Condé Nast*
CATEGORY:	*Single Page/Spread—Photography*
TITLE:	*"Greentree"*
AWARD:	*Merit*

MONSIEUR MODERNE

Mallet-Stevens, the Parisian architect who gave modern design the chic of the new

BY MARTIN FILLER
PHOTOGRAPHS BY DAVID MASSEY

STYLISH CIRCLES
Robert Mallet-Stevens, *right*, personified the élan of progressive French architecture between the two world wars. *Opposite*: On the roof terrace of his Villa Martel in Paris, a cylindrical belvedere overlooking the seventh *arrondissement*. *Above*: Grisaille stained-glass window, apartment block, rue Mechain, Paris, 1929.

284

PUBLICATION: *House & Garden*
ART DIRECTOR: *Karen Lee Grant*
DESIGNER: *Lloyd Ziff*
PUBLISHER: *Condé Nast*
CATEGORY: *Single Page/Spread—Design*
TITLE: *"Monsieur Moderne"*
AWARD: *Merit*

LACQUER PERFECT

The art of Jean Dunand reveals the luxurious side of the Art Deco movement

BY CHRISTINA de LIAGRE   PHOTOGRAPHS BY SHEILA METZNER

A baluster-shaped vase, *opposite*, with geometric decorations in black, red, and gold lacquer on a patinated brown ground, circa 1925, against Jean Lambert-Rucki screen, circa 1923. *Above*: Three views of a vase with abstract geometric design in red and black lacquer on an unpatinated ground with traces of silver dotting.

285

PUBLICATION: *House & Garden*
ART DIRECTOR: *Karen Lee Grant*
DESIGNER: *Lloyd Ziff*
PHOTOGRAPHER: *Sheila Metzner*
PUBLISHER: *Condé Nast*
CATEGORY: *Single Page/Spread—Design*
TITLE: *"Lacquer Perfect"*
AWARD: *Merit*

The Third Dimension

April Greiman's economical conversion of industrial space into her own studio exploits contradictions of flatness vs. depth and reality vs. illusion.

They said it couldn't last. The naysayers of New Wave graphic design predicted that the neon-colored chaos would soon pass and Helvetica would return triumphant. But April Greiman, the designer most often credited with inventing the kitsch-sensitive, pastel-popular style (*P.A.*, Sept. 1987, cover and p. 169) that looks the way Los Angeles feels, sees to such demise in the offing. In fact, business is booming.

As the size and scope of the designer's projects expanded, so did her need for studio space. To accommodate the influx of packaging, advertising, furniture, and interior design projects, Greiman decided to stop working at home and start commuting to a former brewery building in downtown L.A.'s industrial district. There, inside a concrete complex of buildings that have been converted to artists' studios, Greiman leased a raw space with dramatically long, narrow, and tall (29 feet) proportions, with a single, 18-foot-square window. Collaborating with architect Steven Bardwell on the rough plan and construction details, Greiman set out to make what she calls a "loose, fluid, and balanced" two-person work environment, using a resourceful economy of means.

Most of the lively character of the studio comes from light, mobile, multipurpose additions: furniture-clad furniture on wheels; tempered, economically useful drafting-area partitions (which Greiman calls "New Wave Japanese screens"); and changing, Ikea-like tableaux of furniture and objects. The main work space is left as open as possible, while the auxiliary areas—camera room, storage, kitchen, etc.—are compressed into a triangular room off the main space, plus a mezzanine-level loft that doubles as a lounge and conference room.

Greiman has applied her fascination with graphic textures to architectural finishes. Moiré-like tables are covered in thin once-laminate and even thinner once-patterned adhesive paper, and some walls are sponge-painted to look like fabrics. Light objects are made from "heavy" materials, while heavy elements are visually lightened. This interest in transitory, trompe surfaces is visible in Greiman's current experiments in freezing video images, digitalizing them into dotted pictures via computer, and using them to print (she has also been doing the opposite—animating still photos into moving videos).

Although Greiman explains that she "has always been making two-dimensional space three-dimensional," she never considered turning into interior and furniture design and she's got a lot to do. Architect Doug Michels (of Ant Farm fame). Transfixed by one of Greiman's complex, multiplanar posters, Michels suggested that she pursue architecture, since her approach was already architectonic. Now, Greiman studies architecture more closely, especially the "minimal but psychological" work of Arata Isozaki. And Los Angeles architects in turn study April Greiman's designs, which have been called "extremely intellectual and extremely emotional at the same time." *Barbara Flanagan*

Looking down at the studio space from the mezzanine (facing page, large photo and bottom left); screens divide individual work areas, and Greiman-designed furniture houses tools, supplies, and even a computer. On the mezzanine loft (facing page, bottom right), with its shoji-screen dividers, are a lounge/conference room, kitchen and bathroom.

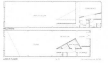

Project: studio for April Greiman, Inc., Los Angeles. **Designer:** April Greiman. **Architect:** Bardwell, Case and Gollett Architects, Los Angeles (Steve Bardwell, principal in charge). **Program:** 1900 sq ft of studio space in a converted brewery. **Structural system:** drywall on steel studs. **Construction coordinator:** Richard Kuhlenschmidt. **Cost:** $26,000, excluding fees. **Photos:** Jayne Odgers.

286

PUBLICATION: *Progressive Architecture*
ART DIRECTOR: *Richelle Huff*
DESIGNER: *Richelle Huff*
PHOTOGRAPHER: *Jayne Odgers*
PUBLISHER: *Penton Publications*
CATEGORY: *Single Page/Spread—Design*
TITLE: *"The Third Dimension"*
AWARD: *Merit*

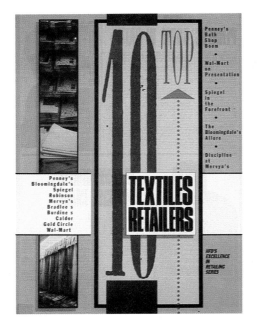

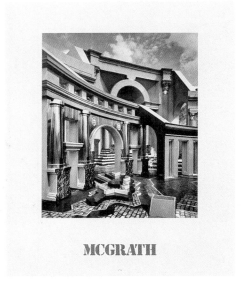

MCGRATH

287

PUBLICATION: *HFD*
ART DIRECTOR: *Jeffery Christensen*
DESIGNER: *Darry L. Turner*
PUBLISHER: *Fairchild Publications*
CATEGORY: *Single Page/Spread—Design*
TITLE: *"10 Top Textile Retailers"*
AWARD: *Merit*

288

PUBLICATION: *HFD*
ART DIRECTOR: *Jeffery Christensen*
DESIGNER: *Jeffery Christensen*
PUBLISHER: *Fairchild Publications*
CATEGORY: *Single Page/Spread—Design*
TITLE: *"Marketing Scandinavia"*
AWARD: *Merit*

289

PUBLICATION: *Mead Annual Report*
ART DIRECTOR: *Bennett Robinson*
DESIGNER: *Bennett Robinson*
AGENCY: *Corporate Graphics, Inc.*
PHOTOGRAPHER: *Norman McGrath*
CLIENT: *Mead Paper Corporation*
CATEGORY: *Single Page/Spread—
                        Photography*
TITLE: *"Wild Johnson on Mead
                        Black and White"*
AWARD: *Merit*

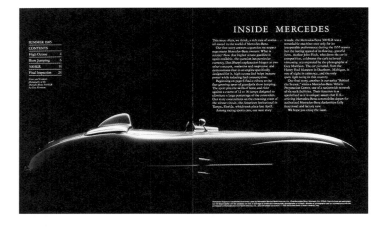

290

PUBLICATION: *American Theatre*
ART DIRECTOR: *Cynthia Friedman*
DESIGNER: *Cynthia Friedman*
PHOTOGRAPHER: *John Menapace*
PUBLISHER: *Theatre Communication
                        Group*
CATEGORY: *Single Page/Spread—Design*
TITLE: *"Center Stage"*
AWARD: *Merit*

291

PUBLICATION: *Mercedes*
ART DIRECTOR: *Peter Morance*
DESIGNER: *Peter Morance*
PHOTOGRAPHER: *Guy Morrison*
AGENCY: *McCaffrey & McCall*
CLIENT: *Mercedes-Benz
                        of North America*
CATEGORY: *Single Page/Spread—Design*
TITLE: *"Inside Mercedes"*
AWARD: *Merit*

Park Nicollet Medical Center

Coronary artery bypass surgery
An HMO perspective

Charles R. Peterson, MD

Preview
How does a major medical center in which conventional and HMO types of payment systems have functioned side by side for more than ten years approach the use of major, expensive procedures such as arteriography and coronary artery bypass surgery? Dr Peterson explains how the indications for these two procedures have evolved at Park Nicollet Medical Center since 1970. He compares the center's results with those of the Coronary Artery Surgery Study, and relates the positive impact the "HMO perspective" has had on care of all patients with coronary artery disease.

Selective coronary arteriography and coronary artery bypass surgery have been used in management of coronary artery disease (CAD) for almost two decades. Yet controversy still exists about how extensively these procedures should be used in diagnosis and treatment. The continuing need to examine treatment alternatives is emphasized by the apparent decrease in recent years in mortality from CAD, the introduction of new drugs and procedures for treating angina, and the accelerating costs of invasive diagnostic and therapeutic techniques. In addition, prospective payment systems such as diagnosis-related groups (DRGs) and health maintenance organizations (HMOs) create incentives for physicians to avoid overutilizing expensive procedures but also cause concern about potential negative impacts of underutilization on the quality of medical care.

Most of the patients referred to the cardiologists and cardiac surgeons at Park Nicollet Medical Center, Minneapolis, have had a fee-for-service type of medical insurance. However, for addition to our clinic of MedCenters Health Plan (MHP), a prospective-payment comprehensive health care plan, has given a "health maintenance" perspective to our care of CAD patients. Thus, in the more than ten years since the introduction of MHP, we have been increasingly concerned with longitudinal cost-effective and consistent management of all CAD patients, no matter what the referral source or type of medical insurance.

During the past 15 years, we have recommended arteriography for consideration of bypass surgery primarily for patients who had symptoms of angina and significant ischemic electrocardiographic changes at low levels of exercise or at rest, preferably after a reasonable period of medical treatment. Patients who are mildly symptomatic and have good exercise capacity have not been considered likely to benefit significantly from bypass surgery.

This article reviews the early studies that helped formulate our approach to selecting patients for arteriography and bypass surgery, presents the findings of a preliminary study of this selection process in a representative population of CAD patients in an HMO plan, and compares our experience with the Coronary Artery Surgery Study (CASS).

Early experience
We first began recommending bypass surgery for patients in 1970. Thus same year, a follow-up study was begun of consecutive patients evaluated for non-specific chest pain or known CAD with mild to severe angina. Six hundred eighty patients were classified into one of three symptomatic groups at the time of initial evaluation. (1) atypical chest pain, (2) minimally symptomatic CAD, or (3) CAD with New York Heart Association functional class II or IV angina pectoris (table 1). [1] Excluded were patients over age 70, patients with significant valvular heart disease, and patients with heart failure requiring digitalis or diuretic treatment. Figure 1 shows three-year survival
continued

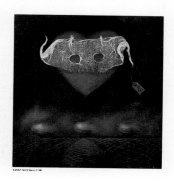

Platelet-inhibitor therapy in cardiovascular disease
Effective defense against thromboembolism

James H. Chesebro, MD,   Peter M. Steele, MBBS,   Valentín Fuster, MD

Preview
The advisability of anticoagulant and antiplatelet therapy in patients with cardiovascular disease is a subject of great importance in clinical practice, as the drugs may be effective in preventing thromboembolism and occlusion. Dr Chesebro and his colleagues, who have extensive experience in this area, give practical therapeutic approaches for use of the agents in patients with a prosthetic heart valve, aortocoronary bypass graft, or atherosclerosis and in those undergoing arterial angioplasty.

Platelet deposition occurs in regions of vascular damage where vessels have lost their antithrombotic protection because of endothelial damage, exposure of subendothelial connective tissue or both. [1] Similarly, platelets may adhere to prosthetic materials in the circulatory system, such as prosthetic heart valves or vascular grafts. Thrombus formation follows platelet deposition and may lead to clinically evident thromboses or to arterial embolization. [2] Arterial thromboembolism is a dynamic process involving aggregation and disaggregation of platelets that precedes and follows a clinical event, resulting in increased platelet consumption or shortening of platelet half-life. [3]

Prosthetic heart valves
The percentage of patients free of thromboembolism after receiving a prosthetic heart valve continues to decrease over time, as

shown by results of a recent study (figure 1). [4] In spite of oral anticoagulant therapy, only 60% and 58% of the patients studied were free of thromboembolism at 10 and 15 years, respectively.

Of the arterial emboli that develop after replacement of a heart valve, 85% go to the brain; approximately half of these arterial emboli lead to permanent neurologic deficit, and 10% lead to death. About one fourth of patients experiencing a thromboembolic event have more than one such event. [5]

Risk factors for systemic embolism, listed in table 1, have been discussed elsewhere. [6] In addition to the factors given, severe left ventricular dysfunction from dilated cardiomyopathy without valvular disease also predisposes to arterial thromboembolism. This can be prevented with warfarin (Athrombin-K, Coumadin, Panwarfin) therapy. [7]

The decreasing risk of thromboembolism after valve replace-

ment in recent years is probably the result of factors involving both patients and valves. Patients now are usually operated on when their disease is less advanced than in the past. This means that the incidence of atrial fibrillation is generally lower, left atrial size smaller, and left ventricular function better at operation. Also, the valves themselves have been improved, with design modifications that result in less turbulent flow and that use new materials with decreased thrombogenicity.

Because of the merits and risk of thromboembolism during oral anticoagulant therapy, trials of oral anticoagulant plus a platelet inhibitor have been conducted (table 2). In four trials, [8-11] oral anticoagulant plus dipyridamole (Persantine) decreased the incidence of thromboembolism when compared with oral anticoagulant alone. The dipyridamole dosage of 300 to 400 mg/day, or 5 to 6 mg/kg/day, in these studies was chosen because it maximally prolonged the shortened platelet survival in patients with a prosthetic heart valve. [2] In two trials, [10,11] oral anticoagulant was used with and without aspirin. Thromboembolism was reduced with the addition of aspirin, but gastrointestinal bleeding increased significantly with an aspirin dosage of 1 gm/day and the incidence of anemia was slightly increased with
continued

292

PUBLICATION:	*Postgraduate Medicine*
ART DIRECTOR:	*Tina Adamek*
ILLUSTRATOR:	*Sandra Filippucci*
PUBLISHER:	*McGraw-Hill*
CATEGORY:	*Single Page/Spread— Illustration*
TITLE:	*"Bypass Surgery"*
AWARD:	*Merit*

293

PUBLICATION:	*Postgraduate Medicine*
ART DIRECTOR:	*Tina Adamek*
ILLUSTRATOR:	*Enid Hatton*
PUBLISHER:	*McGraw-Hill*
CATEGORY:	*Single Page/Spread— Illustration*
TITLE:	*"Platelet Inhibitors"*
AWARD:	*Merit*

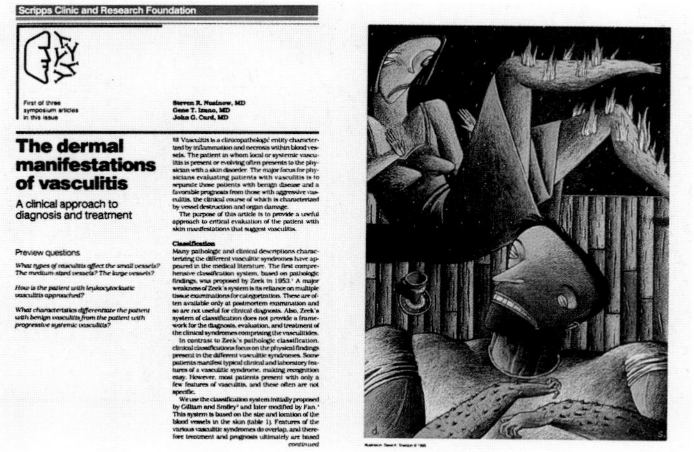

Scripps Clinic and Research Foundation

First of three symposium articles in this issue

Steven R. Mostow, MD
Gene T. Izuno, MD
John G. Curd, MD

The dermal manifestations of vasculitis
A clinical approach to diagnosis and treatment

Preview questions

What types of vasculitis affect the small vessels? The medium-sized vessels? The large vessels?

How is the patient with leukocytoclastic vasculitis approached?

What characteristics differentiate the patient with benign vasculitis from the patient with progressive systemic vasculitis?

■ Vasculitis is a clinicopathologic entity characterized by inflammation and necrosis within blood vessels. The patient in whom local or systemic vasculitis is present or evolving often presents to the physician with a skin disorder. The surge factor the physicians evaluating patients with vasculitis is to separate those patients with benign disease and a favorable prognosis from those with aggressive vasculitis, the clinical course of which is characterized by vessel destruction and organ damage.

The purpose of this article is to provide a useful approach to critical evaluation of the patient with skin manifestations that suggest vasculitis.

Classification
Many pathologic and clinical descriptions characterizing the different vasculitic syndromes have appeared in the medical literature. The first comprehensive classification system, based on pathologic findings, was proposed by Zeek in 1953. [1] A major weakness of Zeek's system is its reliance on multiple tissue examinations for categorization. These are often available only at postmortem examination and so are not useful for clinical diagnosis. Also, Zeek's system of classification does not provide a framework for the diagnosis, evaluation, and treatment of the clinical syndromes comprising the vasculitides.

In contrast to Zeek's pathologic classification, clinical classifications focus on the physical findings present in the different vasculitic syndromes. Some patients manifest typical clinical and laboratory features of a vasculitic syndrome, making recognition easy. However, most patients present with only a few features of vasculitis, and these often are not specific.

We use the classification system initially proposed by Gilliam and Smiley [2] and later modified by Fan. [3] This system is based on the size and location of the blood vessels in the skin (table 1). Features of the various vasculitic syndromes do overlap, and therefore treatment and prognosis ultimately are based
continued

First of three symposium articles in this issue

Charles Bernick, MD
Lawrence Z. Stern, MD

Neurologic complaints in the elderly
The challenge of diagnosis

Preview questions

What reversible dementing processes are sometimes overlooked in the elderly because of organic presentation?

Why is one likely to get a false impression of weakness on clinical testing of muscle strength in the elderly patient?

What condition has replaced syphilis as the "great masquerader" in elderly patients?

■ Evaluation of neurologic complaints in the elderly is made challenging by several factors. First, the aging nervous system is not only prone to primary disease but is also exquisitely sensitive to disturbances of other major organ systems. Frequently, neurologic problems in the elderly are manifestations of more diffuse disease. The history obtained from the patient is often more confusing than clarifying. Furthermore, the physical signs of acute disease may be blunted in the elderly. Finally, once information is gathered, the clinician must decide whether the patient's condition is related to the normal aging process or to disease.

Modern diagnostic technology is quite helpful in elucidating rather ambiguous conditions. Yet, even computed tomography (CT) has its limits; ultimately, diagnosis becomes a test of the physician's clinical skills.

Books have been written on the subject of neurology and aging, and the reader is referred to these and to the articles cited here for a more thorough discussion. [1] The purpose of this article is to review the more common neurologic complaints seen by the primary care physician and to point out possible diagnostic clues and pitfalls.

Changes in mental status
Disorders of behavior and intellect are usually discerned by family members, who bring the patient to medical attention. These disturbances have been categorized as delirium and dementia, states based on temporal profile and level of consciousness and usually distinguishable on clinical grounds (although overlap may occur).

Delirium refers to a transient disorder of widespread cognitive functions manifested by inattentiveness, sensory misperception, disturbed stream of thought, and either increased or decreased psychomotor activity. [2] Onset is rapid. The disorder is common in elderly patients, particularly those with underlying CNS damage who sustain an acute
continued

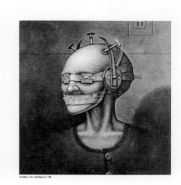

294

PUBLICATION:	*Postgraduate Medicine*
ART DIRECTOR:	*Tina Adamek*
ILLUSTRATOR:	*David K. Sheldon*
PUBLISHER:	*McGraw-Hill*
CATEGORY:	*Single Page/Spread— Illustration*
TITLE:	*"Vasculitis"*
AWARD:	*Merit*

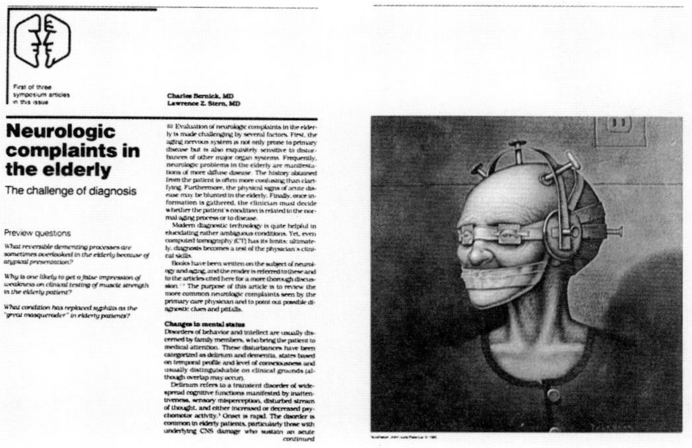

295

PUBLICATION:	*Postgraduate Medicine*
ART DIRECTOR:	*Tina Adamek*
ILLUSTRATOR:	*John Jude Palencar*
PUBLISHER:	*McGraw-Hill*
CATEGORY:	*Single Page/Spread— Illustration*
TITLE:	*"Neurologic Problems"*
AWARD:	*Merit*

The IPMA POSTGRADUATE MEDICINE Lecture

Appetite regulation
Modern concepts offering food for thought

John E. Morley, MB, BCh.   Allen S. Levine, PhD

First of three
symposium articles
in this issue

A. Richard Kendall, MD
Barry S. Stein, MD

Benign prostatic hyperplasia
Evaluation, management, and operative indications

Preview questions

How prevalent is benign prostatic hyperplasia?

How should this condition be managed if symptoms are mild and complaints minimal?

When surgery is required, what procedure is preferred? Why?

296

297

High Blood Pressure in the Competitive Athlete: Guidelines and Recommendations

Raymond J. Walther, MD
Charles P. Tifft, MD

Practical Assessment of Body Composition

Andrew S. Jackson, PED
Michael L. Pollock, PhD

298

299

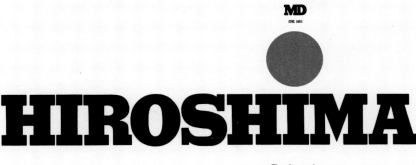

MD

JUNE 1985

HIROSHIMA

The diary of a
Japanese physician
who was there
when the bomb hit

By Michihiko Hachiya, M.D.
Illustrations by John Groth

300

PUBLICATION: *MD*
ART DIRECTOR: *Merrill Cason*
DESIGNER: *Al Foti*
PUBLISHER: *MD Publications, Inc.*
CATEGORY: *Single Page/Spread—Design*
TITLE: *"Hiroshima"*
AWARD: *Merit*

CHELATION CONTROVERSY

Patients say this new
treatment for heart disease
and circulatory problems is
the kiss of life. The medical
profession is divided: some
call it quackery—a placebo,
at best—while the more
than one thousand
physicians who practice
chelation consider it a
medical breakthrough.

by Judith Glassman

AFTER my angina came back, I
thought, This is the end for me,
I sold my big house, sold the
plastics business I had been in
for thirty years, did a lot of
cleaning up to make life easier for my
wife after I was gone," fifty-nine year
old John Fiore of New Jersey says.
"When I first started EDTA chelation
therapy, I was planning on dying."

Fiore had had a triple bypass three-
and-a-half years earlier, but when the
chest pain returned and an angiogram
revealed that his grafted arteries had
closed up, he refused to even consider
more heart surgery. "That operation
was the most awful thing in my life,"
he recalls. "I'd die before I'd do that
again."

Instead, Fiore began an unconven-
tional treatment—and thrived. At the
urging of a neighbor, he began seeing
New York City holistic physician

*Judith Glassman writes frequently on health
and alternative medicine.*
ILLUSTRATION: KISSING IMG ALEX GREY

Warren Levin, who gave him a detailed
medical workup, then recommended a
drastic change in diet, nutritional
supplements, and treatment with the
controversial drug ethylene-diamine-
tetra acetic acid, a manmade amino
acid commonly known as EDTA.

The treatment consists of a series of
intravenous infusions given two to
three times a week for a total of 20-40
infusions or more, depending on the
particular case. The infusions usually
last three-and-a-half to four hours, and
each generally contains three grams
of EDTA.

When Fiore began the therapy, he
had trouble walking the short distance
from the train station to Levin's office.
"I couldn't walk a block. My legs felt
as though they were going to collapse."
But after about fifteen treatments, his
chest and leg pain had totally disappeared. "I feel terrific," he says now.
"I even look younger—I don't have
any more facile wrinkles around my
eyes. Chelation has given me a new
lease on life."

Since the '50s, 400,000 people like
John Fiore have undergone chelation
therapy for a staggering variety of ailments, including angina pains, peri-
pheral vascular disease, gangrene,
memory loss, senility, chronic skin
ulcers, and retina damage from diabetes. Many of them have pronounced
it a miracle cure.

The 1,000 M.D.'s who practice chelation claim it has valid long-term
effects. These physicians maintain
that EDTA has an extraordinary success rate—long-lasting subjective im-
provement in 75-90 percent of all
patients. Says Elmer Cranton, former
president of his county medical society
and author of a recently published
book called *Bypassing Bypass*. "My
patients don't all get completely well.
But 85 percent improve enough so

that they're happy with the treatment." Furthermore, Cranton and his
colleagues claim that when administered according to established protocol,
EDTA is one of today's safest medica-
tions, less toxic than aspirin.

If reports such as Fiore's, Cranton's,
and others are accurate, chelation
ranks as one of the greatest medical
discoveries of all time. Most of the
ailments chelationists claim to treat
successfully stem from impaired cir-
culation, often caused by arterioscle-
rosis—the progressive accumulation
of arterial plaque that clogs and stif-
fens arteries, leading inevitably to
heart attacks and strokes. Arterioscle-
rosis affects up to 100 million people
in the United States, and modern
medicine offers no cure. Drugs and
surgery temporarily relieve symptoms
but do nothing to stop the progress of
the disease.

Still, not everyone shares chelationists' enthusiasm. The treatment is at the
center of a whirlwind of medical controversy, with the big guns of mainstream medicine—the American Medical Association, American Heart
Association, American College of Physicians, American Academy of Family
Physicians, and the American Osteo-
pathic Association—maintaining that
EDTA is useless to treat cardiovascular diseases. Even the most open
minded physicians—like William Castelli, medical director of Framingham
Heart Study, the longest-running
analysis of the relationship between
diet and heart disease—are skeptical.
Castelli concludes, "I know of no
objective evidence whatsoever that
EDTA is of any value."

Many physicians believe that chelation therapy is not only useless, but
hazardous as well. Alfred Soffer, editor in chief of the medical journal
Chest and executive director of the

301

PUBLICATION: *New Age Journal*
ART DIRECTOR: *Greg Paul*
DESIGNER: *Chris Frame*
ILLUSTRATOR: *Alex Grey*
PUBLISHER: *New Age Journal*
CATEGORY: *Single Page/Spread—
Illustration*
TITLE: *"Chelation"*
AWARD: *Merit*

BOTTLE BABIES

Whether they drink or not, the children of alcoholics have a unique set of emotional problems that
haunt them well into adulthood. Only by facing the family trauma can they begin to heal the scars.

By Stephen Phillip Policoff

WHEN I was eleven,
my best friend,
whom I'll call Ted
Griffin, had a sleep-
over party for five
of the guys in the complacent suburbs
of Albany, New York. My parents were
not enthusiastic about this invitation.
I did not know why, though I knew
that Ted's mother was dead and that
his father figured heavily in local gossip.

The party itself was a great success—
until midnight, when Ted and I crept
downstairs to raid the kitchen. As we
pushed open the swinging door, Ted
stopped short, murmuring, "We'd better not." He dashed back upstairs. I
followed, but not before glancing into
the kitchen, where I saw Dr. Griffin
slumped down in the breakfast nook, a
bottle clasped in one rigid fist.

*Stephen Phillip Policoff is a playwright and freelance
writer living in New York City.*
PHOTOGRAPH: MARTIN PAUL

The following morning Dr. Griffin
was supposed to take us to a ball
game, but the housekeeper said he
was ill. For reasons I could not fathom,
this news sent Ted running upstairs,
pale as death.

I had a number of occasions to recall
that fearful look: when Ted, in eighth
grade, became antagonistic toward
teachers, classmates, even me; when
Ted dropped out of school in ninth
grade; when, in 1969, he tried to com-
mit suicide; and years later, when I
heard that Ted was a heroin addict
and that his father had died from cir-
rhosis of the liver.

It baffled me that Dr. Griffin had let
his life be overshadowed by alcohol. It
baffled me more that the darkness
engulfed his son. I had no way of
knowing then how fiercely alcoholism
holds families in its grip—not letting
go for generations.

Ted had been critically injured in a

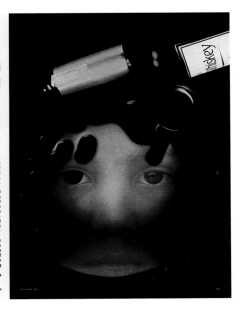

302

PUBLICATION: *New Age Journal*
ART DIRECTOR: *Greg Paul*
DESIGNER: *Greg Paul*
PHOTOGRAPHER: *Martin Paul*
PUBLISHER: *New Age Journal*
CATEGORY: *Single Page/Spread—Design*
TITLE: *"Bottle Babies"*
AWARD: *Merit*

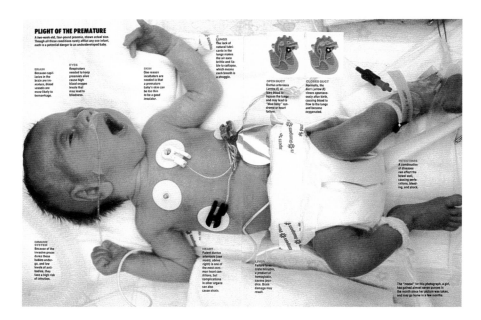

PLIGHT OF THE PREMATURE
A two-week-old, four-pound preemie, shown actual size. Though all these conditions rarely affect any one infant, each is a potential danger to an underdeveloped baby.

303

PUBLICATION:	*Discover*
ART DIRECTOR:	*Eric Seidman*
DESIGNER:	*Robert Daniels*
PUBLISHER:	*Time Inc.*
CATEGORY:	*Single Page/Spread—Design*
TITLE:	*"Preemies: A $2 Billion Dilemma"*
AWARD:	*Merit*

CHEMISTRY

CHINA SPLITS THE NOODLE

A master takes advantage of the peculiarities of dough molecules to turn a single lump into 2,048 delicate strands

BY FRANZ LIDZ

304

PUBLICATION:	*Discover*
ART DIRECTOR:	*Eric Seidman*
DESIGNER:	*Sandra Di Pasqua*
PHOTOGRAPHER:	*Fred Conrad*
PUBLISHER:	*Time Inc.*
CATEGORY:	*Single Page/Spread—Design*
TITLE:	*"China Splits the Noodle"*
AWARD:	*Merit*

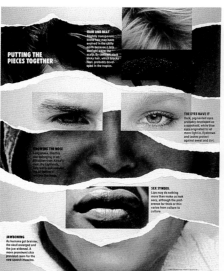

PUTTING THE PIECES TOGETHER

EVOLUTION

WHAT'S IN A FACE

If you thought yours was only pretty or ugly or somewhere in between, look again. Scientists are finding that our faces reveal much more than meets the eye

BY SHANNON BROWNLEE

305

PUBLICATION:	*Discover*
ART DIRECTOR:	*Eric Seidman*
DESIGNER:	*Sandra DiPasqua*
PUBLISHER:	*Time Inc.*
CATEGORY:	*Single Page/Spread—Design*
TITLE:	*"What's in a Face"*
AWARD:	*Merit*

MERIT

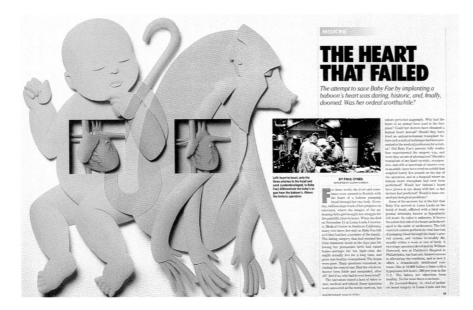

306

PUBLICATION:	*Discover*
ART DIRECTOR:	*Eric Seidman*
DESIGNER:	*Robert Daniels*
ILLUSTRATOR:	*Sally Jo Vitsky*
PUBLISHER:	*Time Inc.*
CATEGORY:	*Single Page/Spread—Design*
TITLE:	*"The Heart That Failed"*
AWARD:	*Merit*

307

PUBLICATION:	*Science '85*
ART DIRECTOR:	*John Isley*
DESIGNER:	*John Isley*
ILLUSTRATOR:	*Steven Guarnaccia*
PUBLISHER:	*Science '85/American Association for the Advancement of Science*
CATEGORY:	*Single Page/Spread— Illustration*
TITLE:	*"Risky Business"*
AWARD:	*Merit*

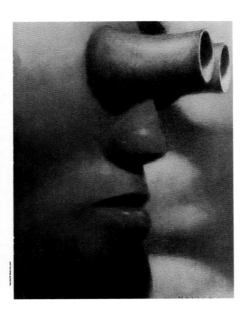

308

PUBLICATION:	*Science '85*
ART DIRECTOR:	*Wayne Fitzpatrick*
DESIGNER:	*Wayne Fitzpatrick*
ILLUSTRATOR:	*Brad Holland*
PUBLISHER:	*Science '85/American Association for the Advancement of Science*
CATEGORY:	*Single Page/Spread— Illustration*
TITLE:	*"The Inspectors"*
AWARD:	*Merit*

MERIT

breaking with

The highest-ranking Soviet official ever to defect tells the extraordinary story of his rejection of the Communist system, and of the frightening world of espionage into which he was drawn.

moscow

by arkady n. shevchenko

309

PUBLICATION: *Literary Cavalcade*
ART DIRECTOR: *James Serfati*
DESIGNER: *James Serfati*
ILLUSTRATOR: *Gene Greif*
PUBLISHER: *Scholastic, Inc.*
CATEGORY: *Single Page/Spread—Design*
TITLE: *"Breaking With Moscow"*
AWARD: *Merit*

THE
SAILOR BOYS' TALE

BY
ISAK DINESEN

"He had killed a man, and had kissed a girl.
He did not demand any more from life."

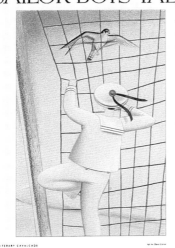

310

PUBLICATION: *Literary Cavalcade*
ART DIRECTOR: *James Serfati*
DESIGNER: *James Serfati*
ILLUSTRATOR: *Dave Calver*
PUBLISHER: *Scholastic, Inc.*
CATEGORY: *Single Page/Spread—Design*
TITLE: *"Sailor"*
AWARD: *Merit*

MONSTER POEMS!

● POETRY: ORAL EXPRESSION ●

These poems are fun to read aloud for Halloween. Get into the right mood. Read them with expression. Pick the words you want to stress. Make your voice sound spooky. Then treat your friends to some *monster-ious* rhymes!

What's That?
What's that
Who's there?
There's a great huge horrible *horrible*
creeping up the stair!
A huge big terrible *terrible*
with creepy crawly hair!
There's a ghastly grisly *ghastly*
with seven slimy eyes!
And flabby grabby tentacles
of a gigantic size!
He's crept into my room now,
he's leaning over me.
I wonder if he's thinking
how delicious I will be.
—Florence Parry Heide

The Monster's Pet
What kind of pet
Would a monster get
If a monster set
His mind on a pet?
Would it snuffle and wuffle
Or snackle and snore?
Would it slither and dither
Or rattle and roar?
Would it dribble and bribble
In manner horr-rible
Or squbble and squirm
Like a worm?
And every day
In pleasant weather,
Would they go out
For a walk together?
—Lilian Moore

Monster Madness!
Think up your own Halloween monster, draw a picture of it, and give it a name. Then choose or make up words to describe . . .

how it looks: _____

how it moves: _____

the noises it makes: _____

311

PUBLICATION: *Scholastic Sprint*
ART DIRECTOR: *Lisa Francella*
DESIGNER: *Joan Michaels*
ILLUSTRATOR: *Bill Mayer*
PUBLISHER: *Scholastic, Inc.*
CATEGORY: *Single Page/Spread—Illustration*
TITLE: *"Monster Poems"*
AWARD: *Merit*

312

PUBLICATION:	*Texas Monthly*
ART DIRECTOR:	*Fred Woodward*
DESIGNERS:	*Fred Woodward/*
	David Kampa
PHOTOGRAPHER:	*George Kern*
PUBLISHER:	*Texas Monthly, Inc.*
CATEGORY:	*Single Page/Spread—Design*
TITLE:	*"Art & Sole"*
AWARD:	*Merit*

313

PUBLICATION:	*Texas Monthly*
ART DIRECTOR:	*Fred Woodward*
DESIGNER:	*Fred Woodward*
PHOTOGRAPHER:	*M.K. Simqu*
PUBLISHER:	*Texas Monthly, Inc.*
CATEGORY:	*Single Page/Spread—Design*
TITLE:	*"105°"*
AWARD:	*Merit*

314

PUBLICATION:	*Texas Monthly*
ART DIRECTOR:	*Nancy F. McMillen*
ILLUSTRATOR:	*Richard McNeel*
PUBLISHER:	*Texas Monthly, Inc.*
CATEGORY:	*Single Page/Spread—*
	Illustration
TITLE:	*"The Hi Sign"*
AWARD:	*Merit*

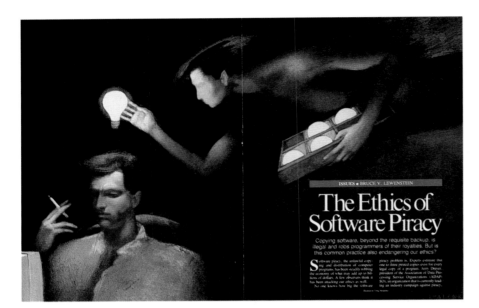

315

PUBLICATION:	*PC*
ART DIRECTOR:	*Mary Zisk*
DESIGNER:	*Louise White*
ILLUSTRATOR:	*Greg Spalenka*
PUBLISHER:	*Ziff Davis*
CATEGORY:	*Single Page/Spread—Illustration*
TITLE:	*"The Ethics of Software Piracy"*
AWARD:	*Merit*

316

PUBLICATION:	*PC*
ART DIRECTOR:	*Mary Zisk*
DESIGNER:	*Louise White*
ILLUSTRATOR:	*Mark Penberthy*
PUBLISHER:	*Ziff Davis*
CATEGORY:	*Single Page/Spread—Illustration*
TITLE:	*"Enable Does it Right"*
AWARD:	*Merit*

317

PUBLICATION:	*PC*
ART DIRECTOR:	*Mary Zisk*
DESIGNER:	*Mark Jensen*
ILLUSTRATOR:	*Jeffery Schrier*
PUBLISHER:	*Ziff Davis*
CATEGORY:	*Single Page/Spread—Illustration*
TITLE:	*"Talking Software for the Visually Impaired"*
AWARD:	*Merit*

MERIT

318

PUBLICATION: *PC*
ART DIRECTOR: *Mary Zisk*
DESIGNERS: *Ilissa Goodheart/*
Monique Cubicciotti
ILLUSTRATOR: *Carter Goodrich*
PUBLISHER: *Ziff Davis*
CATEGORY: *Single Page/Spread—*
Illustration
TITLE: *"Accounting for Individual*
Tastes"
AWARD: *Merit*

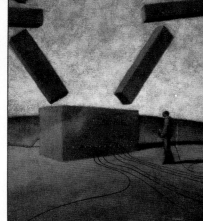

319

PUBLICATION: *Byte*
ART DIRECTOR: *Nancy S. Rice*
ILLUSTRATOR: *Rob Colvin*
PUBLISHER: *Byte*
CATEGORY: *Single Page/Spread—*
Illustration
TITLE: *"A Simpl Compiler"*
AWARD: *Merit*

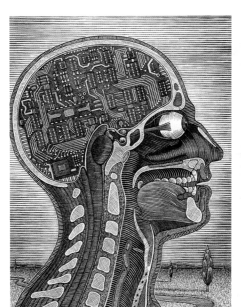

320

PUBLICATION: *Byte*
ART DIRECTOR: *Rosslyn A. Frick*
ILLUSTRATOR: *Douglas Smith*
PUBLISHER: *Byte*
CATEGORY: *Single Page/Spread—*
Illustration
TITLE: *"Theme Introduction"*
AWARD: *Merit*

A SPECIAL REPORT

INDUSTRIAL AUTOMATION

Electronic devices and computers will be as integral to the Factory of the Future as water power was in the early stages of the Industrial Revolution. Those devices and computers represent an opportunity for U.S. industry to reassert itself in the worldwide industrial community. Although the arrival of the electronic factory is inevitable, the rate at which the electronic overhaul develops and the identity of major beneficiaries of the computer-driven workplace are far more uncertain. The following special report, more than a year in the making, analyzes the emergence of the electronic-based factory and forecasts what that emergence will mean to the electronics and computer industry.

72 Galvanizing the Rust Bowl

80 IBM's industrial automation plans

82 Computer-integrated manufacturing glossary

94 INI maps out a factory-networking strategy

96 Artificial intelligence for IA

102 Programmable controllers

108 Computer-assisted maintenance

113 The CIM sell: A boardroom decision

120 Comment: D. Bruce Merrifield,
     U.S. Dept. of Commerce

174 Comment: John Kerr

70 ELECTRONIC BUSINESS   NOVEMBER 15, 1985   NOVEMBER 15, 1985   ELECTRONIC BUSINESS 71

321

PUBLICATION:	*Electronic Business*
ART DIRECTOR:	*Bill Cooke*
DESIGNER:	*Bill Cooke*
ILLUSTRATOR:	*Douglas Fraser*
PUBLISHER:	*CES Publishing*
CATEGORY:	*Single Page/Spread—* *Illustration*
TITLE:	*"Industrial Automation"*
AWARD:	*Merit*

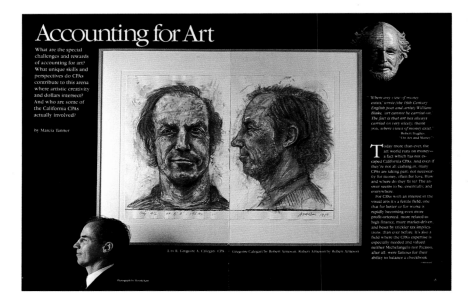

Accounting for Art

What are the special challenges and rewards of accounting for art? What unique skills and perspectives do CPAs contribute to this arena where artistic creativity and dollars intersect? And who are some of the California CPAs actually involved?

by Marcia Tanner

L to R: Gregory A. Calegari, CPA   Gregory Calegari by Robert Arneson; Robert Arneson by Robert Arneson

Photograph by Hendrik Kam

322

PUBLICATION:	*Outlook*
ART DIRECTOR:	*Mike Shenon*
DESIGNER:	*Mike Shenon*
AGENCY:	*Mike Shenon Design*
PHOTOGRAPHER:	*Hendrik Kam*
CLIENT:	*California Society of CPAs*
CATEGORY:	*Single Page/Spread—Design*
TITLE:	*"Accounting for Art"*
AWARD:	*Merit*

CLIENTS BEWARE

USE OF THIS ONCE-GREAT KING OF TORTS AND HIS EVER-CHANGING BAND OF ASSOCIATES MAY BE HAZARDOUS TO YOUR CASE

BY ELLEN JOAN POLLOCK

102 THE AMERICAN LAWYER   THE AMERICAN LAWYER 103

323

PUBLICATION:	*American Lawyer*
ART DIRECTOR:	*John Belknap*
DESIGNER:	*John Belknap*
PHOTOGRAPHER:	*Ed Kashi*
PUBLISHER:	*AmLaw Publishing* *Corporation*
CATEGORY:	*Single Page/Spread—Design*
TITLE:	*"Clients Beware"*
AWARD:	*Merit*

324

PUBLICATION: *The Newsday Magazine*
ART DIRECTOR: *Miriam Smith*
ILLUSTRATOR: *Ned Levine*
PUBLISHER: *Times-Mirror, Inc.*
CATEGORY: *Single Page/Spread—*
Illustration
TITLE: *"Friendship, Sex and the*
Office"
AWARD: *Merit*

325

PUBLICATION: *The Newsday Magazine*
ART DIRECTOR: *Miriam Smith*
ILLUSTRATOR: *Gary Viskupic*
PUBLISHER: *Times-Mirror, Inc.*
CATEGORY: *Single Page/Spread—*
Illustration
TITLE: *"Crisis PR"*
AWARD: *Merit*

326

PUBLICATION: *The Newsday Magazine*
ART DIRECTOR: *Miriam Smith*
DESIGNER: *Miriam Smith*
ILLUSTRATOR: *Greg Spalenka*
PUBLISHER: *Times-Mirror, Inc.*
CATEGORY: *Single Page/Spread—Design*
TITLE: *"In Defense of Boxing"*
AWARD: *Merit*

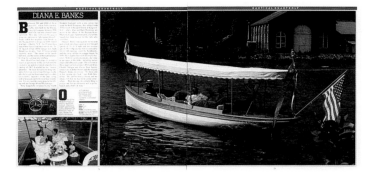

327

PUBLICATION:	*Nautical Quarterly*
ART DIRECTOR:	*Clare Cunningham*
DESIGNER:	*Clare Cunningham*
PHOTOGRAPHER:	*Feadship*
PUBLISHER:	*Nautical Quarterly*
CATEGORY:	*Single Page/Spread—Design*
TITLE:	*"Megayachts"*
AWARD:	*Merit*

328

PUBLICATION:	*Nautical Quarterly*
ART DIRECTOR:	*Marilyn Rose*
DESIGNER:	*Marilyn Rose*
PHOTOGRAPHER:	*Jim Brown*
PUBLISHER:	*Nautical Quarterly*
CATEGORY:	*Single Page/Spread—Design*
TITLE:	*"ELCO"*
AWARD:	*Merit*

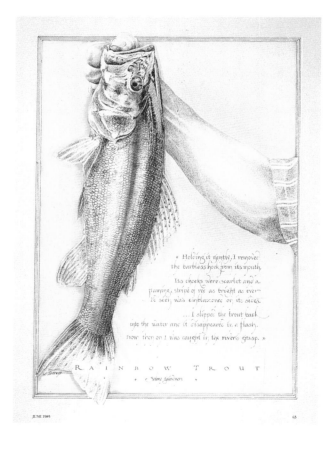

329

PUBLICATION:	*San Francisco Focus*
ART DIRECTOR:	*Laura Lamar*
DESIGNER:	*Dugald Stermer*
ILLUSTRATOR:	*Dugald Stermer*
PUBLISHER:	*San Francisco Focus*
CATEGORY:	*Single Page/Spread— Illustration*
TITLE:	*"Rainbow Trout"*
AWARD:	*Merit*

Judging a Promotion's Success

[body text of article, multiple columns]

Promos are a fact of life for buyers. While the details are still fresh in your mind, analyze your latest sale to learn how you did it or why you shouldn't have tried. The answer could make a difference in your purchasing plans.

By David Habercom

David Habercom is a freelance writer based in Knoxville, Tennessee.

330

PUBLICATION:	*Buy*
ART DIRECTORS:	*Bett McLean/ Lawrence Arnett*
DESIGNER:	*Lawrence Arnett*
PHOTOGRAPHER:	*Howard Bjornsen*
PUBLISHER:	*13-30 Corporation*
CATEGORY:	*Single Page/Spread—Design*
TITLE:	*"Judging a Promotion's Success"*
AWARD:	*Merit*

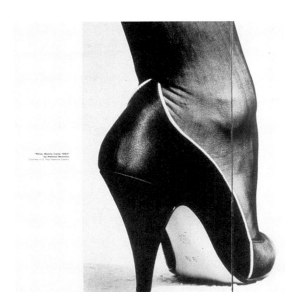

HELMUT NEWTON

Man Behind the Camera

331

PUBLICATION:	*Designers West*
ART DIRECTOR:	*Nan Oshin*
DESIGNER:	*Nan Oshin*
PHOTOGRAPHER:	*Helmut Newton*
PUBLISHER:	*Designers West*
CATEGORY:	*Single Page/Spread—Design*
TITLE:	*"Art and Artisan"*
AWARD:	*Merit*

MERIT

332

PUBLICATION: *Enterprise*
ART DIRECTOR: *Douglas Wolfe*
DESIGNER: *Douglas Wolfe*
ILLUSTRATOR: *Barry Root*
AGENCY: *Hawthorne/Wolfe Design*
CLIENT: *Southwestern Bell Corporation*
CATEGORY: *Single Page/Spread—Design*
TITLE: *"Unlock Your Mind and a Batch of New Ideas Will Pour Forth"*
AWARD: *Merit*

333

PUBLICATION: *Enterprise*
ART DIRECTOR: *Douglas Wolfe*
DESIGNERS: *Douglas Wolfe/John Howze*
ILLUSTRATOR: *Eric Dinyer*
AGENCY: *Hawthorne/Wolfe Design*
CLIENT: *Southwestern Bell Corporation*
CATEGORY: *Single Page/Spread—Design*
TITLE: *"Don't Let the Weight of Someone Else's Drug Problem Pull You Down"*
AWARD: *Merit*

334

PUBLICATION: *Enterprise*
ART DIRECTOR: *Douglas Wolfe*
DESIGNER: *Douglas Wolfe*
ILLUSTRATOR: *Michel Guiré Vaka*
AGENCY: *Hawthorne/Wolfe Design*
CLIENT: *Southwestern Bell Corporation*
CATEGORY: *Single Page/Spread—Design*
TITLE: *"SHHHH!"*
AWARD: *Merit*

MERIT

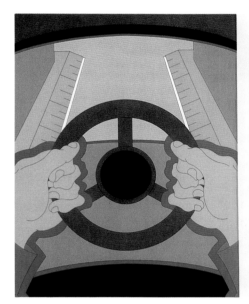

by Donald B. Johnston
Marketing Director, IIL

The Problem Of Evaluating Route Performance

Every industrial launderer deals with the problem of evaluating the performance of route sales people. The problem is often a perplexing one because of a variety of factors. First, the route sales representative is away from the plant while completing his or her tasks, so there is no direct supervision. Second, the route sales representative is expected to do an excellent job of providing service to the customer while at the same time adhering to certain controls demanded by the company. Such circumstances often result in direct conflict. Third, the route sales representative is expected, in most cases, to sell services as well as servicing his or her customers.

These characteristics of the route sales representative's activities make the job of fair evaluation a difficult one. The Route Operation Subcommittee of the Service & Distribution Committee is currently embarked upon a program to develop a series of true life adventures articles for Industrial Launderer which describe the route evaluation methods used by the subcommittee members and others. The article which follows is the first in this series. It is based upon the methods employed by several IIL members and currently published by the IIL in An Industrial Launderer's Guide for Establishing Route Standards. This booklet is only available through attendance at the Institute's Route Efficiency Training Course. The material in Section II Work Activity Standards with some editing follows.

The standards discussed in this Article II are really route salesperson performance goals. They are generally set by management alone or in consultation with the route sales representative. These are performance goals which deal with the activities on the routes over and above delivering merchandise over which the route sales representative exercises some control. Just as running a route according to a reasonable time schedule contributes to the ultimate profitability of the route (delivering the most dollar volume at the lowest costs), so too does the attainment of performance goals contribute to the profitability of each route.

Different companies deal with the setting of performance goals in a variety of route activities in different ways. Some use the performance goals as minimum standards of performance for the route salesperson. If that person continually fails to meet these performance goals, a detailed consultation

should take place to determine the reasons for non-performance. This final management reaction is to continued non-performance — termination.

The idea is that a certain level of proficiency must be reached in order to continue in the job. In practice the inability of a route sales representative to reach performance goals attached by others acts as a red flag to signal management to investigate and to help the route sales representative reach the goals it provides. The natural and intelligent response to non-attainment of goals is to assist the person to improve his or her performance.

Some industrial launderers use these performance goals as minimum work requirements but they carry things a little further by providing bonuses of one sort or another for exceeding the standards. The use of bonuses for exceeding standards stresses the positive rather than the negative. At the very least, the work activity performance goals should present a guideline to both the route sales representative and management as to how successfully the route is being run.

The first step in developing performance goals is to decide which route activities should be included. The route activities for which performance goals are set are those over which the route sales representative actually exercises some control. Though the route sales representative exercises some control over a variety of activities on the route, most IIL members set performance goals primarily on the following activities:

1. Credit
2. Rental sales increase from current accounts
3. Rental sales increase from new accounts
4. Rental sales decreases in current accounts
5. Rental accounts lost
6. Special invoicing
7. Garment replacement
8. Retrieval of garments or money
9. "Cuff" or bank
10. Accounts receivable

These are the route activities for which performance goals are most often established. Obviously, a given company can choose to establish performance goals for other activities over which the route sales representative in that company has some control. The activities for which performance goals are set depend to some

NOVEMBER 1988

335

PUBLICATION:	*Industrial Launderer*
ART DIRECTOR:	*Jack Lefkowitz*
DESIGNER:	*Jack Lefkowitz*
ILLUSTRATOR:	*Virginia Strnad*
PUBLISHER:	*Institute of Industrial Launderers*
CATEGORY:	*Single Page/Spread—Design*
TITLE:	*"The Problem"*
AWARD:	*Merit*

The Old Oak

Marking time and change for three centuries

The owner of the property stopped and faced the field. He squinted into the sun, aligning himself with a distant object. He pointed his finger to the horizon, looking down his arm as if it were a surveyor's sight, and marked the boundary with an imaginary line. "That big tree back there sits right on the property line."

The prospective buyer liked the piece of ground out in Middleburgh Township and bought it on that day in 1912.

Each spring Edwin Busse disced the ground, sending up clouds of dust as he worked the field, cutting wide around the big tree that marked the property line. On hot days he took rests beneath its low branches. One mid-summer day the tree was threatened by strikes of lightning as Busse labored to beat an oncoming storm. But it survived and so did he, working the land another 40 years until he retired.

He sold the ground to William Novak, attaching only one condition to the sale. "I only ask that you leave that old oak tree standing," Busse said, pointing toward the big tree that still marked the property line. Novak shook hands with Busse and closed the deal.

Even then the proportions of the tree couldn't be appreciated from the road. Up close, its bottom tier of gnarled limbs spanned an 80-foot circle and rose 70 feet into the air from the massive 5-foot-thick trunk. The tree was old. It was 150 years old in 1796 when surveyors of the Connecticut Land Co. hacked township lines through 3 million Ohio acres.

Sometime in the 17th century the acorn of a Quercus alba sprouted on the well-drained knoll of woods rising out of the bogs and lowlands in the wilderness west of the Cuyahoga River. It plunged its taproot through the humusy top soil and into the firm clay below. *Continued on Page 11*

By Marjorie Pilarczyk Hertelendy

ILLUSTRATION BY ERIC DONELAN

THE PLAIN DEALER MAGAZINE   8   SUNDAY, DECEMBER 4, 1988
THE PLAIN DEALER MAGAZINE   9   SUNDAY, DECEMBER 4, 1988

336

PUBLICATION:	*The Plain Dealer Magazine*
ART DIRECTOR:	*Gerard Sealy*
DESIGNER:	*Gerard Sealy*
ILLUSTRATOR:	*Eric Donelan*
PUBLISHER:	*Plain Dealer Publishing Co.*
CATEGORY:	*Single Page/Spread—Design*
TITLE:	*"Old Oak"*
AWARD:	*Merit*

MERIT

Photographing a

DREAM

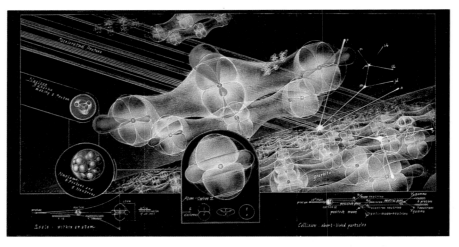

337

PUBLICATION:	*nbeye*
ART DIRECTOR:	*Don Johnson*
DESIGNER:	*Cathy Brennan*
ILLUSTRATOR:	*Steve Henry*
CLIENT:	*Nabisco Brands, Inc.*
CATEGORY:	*Single Page/Spread—Design*
TITLE:	*"Laughter is the Sun…"*
AWARD:	*Merit*

338

PUBLICATION:	*nbeye*
ART DIRECTOR:	*Don Johnson*
DESIGNER:	*Cathy Brennan*
CLIENT:	*Nabisco Brands, Inc.*
CATEGORY:	*Single Page/Spread—Design*
TITLE:	*"Photographing a Dream"*
AWARD:	*Merit*

339

PUBLICATION:	*National Geographic*
ART DIRECTOR:	*Jan Adkins*
DESIGNER:	*Howard Paine*
ILLUSTRATOR:	*Barron Storey*
PUBLISHER:	*National Geographic Society*
CATEGORY:	*Single Page/Spread— Illustration*
TITLE:	*"Inside the Atom"*
AWARD:	*Merit*

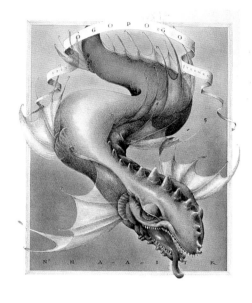

341

PUBLICATION:	*Pacific Northwest*
ART DIRECTOR:	*Steve Bialer*
DESIGNER:	*Dugald Stermer*
PHOTOGRAPHER:	*Dugald Stermer*
PUBLISHER:	*Pacific Northwest*
CATEGORY:	*Single Page/Spread—*
	Illustration
TITLE:	*"Ogopogo"*
AWARD:	*Merit*

340

PUBLICATION:	*Success*
ART DIRECTOR:	*Louis Cruz*
PHOTOGRAPHER:	*Carl Fisher*
PUBLISHER:	*Success Magazine, Inc.*
CATEGORY:	*Single Page/Spread—Design*
TITLE:	*"OMIGOD, I've Hired a*
	Turkey!"
AWARD:	*Merit*

342

PUBLICATION:	*Picture Week*
ART DIRECTOR:	*Mary K. Baumann*
DESIGNER:	*Sandra Di Pasqua*
PUBLISHER:	*Time Inc.*
CATEGORY:	*Single Page/Spread—Design*
TITLE:	*"Blackout"*
AWARD:	*Merit*

▶This Week in History

DISNEY

LONG AFTER HIS DEATH, HIS ARTISTIC–AND BUSINESS–GENIUS STILL ENTERTAINS US

Walt showed his skill with a camera during a 1941 business trip to Rio de Janeiro.

343

PUBLICATION: *Picture Week*
ART DIRECTOR: *Mary K. Baumann*
DESIGNER: *Linda Nussbaum*
PUBLISHER: *Time Inc.*
CATEGORY: *Single Page/Spread—Design*
TITLE: *"Disney"*
AWARD: *Merit*

This Week in History◀

HOUDINI

EVERY YEAR, FOLLOWERS OF THE MOST FAMOUS MAGICIAN OF ALL TIME TRY TO COMMUNE WITH HIM ACROSS THE GRAVE

344

PUBLICATION: *Picture Week*
ART DIRECTOR: *Mary K. Baumann*
DESIGNER: *Linda Nussbaum*
PUBLISHER: *Time Inc.*
CATEGORY: *Single Page/Spread—Design*
TITLE: *"Houdini"*
AWARD: *Merit*

▶Cover Story

UP IN ARMS

WOMEN NOW OWN SOME 7 MILLION OF THE NATION'S LEGAL HANDGUNS

345

PUBLICATION: *Picture Week*
ART DIRECTOR: *Mary K. Baumann*
DESIGNER: *Murray Greenfield*
PHOTOGRAPHER: *Tony Costa*
PUBLISHER: *Time Inc.*
CATEGORY: *Single Page/Spread—Design*
TITLE: *"Up in Arms"*
AWARD: *Merit*

MERIT

346

PUBLICATION: *Time*
ART DIRECTOR: *Rudy Hoglund*
DESIGNER: *Tom Bentkowski*
PUBLISHER: *Time Inc.*
CATEGORY: *Single Page/Spread—Design*
TITLE: *"Vietnam—The Battle of Hue"*
AWARD: *Merit*

347

PUBLICATION: *Time*
ART DIRECTOR: *Rudy Hoglund*
DESIGNER: *Irene Ramp*
PHOTOGRAPHER: *Eddie Adams*
PUBLISHER: *Time Inc.*
CATEGORY: *Single Page/Spread—Design*
TITLE: *"A Global Family Album"*
AWARD: *Merit*

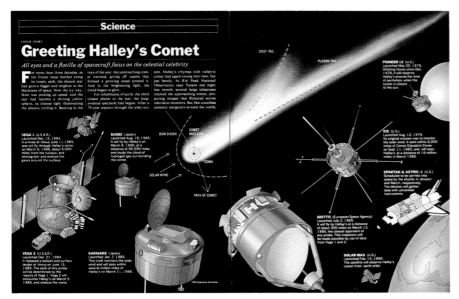

348

PUBLICATION: *Time*
ART DIRECTOR: *Rudy Hoglund*
DESIGNERS: *Billy Powers/Joe Lertola*
ILLUSTRATOR: *Joe Lertola*
PUBLISHER: *Time Inc.*
CATEGORY: *Single Page/Spread—Design*
TITLE: *"Greeting Halley's Comet"*
AWARD: *Merit*

STORY PRESENTATIONS

GOLD

349

PUBLICATION: *Manhattan, inc.*
ART DIRECTOR: *Nancy Butkus*
DESIGNER: *Nancy Butkus*
PHOTOGRAPHER: *George Lange*
PUBLISHER: *Metrocorp*
CATEGORY: *Story Presentation—*
Photography
TITLE: *"Trump—The Ultimate Deal"*
AWARD: *Gold*

Corner Table

TRUMP: THE ULTIMATE DEAL

BY RON ROSENBAUM

At first Trump was as enthusiastic about
discussing The Subject. But then he
had severe second thoughts about it.
He wanted to cancel the lunch.

Trump was worried about revealing
the full extent of his involvement in
the delicate—and explosive—subject. "I'm
dealing at a very high level on this."

Trump is a bit like the Ancient Mariner
here at "21," a stranger at the feast.
Will the dove of peace
become his albatross?

350

PUBLICATION: *The New York Times Magazine*
ART DIRECTOR: *Ken Kendrick*
DESIGNER: *Ken Kendrick*
ILLUSTRATOR: *Anita Kunz*
PUBLISHER: *The New York Times*
CATEGORY: *Story Presentation—
Illustration*
TITLE: *"Women's Movement"*
AWARD: *Gold*

How to Get the Women's Movement Moving Again

By Betty Friedan

The new generation, says the author, must rally to save the rights it now takes for granted.

GOLD

351

PUBLICATION: *Sports Illustrated*
ART DIRECTOR: *Michael Grossman*
PUBLISHER: *Time Inc.*
CATEGORY: *Story Presentation—Design*
TITLE: *"The Boxer and the Blonde"*
AWARD: *Gold*

THE BOXER AND THE BLONDE

T

This is the story of Billy Conn, who won the girl he loved but lost the best fight ever

BY FRANK DEFORD

GOLD

Portraits in POWER

Photography by HELMUT NEWTON

352

PUBLICATION: *Texas Monthly*
ART DIRECTOR: *Fred Woodward*
DESIGNER: *Fred Woodward*
PHOTOGRAPHER: *Helmut Newton*
PUBLISHER: *Texas Monthly, Inc.*
CATEGORY: *Story Presentation—Design*
TITLE: *"Portraits in Power"*
AWARD: *Gold*

353

PUBLICATION:	*The New York Times Magazine*
ART DIRECTOR:	*Ellen Burnie*
DESIGNER:	*Ellen Burnie*
PHOTOGRAPHER:	*Peter Lindbergh*
PUBLISHER:	*The New York Times*
CATEGORY:	*Story Presentation— Photography*
TITLE:	*"Fashions of the Times"*
AWARD:	*Silver*

354

PUBLICATION:	*The New York Times Magazine*
ART DIRECTOR:	*Ken Kendrick*
DESIGNER:	*Ken Kendrick*
PHOTOGRAPHERS:	*Barbara Wal/Martha Swope*
PUBLISHER:	*The New York Times*
CATEGORY:	*Story Presentation— Photography*
TITLE:	*"The Public and Private Joe Papp"*
AWARD:	*Silver*

355

PUBLICATION:	*The New York Times Magazine*
ART DIRECTOR:	*Ken Kendrick*
DESIGNER:	*Nancy Hoefig*
PHOTOGRAPHERS:	*Ricardo Salas, New-York Historical Society*
PUBLISHER:	*The New York Times*
CATEGORY:	*Story Presentation—Design*
TITLE:	*"Audubon"*
AWARD:	*Silver*

356

PUBLICATION:	*The New York Times Magazine*
ART DIRECTOR:	*Ken Kendrick*
DESIGNER:	*Diana LaGuardia*
PHOTO EDITOR:	*Peter Howe*
PHOTOGRAPHER:	*Various*
PUBLISHER:	*The New York Times*
CATEGORY:	*Story Presentation—Design*
TITLE:	*"How We See Each Other"*
AWARD:	*Silver*

357

PUBLICATION:	*US*
ART DIRECTOR:	*Robert Priest*
DESIGNER:	*Janet Waegel*
PHOTOGRAPHER:	*Mark Hanauer*
PUBLISHER:	*Straight Arrow Publications*
CATEGORY:	*Story Presentation—*
	Photography
TITLE:	*"The New Short Kid*
	Hits It Big"
AWARD:	*Silver*

358

PUBLICATION:	*US*
ART DIRECTOR:	*Robert Priest*
DESIGNER:	*Janet Waegel*
PHOTOGRAPHER:	*Michael Comte*
PUBLISHER:	*Straight Arrow Publications*
CATEGORY:	*Story Presentation—*
	Photography
TITLE:	*"Dustin Does TV"*
AWARD:	*Silver*

360

PUBLICATION:	*GQ*
ART DIRECTOR:	*Mary Shanahan*
DESIGNER:	*Fabien Baron*
PHOTOGRAPHER:	*Dennis Piel*
PUBLISHER:	*Condé Nast*
CATEGORY:	*Story Presentation—Design*
TITLE:	*"Decent Exposure"*
AWARD:	*Silver*

SILVER

HOW THEY RUINED OUR
PRISONS

Judge Justice is wrong. The governor is wrong. The Legislature is wrong. And the reformers are wrong. The answer to the Texas prison crisis is to run the jails the same way we did twenty years ago.

BY DICK J. REAVIS

In the file room of the fifth floor of the federal courthouse in downtown Houston, there's a sheet of paper that has eclipsed the Texas constitution, the laws of our Legislature, and traditions that have guided us since the days of the Republic. It's an ordinary piece of paper, a white sheet of onionskin, legal size. Words formed of black letters are written across its face, in ballpoint ink so pale that it appears to be gray. The handwriting is steady and careful; the writer apparently used a slip of pasteboard to guide his hand, because the bottoms of his letters all stop at precisely the same point, as if on an invisible line. The first words written on the page are those of a pauper's oath, "Motion To Proceed In Forma Pauperis." They were not intended to be but they have become words of irony. In the past five years, that sheet of paper and thousands of others indexed to it—the text and proceedings of the *Ruiz v. Estelle* case—have cost Texas taxpayers more than $150 million, including $4 million in legal fees alone. During the next ten years the suit could cost the state nearly $1 billion more.

The man whose signature appears beneath the writing is David R. Ruiz, a diminutive, intense convict with only seven years of formal education. In June 1972, when he penned his suit against employees of the Texas Department of Corrections (TDC), the nation's largest prison system, he was only 29. In the years since then, Ruiz has become a symbol of courage and tenacity, a figure mentioned almost daily in our press. In some quarters he's a folk hero, the little man who beat a big, oppressive system; a David who brought a Goliath low. David Ruiz is the kind of man whom the *Austin American-Statesman*, without any cynicism, could quote describing himself as "a person whose only aims, hopes and desires are to improve, always to improve, and to contribute to humanity." He is the standardbearer of the Texas movement for penal reform.

But David Ruiz is no hero. He's hardly deserving of admiration at all. In 1972 he already had a long prison record, for robberies he later admitted he had committed. After four stretches in reform school, Ruiz first

went to prison in 1960 on an armed robbery charge. Released in 1968, he returned before the close of the year with three concurrent sentences, for another ill-fated mugging and two counts of robbery by assault. In June 1972 he was also wanted for murder on a warrant out of Ohio, where he had spent a part of the brief seven months between his prison terms. David Resendez Ruiz had not, as the wardens would say, been sent to prison for singing too loud in church.

He'd been less than a choirboy while wearing the white uniform of a Texas convict, too. During the trial of his lawsuit, he admitted that he had stabbed "approximately three or four" of his fellow inmates. He had escaped once and had several times been found with weapons. He had been put in solitary confinement some fifteen times for assaultiveness and had been denied parole for the same reason. David Ruiz didn't show much respect for the law or for the rights of others. His explanation for one of the stabbings was "He had his hand in his pocket. I didn't know what he had in his

pocket, so I had a knife myself, and I used it." Yet during his career as a convict, he'd filed a dozen suits alleging that the Texas Department of Corrections had engaged in unlawful practices and violated his rights. David Ruiz hasn't shown much regard for the truth either. He is now back in prison, this time for aggravated perjury. Some of the charges he made in his petition weren't credible, even by the farthest stretch of the imagination. For example, he asserted that the cells in which he had been confined—in various unair-conditioned Texas prisons—were cold in May, August, and September. The question his suit raised was, Does a man like this, a hardened criminal, deserve the rights the rest of us have?

But Ruiz wasn't the first or only convict to see the Texas prison system, and in April 1974, after federal district judge William Wayne Justice set the *Ruiz* case on his docket, he joined married it to the suits of seven other prisoners. The most important allegations in their petitions concerned punishments administered to disci-

Photography by Matt Mahurin

In the South, convicts had to be taken outside the prison walls to find work, so eyes, ears, whips, and dogs became the chief barriers to escape. In Texas, the prisoners themselves were used to help train packs of guard dogs.

thrived so long as discipline was harsh and summary. "The old system," a veteran warden told me, "ran on fear." Then he paused, as if in nostalgia for a boyhood sweetheart. "But you know what?" he continued. "It worked. We kept order that way."

However ugly, the system did most of the things we can realistically expect a prison system to do. It did them well, and it did them cheaply. Before the trial of *Ruiz v. Estelle*, prisons in Texas were the safest, most productive, and most economical in the nation. Today, they are the most dangerous, yet their cost has more than quadrupled. Growing indiscipline has set new records and created new categories of cost. For example, last year so many convicts turned cafeteria spoons into shanks, or jailhouse knives, that the prisons had to abandon the metal dinnerware that had been in use for years and spend more than $30,000 to purchase disposable plastic utensils. At the system's Coffield Unit alone, near Dallas, convicts who couldn't be controlled by the new, *Ruiz*-era disciplinary code last year broke six thousand window panes, and convicts across the state vandalized...

(Continued on page 232)

Throughout the system's history, despite the efforts of reformers within and without, guards indulged in simple, straightforward, punitive assault. Apologists said that such abuse was inevitable in any system of authority.

plinary violators in prison, an issue that federal judges had come to regard during the sixties as invoking constitutional protection. Using the prisoners' petitions as a basis, Judge Justice engineered a proceeding—it isn't over yet—in which issues not mentioned by the petitioners, like living space, recreation programs, and even prison landfill operations, also came under his review. As if the expert lawyers he appointed to represent the plaintiffs were not enough, the judge also brought in the United States Department of Justice as an adversary to the State of Texas. The trial of *Ruiz v. Estelle*, the most thorough in penal history, lasted eight months and heard 349 witnesses, most of them convicts. The result was a lengthy opinion from Judge Justice, followed by teams of court-approved settlement agreements, all aimed at reforming the prison system.

If you have ever visited a prison, it is easy to comprehend the desire for reform. Prisons are ugly, frightening places, and there is something fundamental in human nature that recoils from the idea of men and women locked up. I have toured all 27 Texas prison units. I talked to wardens, guards, sheep and field supervisors,

361

PUBLICATION: *Texas Monthly*
ART DIRECTOR: *Fred Woodward*
DESIGNER: *Fred Woodward*
PHOTOGRAPHER: *Matt Mahurin*
PUBLISHER: *Texas Monthly, Inc.*
CATEGORY: *Story Presentation—Photography*
TITLE: *"How They Ruined Our Prisons"*
AWARD: *Silver*

WHEN PICASSO WAS A TEXAN

And Dalí. And Matisse. And Degas. And Van Gogh. And…

At first they tried to shoo him away. The bent, wizened old man appeared at the door of the Alamo library carrying a number of paintings under one arm and a stack of old letters and rent receipts under the other. He needed a shave, his clothes were tattered, and, as one librarian put it, he "smelled like a skunk in a feedlot." The man refused to leave until he was allowed to donate his paintings and documents to the library. To get rid of him, they were accepted, and the old man disappeared into the late afternoon never to be seen again. His things were immediately put into the collection box for the Daughters of the Republic of Texas garage sale to benefit the Alamo. Fortunately for us all, a lowly assistant curator from the San Antonio Museum of Art arrived early at the sale and recognized the immense value of the paintings, which he was able to buy for $30. The paintings were proof of a previously unsuspected fact of modern art history—that many of the greatest European painters had spent some of their formative years in Texas. The old man had evidently run a boardinghouse where the artists had stayed, often leaving canvases behind instead of rent. Some of the works were early versions, redolent with Texas iconography, of the later paintings that would make the artists famous. Other than the paintings, we have little evidence of how these artists felt about Texas. One clue, however, was discovered in the old man's papers. "Texas," said a note by Picasso on a rent receipt, "is not a place for squares, but for cubists!"

THE THREE COUNTRY PICKERS

Pablo Picasso painted *The Three Country Pickers* after driving nonstop across Texas with his friend Marcel Duchamp. When their Hispano-Suiza broke down in El Paso, Duchamp took the train to Los Angeles while Picasso checked into the Paso del Norte Hotel and waited for car parts to arrive from Europe. Ever prolific, Picasso bought canvas and paints and set to work in the hotel lobby with a bottle of tequila at his side. Perhaps that is why he saw triple.

Pablo Picasso, Three Musicians, 1921. The Museum of Modern Art, New York. Mrs. Simon Guggenheim Fund.

Illustration by Sean Earley

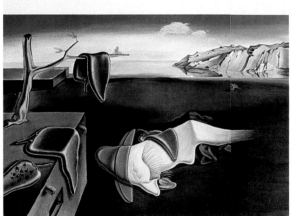

THE PERSISTENCE OF TASTE

Salvador Dalí painted *The Persistence of Taste* in 1929 after his first Mexican dinner at San Antonio, an event that left him indisposed most of a week. The meal was again alluded to in *The Persistence of Memory* when the Spanish surrealist transposed melting clocks and ants for jalapeños and scorpions. Dalí achieved a more universal theme by sacrificing some of the lime in the original work.

Above: Illustration by Stephan Durke. Right: Illustration by Steve Shock

Above: Salvador Dalí, The Persistence of Memory, 1931. The Museum of Modern Art, New York. Given anonymously. Right: Henri Matisse, Icarus, from Jazz, 1947. National Gallery of Art, Washington D.C. Gift of Mr. and Mrs. Andrew S. Keck.

BILLY BOB FROM SWING

Boredom and constraint can be an inspiration for great art. Henri Matisse was visiting his sister in Schneider, Texas (no one Sophie had married a rancher she met during the Great War), when the artist, having no facility for English nor any interest in horses, took up his sister's scissors to amuse himself. "What could I do?" he wrote to his Parisian friend L. "I had wearied of rope tricks and yodeling."

February 1990/Texas Monthly 113

THE ALAMO OF THE PYRENEES

John Wayne commissioned his old friend René Magritte to design a poster for his 1960 film, *The Alamo*, and if you study the painting, it's easy to visualize the Alamo, rock-like, atop the boulder, which floats serenely above the Gulf of Mexico. The Duke, however, couldn't see it and was quoted as saying, "Come on, René, get real"—something the Belgian surrealist never did, at least not in his paintings.

THE CHEERLEADERS

When the authenticity of Edgar Degas' *The Cheerleaders* was established, art historians surmised that the French impressionist had been prescient, somehow anticipating the costume design for the Dallas Cowboys Cheerleaders. It has since been discovered that the painting was at one time on loan to the Adolphus Hotel in Dallas, where it served as an important if unconscious inspiration to Tex Schramm—and a reminder to us that art history is a two-way street.

Left: Edgar Degas, Dancers in Green, 1885. The Museum of Modern Art. Right: René Magritte, The Castle in the Pyrenees, 1959. California. Bottom: Top: Illustration by Gary Kelley. Right: Illustration by Steve Pietzsch

362

PUBLICATION: *Texas Monthly*
ART DIRECTOR: *Fred Woodward*
DESIGNERS: *Fred Woodward, David Kampa*
ILLUSTRATORS: *Sean Earley, Stephan Durke, Steve Shock, Thomas Woodruff, Lee Lee Brazeal, Gary Kelley, Steve Pietzsch*
PUBLISHER: *Texas Monthly, Inc.*
CATEGORY: *Story Presentation—Design*
TITLE: *"When Picasso Was a Texan"*
AWARD: *Silver*

S
W H **O** P
A—T—C
H

Nowhere to Go but Up

Yes, it does look like work, but the Versa-Climber claims to burn up twice the calories of any other exercise. The machine stimulates the motions of climbing a ladder, lifting body weight hand over hand and foot over foot, giving a full body workout, using all the major skeletal groups. The built-in microcomputer has a digital display, showing exercise time plus climbing and step rate. For the truly determined, there's a metronome that keeps the pace. At Hi-Tech Fitness, 617 N. La Cienega Blvd., $1,995 to $2,450.

A Row Is a Row

When it comes to keeping in shape, we're not all in the same boat. But through thick and thin, we can paddle off surplus poundage on the AMF Benchmark rowing machine, a high-tech toner that features a timer and adjustable resistance, plus a special readout that lets you learn how many calories you burn. That should keep you on the straight and narrow. At Nordic Fitness Equipment, 14431 Ventura Blvd., Sherman Oaks, $600.

W
O U T O R K

Gym Dandy

With the versatile Genesis 1000 home fitness center, you get three, three, three gyms in one. You can row, row, row away your bloat, approach the bench-pressing exercises with ease, and watch flab melt away when you go through the motions of cross-country skiing. The single compact unit provides that essential aerobic workout and also lets you focus on conditioning specific muscle groups, so you can vary your exercise routine while you get lean. At High-Tech Fitness, 617 N. La Cienega Blvd., $759.

Easy Rider

So you've had it up to here with the matching leg warmer-and-headband contingent that dominates those disco-fied aerobic dance classes? You say you're sick and tired of exposing your excess avoirdupois to a room full of svelter-than-thou strangers? Pressing against that too, too solid flesh at an overcrowded gym got you down? Is that what's bothering you Bunkie? Well, you don't have to leave home to get fit while you sit on the Ergo-Fit 300 stationary bike. Crafted in West Germany of steel and plastic, it's designed to pedal so smoothly that you won't miss a single heart-wrenching moment of your favorite soap. At Nordic Fitness Equipment, 14431 Ventura Blvd., Sherman Oaks, $1,220.

S
U P
H A P
E

Tone Up, Tune In, Drop Weight

Riding a stationary bike may be good exercise, but it's no fun when you're not going anywhere. For a change of scene, try the Heart Mate 200 computerized bike, the ultimate home-exercise/entertainment center in one. It has a built-in color TV and AM-FM radio to keep you tuned in while you tone up, as well as a speedometer, timer, calorie counter, and heart-rate and pulse monitors to chart your progress. Now we're getting someplace. At High-Tech Fitness, 617 N. La Cienega Blvd., $4,540.

A Run for Your Money

Space-age sweethearts George and Jane Jetson gave each other the runaround on a high-tech treadmill, and now you can run around in circles and reduce in your house, too. There's nothing run-of-the-mill about the Powerjob 60-10, a high-tech treadmill with a built-in computer that measures the speed, time, distance and gradient of your workout. At High-Tech Fitness, 617 N. La Cienega Blvd., $4,495.

363

PUBLICATION: *L.A. Style*
ART DIRECTOR: *Rip Georges*
DESIGNER: *Rip Georges*
PHOTOGRAPHER: *Dan Arsenault*
PUBLISHER: *L.A. Style, Inc.*
CATEGORY: *Story Presentation—Design*
TITLE: *"Shopwatch"*
AWARD: *Silver*

300 SLR

THE MERCEDES-BENZ 300SLR racing sports car enjoyed one brief, glorious season in which it dominated every event it entered. Story by John Fitch, co-winner of the 1955 Irish Tourist Trophy and the car's sole American driver in competition. Photographs by Guy Morrison; car from the collection of the Henry Ford Museum.

364

PUBLICATION:	*Mercedes*
ART DIRECTOR:	*Peter Morance*
DESIGNER:	*Peter Morance*
PHOTOGRAPHER:	*Guy Morrison*
AGENCY:	*McCaffrey, McCall*
CLIENT:	*Mercedes-Benz*
	of North America
CATEGORY:	*Story Presentation—Design*
TITLE:	*"Mercedes-Benz 300 SLR"*
AWARD:	*Silver*

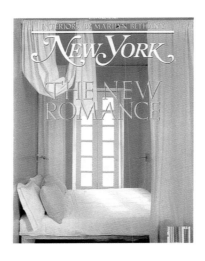

365

PUBLICATION:	*New York*
ART DIRECTOR:	*Robert Best*
PHOTO DIRECTOR:	*Jordan Schaaps*
PHOTOGRAPHER:	*Oberto Gili*
PUBLISHER:	*Murdoch Magazines*
CATEGORY:	*Story Presentation— Photography*
TITLE:	*"The New Romance"*
AWARD:	*Silver*

366

PUBLICATION:	*Time*
ART DIRECTOR:	*Rudy Hoglund*
DESIGNER:	*Tom Bentkowski*
PHOTOGRAPHER:	*Various*
PUBLISHER:	*Time Inc.*
CATEGORY:	*Story Presentation—Design*
TITLE:	*"Images '85"*
AWARD:	*Silver*

SILVER

Pure and Simple
The owners of this apartment are art collectors who've managed brilliantly to avoid the cliché residence as gallery look. Yes, they hired an architect, Mark Zeff, and a contractor, Bill Fares, to clean up their West Side co-op. But the place had a nice bit of character all its own that the design professionals managed to clean around. And yes, they have "important" lighting, also designed by Zeff. But the fixtures make a decorative contribution that's pleasantly uncommercial.

Madonna Louise Ciccone or her Sacred Image — "There is a very modest side to me too."

Rick Nicholas Save March on the Boss — "In his generation, there's no one who can touch Bruce Springsteen as a live performer."

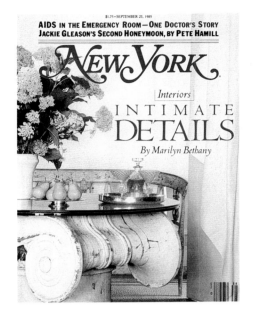

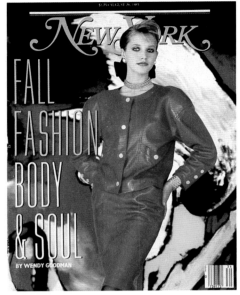

367

PUBLICATION:	*New York*
ART DIRECTOR:	*Robert Best*
DESIGNER:	*Josh Gosfield*
PHOTOGRAPHER:	*Oberto Gili*
PUBLISHER:	*Murdoch Magazines*
CATEGORY:	*Story Presentation—Photography*
TITLE:	*"Intimate Details"*
AWARD:	*Merit*

368

PUBLICATION:	*New York*
ART DIRECTOR:	*Robert Best*
DESIGNERS:	*Josh Gosfield/ Rhonda Rubinstein*
PHOTOGRAPHER:	*Just Loomis*
PUBLISHER:	*Murdoch Magazines*
CATEGORY:	*Story Presentation—Photography*
TITLE:	*"Fall Fashions"*
AWARD:	*Merit*

369

PUBLICATION:	*New York*
ART DIRECTOR:	*Robert Best*
DESIGNER:	*Robert Best*
PUBLISHER:	*Murdoch Magazines*
CATEGORY:	*Story Presentation—Design*
TITLE:	*"That's Italian"*
AWARD:	*Merit*

370

PUBLICATION:	*New York*
ART DIRECTOR:	*Robert Best*
DESIGNERS:	*David Walters,*
	Patricia Von Brachel
ILLUSTRATOR:	*Max Ginzburg*
PUBLISHER:	*Murdoch Magazines*
CATEGORY:	*Story Presentation—*
	Illustration
TITLE:	*"That's Italian"*
AWARD:	*Merit*

THAT'S
ITALIAN

371

PUBLICATION: *New York*
ART DIRECTOR: *Robert Best*
DESIGNER: *Patricia Von Brachel*
ILLUSTRATOR: *James McMullan*
PUBLISHER: *Murdoch Magazines*
CATEGORY: *Story Presentation—Illustration*
TITLE: *"That's Italian II"*
AWARD: *Merit*

372

PUBLICATION: *New York*
ART DIRECTOR: *Robert Best*
DESIGNER: *Robert Best*
PHOTOGRAPHER: *Tohru Nakamura*
PUBLISHER: *Murdoch Magazines*
CATEGORY: *Story Presentation—Design*
TITLE: *"Going for the Gold"*
AWARD: *Merit*

373

PUBLICATION: *New York*
ART DIRECTOR: *Robert Best*
DESIGNERS: *Josh Gosfield,*
Rhonda Rubenstein
PUBLISHER: *Murdoch Magazines*
CATEGORY: *Story Presentation—Design*
TITLE: *"Best of New York"*
AWARD: *Merit*

374

PUBLICATION: *New York*
ART DIRECTOR: *Robert Best*
DESIGNER: *Robert Best*
PHOTOGRAPHER: *Douglas Kirkland*
PUBLISHER: *Murdoch Magazines*
CATEGORY: *Story Presentation—Design*
TITLE: *"Fall Preview '85"*
AWARD: *Merit*

375

PUBLICATION: *New York*
ART DIRECTOR: *Robert Best*
DESIGNER: *Robert Best*
ILLUSTRATOR: *Phillipe Weisbecker*
PUBLISHER: *Murdoch Magazines*
CATEGORY: *Story Presentation—*
Illustration
TITLE: *"Gael Grazes"*
AWARD: *Merit*

376

PUBLICATION:	*New York*
ART DIRECTOR:	*Robert Best*
DESIGNER:	*Josh Gosfield*
ILLUSTRATOR:	*Burt Silverman*
PUBLISHER:	*Murdoch Magazines*
CATEGORY:	*Story Presentation—Design*
TITLE:	*"A Homeless Woman's Story"*
AWARD:	*Merit*

377

PUBLICATION:	*New York*
ART DIRECTOR:	*Robert Best*
DESIGNERS:	*David Walters,*
	Patricia Von Brachel
ILLUSTRATOR:	*Arnold Roth*
PUBLISHER:	*Murdoch Magazines*
CATEGORY:	*Story Presentation—*
	Illustration
TITLE:	*"How to Complain"*
AWARD:	*Merit*

378

PUBLICATION:	*New York*
ART DIRECTOR:	*Robert Best*
DESIGNER:	*Robert Best*
ILLUSTRATOR:	*Alan E. Cober*
PUBLISHER:	*Murdoch Magazines*
CATEGORY:	*Story Presentation—*
	Illustration
TITLE:	*"A New Standard for Libel"*
AWARD:	*Merit*

379

PUBLICATION: *New York*
ART DIRECTOR: *Robert Best*
DESIGNER: *Robert Best*
PHOTOGRAPHER: *Oberto Gili*
PUBLISHER: *Murdoch Magazines*
CATEGORY: *Story Presentation—Design*
TITLE: *"Intimate Details"*
AWARD: *Merit*

380

PUBLICATION: *Rolling Stone*
ART DIRECTOR: *Derek Ungless*
DESIGNER: *Derek Ungless*
PHOTO EDITOR: *Laurie Kratchovil*
PHOTOGRAPHER: *Mary Ellen Mark*
PUBLISHER: *Straight Arrow Publications*
CATEGORY: *Story Presentation—
Photography*
TITLE: *"The New Spain"*
AWARD: *Merit*

381

PUBLICATION: *Rolling Stone*
ART DIRECTOR: *Derek Ungless*
DESIGNER: *Derek Ungless*
PHOTO EDITOR: *Laurie Kratchovil*
PHOTOGRAPHER: *Max Vadukul*
PUBLISHER: *Straight Arrow Publications*
CATEGORY: *Story Presentation—
Photography*
TITLE: *"Loose Springs"*
AWARD: *Merit*

MERIT

382

PUBLICATION: *Designers West*
ART DIRECTOR: *Nan Oshin*
DESIGNER: *Nan Oshin*
PHOTOGRAPHERS: *Bruce Forster, Dick Busher*
PUBLISHER: *Designers West*
CATEGORY: *Story Presentation—Design*
TITLE: *"Profile"*
AWARD: *Merit*

383

PUBLICATION: *Architecture Minnesota*
ART DIRECTOR: *Bruce Rubin*
DESIGNER: *Jim Cordaro*
PHOTOGRAPHER: *George Heinrich*
PUBLISHER: *Minnesota Society, American Institute of Architects*
CATEGORY: *Story Presentation—Design*
TITLE: *"Doors"*
AWARD: *Merit*

D O O R S

Opened to let the cat out, to bring the paper in, to welcome friends. Closed to shut out the cold and noise of the world. Where people live, there are doors. Photography by George Heinrich.

DOORS

384

PUBLICATION: *Architectural Record*
ART DIRECTOR: *Alex H. Stillano*
DESIGNER: *Anna Egger-Schlesinger*
PHOTOGRAPHER: *Paul Warchol*
PUBLISHER: *McGraw-Hill*
CATEGORY: *Story Presentation—Design*
TITLE: *"The French Connection"*
AWARD: *Merit*

385

PUBLICATION: *Connecticut's Finest*
ART DIRECTORS: *Deb Hardison, Bett McLean*
DESIGNER: *Bett McLean*
PHOTOGRAPHER: *Ty Harrington*
PUBLISHER: *13-30 Corporation*
CATEGORY: *Story Presentation—Design*
TITLE: *"Kriz"*
AWARD: *Merit*

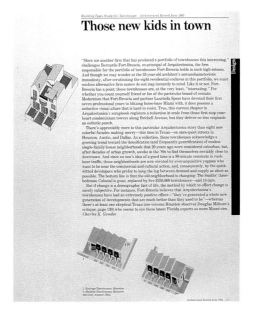

386

PUBLICATION: *Architectural Record*
ART DIRECTOR: *Alex H. Stillano*
DESIGNER: *Alberto Bucchianeri*
PHOTOGRAPHER: *Richard Payne*
PUBLISHER: *McGraw-Hill*
CATEGORY: *Story Presentation—Design*
TITLE: *"Those New Kids in Town"*
AWARD: *Merit*

387

PUBLICATION: *Progressive Architecture*
ART DIRECTOR: *Richelle Huff*
DESIGNER: *Richelle Huff*
PHOTOGRAPHERS: *Rion Rizzo,*
William E. Mathis
PUBLISHER: *Penton Publications*
CATEGORY: *Story Presentation—Design*
TITLE: *"The Spirit of St. Louis"*
AWARD: *Merit*

360

PUBLICATION:	*GQ*
ART DIRECTOR:	*Mary Shanahan*
DESIGNER:	*Fabien Baron*
PHOTOGRAPHER:	*Dennis Piel*
PUBLISHER:	*Condé Nast*
CATEGORY:	*Story Presentation—Design*
TITLE:	*"Decent Exposure"*
AWARD:	*Silver*

SILVER

HOW THEY RUINED OUR
PRISONS

Judge Justice is wrong. The governor is
wrong. The Legislature is wrong. And
the reformers are wrong. The answer to
the Texas prison crisis is to run the jails
the same way we did twenty years ago.

BY DICK J. REAVIS

In the file room of the fifth floor of the federal court-house in downtown Houston, there's a sheet of paper that has eclipsed the Texas constitution, the laws of our Legislature, and traditions that have guided us since the days of the Republic. It's an ordinary piece of paper, a white sheet of onionskin, legal size. Words formed of block letters are written across its face, in ballpoint ink, so pale that it appears to be gray. The handwriting is steady and careful; the writer apparently used a slip of paperboard to guide his hand, because the bottoms of his letters all stop at precisely the same point, as if on an invisible line. The first words written on the page are those of a pauper's oath, "Motion To Proceed In Forma Pauperis." They were not intended to be but they have become words of irony. In the past five years, that sheet of paper and thousands of others indexed to it—the text and proceedings of the Ruiz v. Estelle case—have cost Texas taxpayers more than $150 million, including $4 million in legal fees alone. During the next ten years the suit could cost the state nearly $1 billion more.

The man whose signature appears beneath the writing is David R. Ruiz, a diminutive, intense convict with only seven years of formal education. In June 1972, when he penned his suit against employees of the Texas Department of Corrections (TDC), the nation's largest prison system, he was only 29. In the years since then, Ruiz has become a symbol of courage and tenacity, a figure mentioned almost daily in our press. In some quarters he's a folk hero, the little man who beat a big oppressive system, a David who brought a Goliath low. David Ruiz is the kind of man whom the Austin American-Statesman, without any cynicism, could quote describing himself as "a person whose only aims, hopes and desires are to improve, always to improve, and to contribute to humanity." He is the standard-bearer of the Texas movement for penal reform.

But David Ruiz is no hero. He's hardly deserving of admiration at all. In 1972 he already had a long prison record, for robberies he later admitted he had committed. After four stretches in reform school, Ruiz first

went to prison in 1960 on an armed robbery charge. Released in 1968, he returned before the close of the year with three concurrent sentences, for another ill-fated stickup and two counts of robbery by assault. In June 1972 he was also wanted for murder on a warrant out of Ohio, where he had spent a part of the brief seven months between his prison terms. David Resendez Ruiz had not, as the wardens would say, been sent to prison for singing too loud in church.

He'd been less than a choirboy while wearing the white uniform of a Texas convict, too. During the trial of his lawsuit, he admitted that he had stabbed "approximately three or four" of his fellow inmates. He had escaped once and had several times been found with weapons. He had been put in solitary confinement some fifteen times for assaultiveness and had been denied parole for the same reason. David Ruiz didn't show much respect for the law or for the rights of others. His explanation for one of the stabbings was: "He had his hand in his pocket, I didn't know what he had in his

pocket, so I had a knife myself, and I used it." Yet during his career as a convict, he'd filed a dozen suits alleging that the Texas Department of Corrections had engaged in unlawful practices and violated his rights. David Ruiz hasn't shown much regard for the truth either. He is now back in prison, this time for aggravated perjury. Some of the charges he made in his petition weren't credible, even by the farthest stretch of the imagination. For example, he asserted that the cells in which he had been confined—in various court-conditioned Texas prisons—were cold in May, August, and September. The question he sat naked was, Does a man like this, a hardened criminal, deserve the rights the rest of us have?

But Ruiz wasn't the first or only convict to sue the Texas prison system, and in April 1974, after federal district judge William Wayne Justice set the Ruiz case on his docket, the judge married it to the suits of seven other prisoners. The most important allegations in their petitions concerned punishments administered to disci-

Photography by Matt Mahurin

In the South, convicts had
to be taken outside the prison
walls to find work, so eyes,
ears, whips, and dogs became
the chief barriers to escape.
In Texas, the prisoners themselves were used to help train
packs of guard dogs.

thrived so long as discipline was harsh and summary. "The old system," a veteran warden told me, "ran on fear." Then he paused, as if in nostalgia for a boyhood sweetheart. "But you know what?" he continued. "It worked. We kept order that way."

However ugly, the system did most of the things we can realistically expect a prison system to do. It did them well, and it did them cheaply. Before the trial of Ruiz v. Estelle, prisons in Texas were the safest, most productive, and most economical in the nation. Today they are the most dangerous, yet their cost has more than quadrupled. Growing indiscipline has set new records and created new categories of cost. For example, last year so many convicts turned cafeteria spoons into shanks, or jailhouse knives, that the prisons had to abandon the metal dinnerware that had been in use for years and spend more than $30,000 to purchase disposable plastic utensils. At the system's Coffield Unit alone, near Dallas, convicts who couldn't be controlled by the new, Ruiz-era disciplinary code last year broke six thousand window panes, and convicts across the state van-

(Continued on page 232)

Throughout the system's
history, despite the efforts of
reformers within and without,
guards indulged in simple,
straightforward, punitive assault.
Apologists said that such
abuse was inevitable in any
system of authority.

plinary violators in prison, an issue that federal judges had come to regard during the sixties as involving constitutional protection. Using the prisoners' petitions as a basis, Judge Justice engineered a proceeding—it isn't over yet—in which issues not mentioned by the petitioners, like living space, recreation programs, and even prison layoff operations, also came under his review. As if the expert lawyers he appointed to represent the plaintiffs were not enough, the judge also brought in the United States Department of Justice as an adversary to the State of Texas. The trial of Ruiz v. Estelle, the most thorough in penal history, lasted eight months and heard 349 witnesses, most of them convicts. The result was a lengthy opinion from Judge Justice, followed by reams of court-approved settlement agreements, all aimed at reforming the prison system.

If you have ever visited a prison, it is easy to comprehend the desire for reform. Prisons are ugly, frightening places, and there is something fundamental in human nature that recoils from the idea of men and women locked up. I have toured all 27 Texas prison units. I talked to wardens, guards, and field supervisors.

361

PUBLICATION:	*Texas Monthly*
ART DIRECTOR:	*Fred Woodward*
DESIGNER:	*Fred Woodward*
PHOTOGRAPHER:	*Matt Mahurin*
PUBLISHER:	*Texas Monthly, Inc.*
CATEGORY:	*Story Presentation—Photography*
TITLE:	*"How They Ruined Our Prisons"*
AWARD:	*Silver*

Cincinnati Centerpiece

Procter & Gamble's new headquarters in Cincinnati, Ohio, designed by Kohn Pedersen Fox of New York, is contextual at both urban and architectural levels.

388

PUBLICATION:	*Progressive Architecture*
ART DIRECTOR:	*Richelle Huff*
DESIGNER:	*Richelle Huff*
PUBLISHER:	*Penton Publishing*
CATEGORY:	*Story Presentation—Photography*
TITLE:	*"Cincinnati Centerpiece"*
AWARD:	*Merit*

389

PUBLICATION:	*Progressive Architecture*
ART DIRECTOR:	*Richelle Huff*
DESIGNER:	*Richelle Huff*
PHOTOGRAPHERS:	*Barbara Karant, Peter Aaron, Jack Pottle, Judith Turner, Timothy Hursley*
PUBLISHER:	*Penton Publications*
CATEGORY:	*Story Presentation—Design*
TITLE:	*"Cincinnati Centerpiece"*
AWARD:	*Merit*

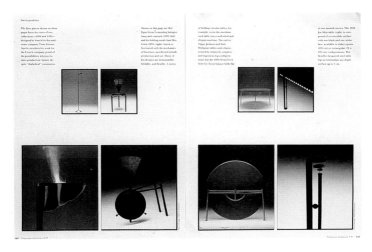

Starck Contrasts

After decades of decline, French design is making a comeback, led by the self-styled enfant terrible Philippe Starck. Shown here: a survey of (relatively!) earlier works and the latest offerings.

390

PUBLICATION:	*Progressive Architecture*
ART DIRECTOR:	*Richelle Huff*
DESIGNER:	*Richelle Huff*
PHOTOGRAPHER:	*Deidi Von Schaewen*
PUBLISHER:	*Penton Publications*
CATEGORY:	*Story Presentation—Design*
TITLE:	*"Starck Contrasts"*
AWARD:	*Merit*

391

PUBLICATION:	*Metropolitan Home*
ART DIRECTOR:	*Michael Jensen*
DESIGNER:	*Don Morris*
PHOTOGRAPHERS:	*Jeff McNamara, Oberto Gili, Langdon Clay, Tom Hooper, John Vaughan*
PUBLISHER:	*Burzon Publishing Co.*
CATEGORY:	*Story Presentation—Design*
TITLE:	*"Elements of Style"*
AWARD:	*Merit*

ELEMENTS
OF
STYLE

NEW CLASSICS

THE HIT PARADE OF 20TH CENTURY DESIGN

THE PHILIPPE FRENCH STARCK ROOTS

The timeless look of the Café Costes. Its functional, minimalist design borrows from the '30s, '50s, '60s—and 2001. Of rising design are Philippe Starck (below) one for steps: "He makes learning from the past a futuristic experience."

IT'S FOUR O'CLOCK in the afternoon at the Café Costes. Out on the terrace, under a low-slung, steamship-style canopy, tourists en route from the Pompidou linger at conical tables, eyeing punks in Japanese black on leatherette-covered chairs. Inside, the focus is equally on being seen. Placed center stage, a dramatic sea-green granite staircase bisects the room, rising to a giant clock Harold Lloyd might have swung from. Dazzling restrooms have translucent glass stalls, and in the men's rooms, the central pissoir (also of glass) resembles a mirrored waterfall. The café's peach stucco walls are also lined with chunks of mirrors to reflect the scene. Young men in broad-shouldered jackets, teenage girls in chiffon hairbows—the cafe accommodates them all on banquettes covered in black Mercedes leatherette. Waiters serve mustard in pots by Achille Castiglioni, bread in baskets by Ettore Sottsass, tea in Richard Sapper teapots. There is a palpable sense that by simply being here you are *brunché*, plugged-in. Hip.

Holding court in the corner over a bottle of champagne is Philippe Starck, the master planner of it all. He has every reason to celebrate. Only 36, Starck is the hottest designer in France at a time when Design has become the new Cinema, and his influence is rapidly spreading. The resolutely modern Starck look—timeless and pared down—has shaped everything from Italian pasta to Mme. Mitterrand's bed-

room at the Elysée Palace, from a Dallas nightclub to Euro-chic chairs now coming on strong at stores in New York, Chicago and Los Angeles. But in designing the Café Costes, Starck has produced the perfect showcase for his alluring hybrid of functional sleekness and Post-Modern wit. The café's curved-wood chairs have only three legs—one of them a steel rod that ends in a pencil-thin point to give the illusion of instability. Starck named the chairs Pratfall I. Is he pulling ours when he insists the *real* point is that there is no fourth leg to trip up waiters? His round synthetic tables are intentionally tiny to encourage customers to communicate, and triangular washbasins in the dazzling men's room were so often misconstrued that management finally posted a sign: *ne pas uriner.*

Café Costes was the first bistro in Paris to make a design statement. And when it opened in 1984, in the midst of Les Halles, it was heralded as an instant

Bye-bye Versailles: Philippe Starck took two rooms of the Elysée Palace, France's presidential habitat, and blew off the cobwebs. A sleek, Starck look (above) for President Mitterrand's conference room, with an up-market version of the three-legged Costes chair. Pratfall II is made of curved wood with black metal tube legs and black Mercedes leatherette cushions.

Mme. Mitterrand says she cannot sleep anywhere but in the room I made for her," boasts Starck. In her Elysée hideaway (left), a painted ceiling by artist Gérard Garouste inspires escape, dreams. The room's functional lower half is for work, Starck's chair is exquisitely crafted of aluminum and leather—a witty take on the traditional club, sans its canvas.

Photographs by Larry Williams.

THE ITALIAN ROOTS NEW YORK

Italian Eurostyle flourishing in a richly detailed period room* Certainly. The new in Italy has always been seen and set against the rich architectural heritage of the past. Here the white background—walls and floors—lets the sculptural furnishings shine like objects in a personal gallery.

MEMPHIS IS JUST the latest thunderbolt from the sky's-the-limit Italian design community. These neo-Renaissance men and women, most of them trained as architects, have been Europe's movers and shakers—particularly the shakers—for 30 years now. After reshaping the Sixties and Seventies with molded plastics and bringing lighting out of the dark ages with the tiny halogen bulb, they continue to sail the cutting edge between technology and invention.

It was Ettore Sottsass' Memphis Group that redefined furniture at the 1981 Milan Furniture Fair. Looking for luxe in all the wrong places—the Fifties, Memphis, Tennessee (home of Elvis)—they found a swivel-hipped international style that banned the Bauhaus, canned Corbu, trashed 50 years of architectural good taste and proclaimed a brave new world where the only rule was that there were no rules.

Today, New York designer Stewart Skolnick builds from Memphis' anything-goes tradition. There are flashbacks to the Fifties in this living room, like the daring shape of Italian designer Paolo Deganello's 1982 Torso lounge chairs, which interact with the sitter. But the Skolnick-designed coffee table throws the Fifties a curve. That boomerang shape (the legacy of artist Isamu Noguchi) is rendered here in glass and cantilevered from a cold white cube made of Italian tile. Each virtuoso piece is in the iconoclastic Italian spirit, each a world unto itself. But in this simple setting, they come together to form a universe.

Produced by Ben Lloyd. Written by Donald M. Young. Design: Stewart Skolnick. Photographs by Norman McGrath.

A freestanding wall of clear glass brick cuts a sinuous corner in a square room, reshaping it and cradling a sleek black electronic clock. Laid diagonally, the oversized Italian tile creates room, stretching great legs. With the bold bridge, the furnishings fit like gloves? Resources, page 130

THE ENGLISH ROOTS TERENCE CONRAN

ENGLAND'S UNIQUE contribution to Eurostyle—a light, eclectic mix of pale color, uncluttered rooms and soft, nostalgic furnishings—owes a large debt to Sir Terence Conran, founder of the European Habitat and American Conran's chains of stores. "I was lucky because when I was a child my mother decided what our house would look like. She achieved great simplicity," says Conran. "I remember big, chunky sofas and good, hand-me-down antique furniture in a real 1930s interior. The few objects that were in it seemed to be in sharp focus, you saw them with an intensity you can't appreciate in a cluttered room. I've tried to re-create that atmosphere of luxurious simplicity ever since." This philosophy is readily evident in these rooms, taken from the forthcoming *Terence Conran's New House Book.*

From *Terence Conran's New House Book,* by Terence Conran. Copyright 1985. To be published by Villard Books in October.

The London living room (right) of Conran's son Jasper is English comfort without the stuffiness. Keys to the look: A spare, confident mix (Thonet table, Tizio lamp) set against 19th century grandeur stripped to its bare, elegant skeleton.

A former billiard room was transformed into the kitchen of the Conran country house. Hints of the sumptuous English manor survive in the generous windows, ceramic tile, stripped wood floors and a tongue-in-groove ceiling covered in high-gloss paint. Resources, page 130

392

PUBLICATION: *Metropolitan Home*
ART DIRECTOR: *Michael Jensen*
DESIGNER: *Don Morris*
PHOTOGRAPHERS: *Tim Street Porter, Ken Kirkwood, Bill Hedrich, Simon Brown, Larry Williams, John Vaughan, François Halard, Bill Helms, Jim Koch, Jeff McNamara, Norman McGrath*
PUBLISHER: *Burzon Publishing Co.*
CATEGORY: *Story Presentation—Design*
TITLE: *"Eurostyle"*
AWARD: *Merit*

393

PUBLICATION:	*House & Garden*
ART DIRECTOR:	*Karen Lee Grant*
DESIGNER:	*Lloyd Ziff*
PHOTOGRAPHER:	*Jacques Dirand*
PUBLISHER:	*Condé Nast*
CATEGORY:	*Story Presentation—Photography*
TITLE:	*"Home of Our Father's Pride"*
AWARD:	*Merit*

394

PUBLICATION:	*House & Garden*
ART DIRECTOR:	*Karen Lee Grant*
DESIGNER:	*Lloyd Ziff*
PHOTOGRAPHER:	*Oberto Gili*
PUBLISHER:	*Condé Nast*
CATEGORY:	*Story Presentation—Design*
TITLE:	*"An Artist's Life, 1985"*
AWARD:	*Merit*

395

PUBLICATION:	*L.A. Style*
ART DIRECTOR:	*Rip Georges*
DESIGNER:	*Rip Georges*
PHOTOGRAPHER:	*Four Eyes*
PUBLISHER:	*L.A. Style, Inc.*
CATEGORY:	*Story Presentation—Photography*
TITLE:	*"Uncommon Adornment"*
AWARD:	*Merit*

396

PUBLICATION:	*Town & Country*
ART DIRECTOR:	*Melissa Tardiff*
DESIGNER:	*Mary Rosen*
PHOTOGRAPHER:	*Henry Wolf*
PUBLISHER:	*Hearst Publications*
CATEGORY:	*Story Presentation—Design*
TITLE:	*"Quintessential New Yorkers"*
AWARD:	*Merit*

MERIT

THE WHITNEY

A lively landmark
for American art
on Madison

BY RICHARD COVINGTON

397

PUBLICATION:	*Travel & Leisure*
ART DIRECTOR:	*Adrian Taylor*
PHOTOGRAPHER:	*Burt Gunn*
PUBLISHER:	*American Express Publishing Co.*
CATEGORY:	*Story Presentation— Photography*
TITLE:	*"Mad for Mad. Ave."*
AWARD:	*Merit*

398

PUBLICATION:	*Travel & Leisure*
ART DIRECTOR:	*Adrian Taylor*
PHOTOGRAPHERS:	*Robert Fereck, Jeff Gnass, David Muench*
PUBLISHER:	*American Express Publishing Co.*
CATEGORY:	*Story Presentation— Photography*
TITLE:	*"Bryce Canyon"*
AWARD:	*Merit*

MERIT

399

PUBLICATION: *Travel & Leisure*
ART DIRECTOR: *Adrian Taylor*
PHOTOGRAPHERS: *Adam Woolfitt,*
Anthony Edgeworth
PUBLISHER: *American Express*
Publishing Co.
CATEGORY: *Story Presentation—*
Photography
TITLE: *"Yorkshire"*
AWARD: *Merit*

400

PUBLICATION: *Travel & Leisure*
ART DIRECTOR: *Adrian Taylor*
PHOTOGRAPHER: *Enrico Ferorelli*
PUBLISHER: *American Express*
Publishing Co.
CATEGORY: *Story Presentation—*
Photography
TITLE: *"The Glorious Hill Town of*
Umbria"
AWARD: *Merit*

401

PUBLICATION:	*European Travel & Life*
ART DIRECTOR:	*Terry Koppel*
DESIGNER:	*Terry Koppel*
PHOTOGRAPHERS:	*Michael O'Neill, Guy Bouchet*
PUBLISHER:	*Inabnit Communications*
CATEGORY:	*Story Presentation—Design*
TITLE:	*"A Sense of Place"*
AWARD:	*Merit*

402

PUBLICATION:	*European Travel & Life*
ART DIRECTOR:	*Terry Koppel*
DESIGNERS:	*Terry Koppel, April Garston*
PHOTOGRAPHER:	*Guy Bouchet*
PUBLISHER:	*Inabnit Communications*
CATEGORY:	*Story Presentation—Design*
TITLE:	*"Italian Style"*
AWARD:	*Merit*

403

PUBLICATION:	*European Travel & Life*
ART DIRECTOR:	*Terry Koppel*
DESIGNER:	*Terry Koppel*
PHOTOGRAPHER:	*Chris Mead*
PUBLISHER:	*Inabnit Communications*
CATEGORY:	*Story Presentation—Design*
TITLE:	*"The Fragrant Harvest"*
AWARD:	*Merit*

404

PUBLICATION:	*European Travel & Life*
ART DIRECTOR:	*Terry Koppel*
DESIGNER:	*Terry Koppel*
PHOTOGRAPHER:	*Harry Gruyaert*
PUBLISHER:	*Inabnit Communications*
CATEGORY:	*Story Presentation—Design*
TITLE:	*"Friends of French Art"*
AWARD:	*Merit*

Photography by Richard Avedon

Faces of the WEST

In these faces you can see the wind, the sun, and the heat. You can see the power of the West.

This is a fictional West. I don't think the West of these portraits is any more conclusive than the West of John Wayne. —RICHARD AVEDON

IN THE SPRING OF 1979 RICHARD Avedon came to Texas and began to make a sequence of portraits. He did not stop in Highland Park or River Oaks, to revisit any of the clothes he had photographed for fashion magazines over the years, but went instead to the Sweetwater Jaycees' Rattlesnake Round-up, where he took a picture of a young man named Boyd Fortin holding a gutted diamondback.

For the next five and a half years, in the summers particularly, Avedon returned to the West. He visited truck stops, rodeos, ranches, mines, and stockyards. He made two remarkable portraits in the San Antonio jail, two more in a mental hospital in New Mexico, several in a Hutterite community in Montana; and four of extraordinary power—in slaughterhouses.

He photographed miners, drifters, cowhands, roughnecks, couples, teenagers, old folks, and many, many people who would probably be content to be described as just folks.

By late October 1984 he had traveled in seventeen states, photographed 752 people, and created, very much on his own terms, his fictional West. All his Westerners were shot against a sheet of white paper and in natural light because Avedon wanted the "source of light to be invisible so as to neutralize its role in the appearance of things." Whether such lighting plays a neutral role may be questioned, but certainly it is consistent, as the Western sun is not; if a fiction is being made, then the fictionist, whether writer or photographer, has a right to the style of his choice.

Avedon stood beside the camera, close to the person or persons being photographed, seeing them but not the image the camera was about to give him. In a lucid and interesting introduction to *In the American West*, the soon-

INTRODUCTION BY LARRY McMURTRY

BOYD FORTIN, THIRTEEN-YEAR-OLD RATTLESNAKE SKINNER

Sweetwater, Texas

146—SEPTEMBER 1985

TEXAS MONTHLY·147

405

PUBLICATION:	*Texas Monthly*
ART DIRECTOR:	*Fred Woodward*
DESIGNER:	*Fred Woodward*
PHOTOGRAPHER:	*Richard Avedon*
PUBLISHER:	*Texas Monthly, Inc.*
CATEGORY:	*Story Presentation—Design*
TITLE:	*"Faces of the West"*
AWARD:	*Merit*

MERIT

AMBIENT COLOR
by Robert A. Widdicombe

‹ PUERTO ANGEL, OAXACA ›

Strangeness is what attracts Robert Widdicombe to Mexico—the vibrating colors, the religious images, the people and their demeanor. To capture his impressions, he takes his photographs at night, using a flash and a slow shutter speed. The flash flattens surfaces and intensifies color, and once the flash fades, the ambient light brings out the shadow images, registering Widdicombe's amazement that just across the border everything can be so different.

‹ CHILAPA, GUERRERO ›

‹ ISLA MUJERES, QUINTANA ROO ›

‹ GUADALAJARA, JALISCO ›

‹ ISLA MUJERES, QUINTANA ROO ›

‹ VILLA DIAZ ORDAZ, OAXACA ›

406

PUBLICATION:	*Texas Monthly*
ART DIRECTOR:	*Fred Woodward*
DESIGNER:	*Fred Woodward*
PHOTOGRAPHER:	*Robert Widdicombe*
PUBLISHER:	*Texas Monthly, Inc.*
CATEGORY:	*Story Presentation— Photography*
TITLE:	*"Ambient Color"*
AWARD:	*Merit*

The Return of the URBAN COWBOY

In the five years since their lives inspired a movie, the urban cowboys who hung out at Gilley's lost their jobs, their marriages, and even the joy of conquering the mechanical bull. Now they're back in the saddle again.

by Aaron Latham

407

PUBLICATION: *Texas Monthly*
ART DIRECTOR: *Fred Woodward*
DESIGNER: *Fred Woodward*
PHOTOGRAPHER: *Brian Smale*
PUBLISHER: *Texas Monthly, Inc.*
CATEGORY: *Story Presentation—
Photography*
TITLE: *"The Return of the Urban
Cowboy"*
AWARD: *Merit*

WHEN PICASSO WAS A TEXAN

And Dali. And Matisse. And Degas. And Van Gogh. And…

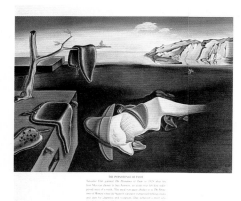

408

PUBLICATION: *Texas Monthly*
ART DIRECTOR: *Fred Woodward*
DESIGNERS: *Fred Woodward,
David Kampa*
ILLUSTRATORS: *Sean Earley, Steve Pietzsch,
Stephen Durke, Steven
Schock, Thomas Woodruff,
LeeLee Brazeal, Gary Kelley*
PUBLISHER: *Texas Monthly, Inc.*
CATEGORY: *Story Presentation—
Illustration*
TITLE: *"When Picasso Was a Texan"*
AWARD: *Merit*

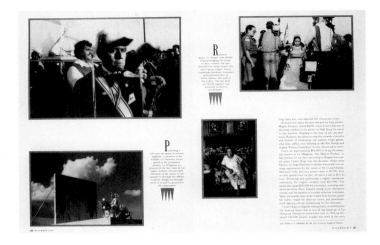

409

PUBLICATION:	*Texas Monthly*
ART DIRECTOR:	*Fred Woodward*
DESIGNERS:	*Fred Woodward,*
	David Kampa
PHOTOGRAPHER:	*Robert Maxham*
PUBLISHER:	*Texas Monthly, Inc.*
CATEGORY:	*Story Presentation—Design*
TITLE:	*"The Week of the Virgin"*
AWARD:	*Merit*

410

PUBLICATION:	*The Providence Journal*
ART DIRECTOR:	*Ray Lomax*
DESIGNER:	*Christian Potter Drury*
PHOTOGRAPHER:	*Mark Patinkin*
PUBLISHER:	*Providence Journal*
CATEGORY:	*Story Presentation—Design*
TITLE:	*"African Journey"*
AWARD:	*Merit*

411

PUBLICATION:	*Daily News Magazine*
ART DIRECTOR:	*Janet Froelich*
DESIGNER:	*Janet Froelich*
ILLUSTRATOR:	*Scott Reynolds*
PUBLISHER:	*New York News, Inc.*
CATEGORY:	*Story Presentation—Design*
TITLE:	*"Murder of a Bag Lady"*
AWARD:	*Merit*

412

PUBLICATION:	*Daily News Magazine*
ART DIRECTOR:	*Janet Froelich*
DESIGNER:	*Janet Froelich*
ILLUSTRATOR:	*Scott Reynolds*
PUBLISHER:	*New York News, Inc.*
CATEGORY:	*Story Presentation—*
	Illustration
TITLE:	*"Murder of a Bag Lady"*
AWARD:	*Merit*

413

PUBLICATION:	*Daily News Magazine*
ART DIRECTOR:	*Janet Froelich*
DESIGNERS:	*Janet Froelich, Zoe Brotman*
PHOTOGRAPHER:	*Bob Murray*
PUBLISHER:	*New York News, Inc.*
CATEGORY:	*Story Presentation—Design*
TITLE:	*"New Wave Yuppie"*
AWARD:	*Merit*

CLOSET KIDS

414

PUBLICATION:	*Daily News Magazine*
ART DIRECTOR:	*Thomas P. Ruis*
DESIGNER:	*Thomas P. Ruis*
PHOTOGRAPHER:	*Janette Beckman*
PUBLISHER:	*New York News, Inc.*
CATEGORY:	*Story Presentation—Design*
TITLE:	*"Closet Kids"*
AWARD:	*Merit*

CLOSET KIDS

The OASIS

FIRESIDE FICTION

AGE of HEROES

NEXT of KIN

415

PUBLICATION:	*The Boston Globe Magazine*
ART DIRECTOR:	*Lynn Staley*
DESIGNER:	*Lynn Staley*
ILLUSTRATOR:	*Merle Nacht*
PUBLISHER:	*The Boston Globe*
CATEGORY:	*Story Presentation—Design*
TITLE:	*"Christmas Greetings"*
AWARD:	*Merit*

MERIT

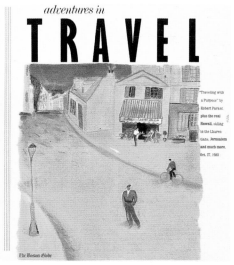

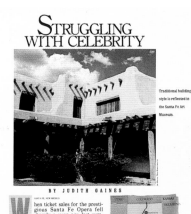

416

PUBLICATION:	*The Boston Globe Magazine*
ART DIRECTOR:	*Ronn Campisi*
DESIGNER:	*Ronn Campisi*
ILLUSTRATOR:	*Vivienne Flescher*
PUBLISHER:	*The Boston Globe*
CATEGORY:	*Story Presentation—Design*
TITLE:	*"Adventures in Travel"*
AWARD:	*Merit*

417

PUBLICATION:	*The Boston Globe Magazine*
ART DIRECTOR:	*Ronn Campisi*
DESIGNER:	*Ronn Campisi*
PHOTOGRAPHER:	*Stan Grossfeld*
PUBLISHER:	*The Boston Globe*
CATEGORY:	*Story Presentation—Design*
TITLE:	*"40 Days on the Mississippi"*
AWARD:	*Merit*

418

PUBLICATION:	*Chicago*
ART DIRECTOR:	*Robert Post*
DESIGNER:	*Cynthia Hoffman*
PHOTOGRAPHER:	*Victor Skrebneski*
CATEGORY:	*Story Presentation— Photography*
TITLE:	*"Rain"*
AWARD:	*Merit*

MERIT

CHILDREN OF POVERTY

The faces of those who have seen too much to remain young
Photographs by Stephen Shames   Text by Alex Kotlowitz

419

PUBLICATION: *Chicago*
ART DIRECTOR: *Robert Post*
DESIGNER: *Robert Post*
PHOTOGRAPHER: *Stephen Shames*
CATEGORY: *Story Presentation—*
               Photography
TITLE: *"Children of Poverty"*
AWARD: *Merit*

420

PUBLICATION: *Style*
ART DIRECTOR: *Ed Barnett*
DESIGNER: *Barbara Bose*
ILLUSTRATOR: *Barbara Bose*
PHOTOGRAPHER: *Ted Ancher*
PUBLISHER: *The Boston Herald*
CATEGORY: *Story Presentation—Design*
TITLE: *"Sashimi"*
AWARD: *Merit*

421

PUBLICATION: *Washington*
ART DIRECTOR: *Elizabeth Watson*
DESIGNER: *Elizabeth Watson*
PHOTOGRAPHER: *David Watanabe*
PUBLISHER: *Washington Magazine*
CATEGORY: *Story Presentation—Design*
TITLE: *"Mudders"*
AWARD: *Merit*

422

PUBLICATION:	*The New York Times Magazine*
ART DIRECTOR:	*Ken Kendrick*
DESIGNER:	*Diana LaGuardia*
ILLUSTRATOR:	*Bannu (Ved Pal Sharma)*
	from "A Second Paradise"
	by S.C. Welch
PUBLISHER:	*The New York Times*
CATEGORY:	*Story Presentation—Design*
TITLE:	*"India"*
AWARD:	*Merit*

423

PUBLICATION:	*The New York Times Magazine*
ART DIRECTOR:	*Ken Kendrick*
DESIGNER:	*Audrone Razgaitis*
ILLUSTRATOR:	*Harvey Dinnerstein*
PHOTOGRAPHER:	*Jules Allen*
PUBLISHER:	*The New York Times*
CATEGORY:	*Story Presentation—Design*
TITLE:	*"Boxing"*
AWARD:	*Merit*

424

PUBLICATION:	*The New York Times Magazine*
ART DIRECTOR:	*Ken Kendrick*
DESIGNER:	*Diana LaGuardia*
PHOTOGRAPHERS:	*Huynh Congut, Kyoichi Sawada, Sara Krulwich, Eddie Adams, Paul Fusco, Steve Northrup, Catherine LeRoy*
PUBLISHER:	*The New York Times*
CATEGORY:	*Story Presentation—Design*
TITLE:	*"Vietnam in America"*
AWARD:	*Merit*

425

PUBLICATION:	*The New York Times Magazine*
ART DIRECTOR:	*Ellen Burnie*
DESIGNER:	*Ellen Burnie*
PHOTOGRAPHER:	*Peter Lindbergh*
PUBLISHER:	*The New York Times*
CATEGORY:	*Story Presentation—Design*
TITLE:	*"Fashions of the Times"*
AWARD:	*Merit*

CRIME
How It Destroys, What Can Be Done

By Roger Starr

E ach city must focus anticrime efforts on one special target. In New York, that means the subways.

426

PUBLICATION: *The New York Times Magazine*
ART DIRECTOR: *Ken Kendrick*
DESIGNER: *Richard Samperi*
PHOTOGRAPHER: *Angel Franco*
PUBLISHER: *The New York Times*
CATEGORY: *Story Presentation—
Photography*
TITLE: *"Crime"*
AWARD: *Merit*

427

PUBLICATION: *The New York Times Magazine*
ART DIRECTOR: *Ken Kendrick*
DESIGNER: *Audrone Razgaitis*
PHOTOGRAPHERS: *Wayne Sorce,
Christopher Morris*
PUBLISHER: *The New York Times*
CATEGORY: *Story Presentation—
Photography*
TITLE: *"Inside the Philippine
Insurgency"*
AWARD: *Merit*

Inside the Philippine Insurgency

As the political and economic crises continue, the guerrillas are winning support.

By Steve Lohr

AREAS OF GUERRILLA ACTIVITY

Insurgent groups espousing various causes have come and gone in the Philippines for nearly 400 years.

MERIT

428

PUBLICATION: *The New York Times Magazine*
ART DIRECTOR: *Tom Bodkin*
DESIGNER: *Tom Bodkin*
PHOTOGRAPHERS: *Various*
PUBLISHER: *The New York Times*
CATEGORY: *Story Presentation—Design*
TITLE: *"World of New York/*
101 Reasons"
AWARD: *Merit*

429

PUBLICATION: *The New York Times Magazine*
ART DIRECTOR: *Ken Kendrick*
DESIGNER: *Ken Kendrick*
PHOTOGRAPHERS: *Lizzie Himmel,*
Gianfranco Gorgoni
PUBLISHER: *The New York Times*
CATEGORY: *Story Presentation—*
Photography
TITLE: *"New Art/New Money"*
AWARD: *Merit*

The audience for art is
larger than ever; collecting is no longer the sole province of the rich.

NEW ART, NEW MONEY
The Marketing of an American Artist

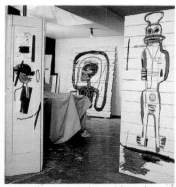

Just a few years ago,
the demand for contemporary art began to climb; prices have soared.

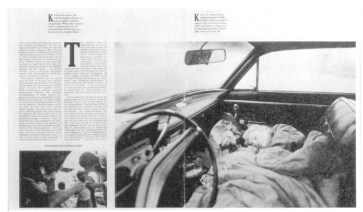

HUNGER IN AMERICA

The Safety Net Has Shrunk But It's Still in Place

430

PUBLICATION:	*The New York Times Magazine*
ART DIRECTOR:	*Ken Kendrick*
DESIGNER:	*Diana LaGuardia*
PHOTOGRAPHER:	*Stephen Shames*
PUBLISHER:	*The New York Times*
CATEGORY:	*Story Presentation—*
	Photography
TITLE:	*"Hunger in America"*
AWARD:	*Merit*

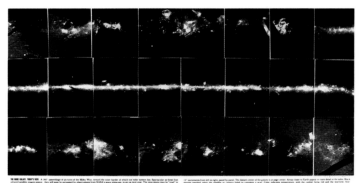

TO THE EDGE OF THE UNIVERSE THE NEW AGE OF ASTRONOMY

431

PUBLICATION:	*The New York Times Magazine*
ART DIRECTOR:	*Diana LaGuardia*
DESIGNER:	*Diana LaGuardia*
ILLUSTRATORS:	*Bob Conrad, Izumi Inoue*
PUBLISHER:	*The New York Times*
CATEGORY:	*Story Presentation—Design*
TITLE:	*"Universe"*
AWARD:	*Merit*

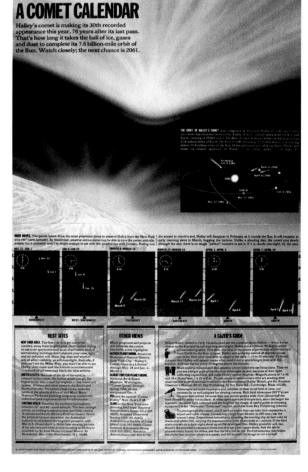

A COMET CALENDAR

Halley's comet is making its 30th recorded appearance this year, 76 years after its last pass. That's how long it takes the ball of ice, gases and dust to complete its 7.6 billion-mile orbit of the Sun. Watch closely; the next chance is 2061.

SOUTH AFRICA: DREAM AND REALITY

A returning journalist examines the white fantasies that define apartheid.

By Joseph Lelyveld

432

PUBLICATION: *The New York Times Magazine*
ART DIRECTOR: *Ken Kendrick*
DESIGNER: *Audrone Razgaitis*
PHOTOGRAPHER: *John F. Conn*
PUBLISHER: *The New York Times*
CATEGORY: *Story Presentation—*
                 Photography
TITLE: *"South Africa: Dream and*
                 Reality"
AWARD: *Merit*

YOUTH·ART·HYPE
A Different Bohemia

By Maureen Dowd

Young artists are asked to explain why a product that looks like fun should be taken seriously.

433

PUBLICATION: *The New York Times Magazine*
ART DIRECTOR: *Ken Kendrick*
DESIGNER: *Audrone Razgaitis*
PHOTOGRAPHER: *Arlene Gottfried*
PUBLISHER: *The New York Times*
CATEGORY: *Story Presentation—*
                 Photography
TITLE: *"A Different Bohemia"*
AWARD: *Merit*

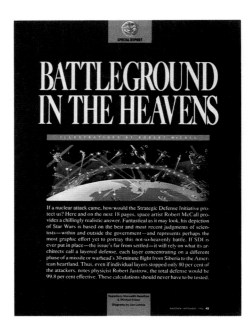

BATTLEGROUND IN THE HEAVENS

ILLUSTRATIONS BY ROBERT McCALL

If a nuclear attack came, how would the Strategic Defense Initiative protect us? Here and on the next 18 pages, space artist Robert McCall provides a chillingly realistic answer. Fantastical as it may look, his depiction of Star Wars is based on the best and most recent judgments of scientists—within and outside the government—and represents perhaps the most graphic effort yet to portray this not-so-heavenly battle. If SDI is ever put in place—the issue's far from settled—it will rely on what its architects call a layered defense, each layer concentrating on a different phase of a missile or warhead's 30-minute flight from Siberia to the American heartland. Thus, even if individual layers stopped only 80 per cent of the attackers, notes physicist Robert Jastrow, the total defense would be 99.8 per cent effective. These calculations should never have to be tested.

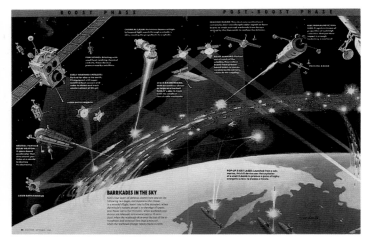

BARRICADES IN THE SKY

434

PUBLICATION: *Discover*
ART DIRECTOR: *Eric Seidman*
DESIGNER: *Sandra DiPasqua*
ILLUSTRATOR: *Robert McCall*
PUBLISHER: *Time Inc.*
CATEGORY: *Story Presentation—Design*
TITLE: *"Battleground in the Heavens"*
AWARD: *Merit*

THE LAST STAND

BY DAVID WESTERN

Slaughtered for its horn, the black rhino is plunging toward extinction. It can be saved—if we act now

The reason for the rhino's demise is a jarring mix of Asia's growing prosperity and Africa's desperate poverty

435

PUBLICATION: *Discover*
ART DIRECTOR: *Eric Seidman*
DESIGNER: *Sandra Di Pasqua*
PUBLISHER: *Time Inc.*
CATEGORY: *Story Presentation—Design*
TITLE: *"The Last Stand"*
AWARD: *Merit*

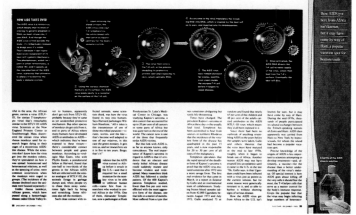

436

PUBLICATION:	*Discover*
ART DIRECTOR:	*Eric Seidman*
DESIGNER:	*Theodore Kalomirakis*
PHOTOGRAPHER:	*Olaf Wahlund*
PUBLISHER:	*Time Inc.*
CATEGORY:	*Story Presentation—Design*
TITLE:	*"AIDS"*
AWARD:	*Merit*

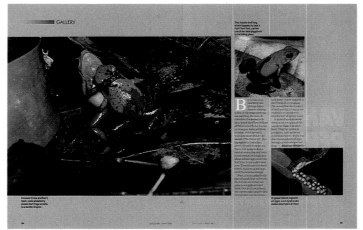

437

PUBLICATION:	*Discover*
ART DIRECTOR:	*Eric Seidman*
DESIGNER:	*Theodore Kalomirakis*
PHOTOGRAPHERS:	*Michael and Patricia Fogden*
PUBLISHER:	*Time Inc.*
CATEGORY:	*Story Presentation—Design*
TITLE:	*"A Frog He Would A-wooing Go"*
AWARD:	*Merit*

MERIT

438

PUBLICATION: *Science '85*
ART DIRECTOR: *John Isley*
DESIGNER: *John Isley*
ILLUSTRATOR: *Steven Guarnaccia*
PUBLISHER: *Science '85/American Association for the Advancement of Science*
CATEGORY: *Story Presentation— Illustration*
TITLE: *"The Compleat Worrier"*
AWARD: *Merit*

439

PUBLICATION: *The Village Voice*
ART DIRECTOR: *C. Carr*
DESIGNER: *Michael Grossman*
ILLUSTRATOR: *Mark Marek*
PUBLISHER: *VV Publishing Corp.*
CATEGORY: *Story Presentation— Illustration*
TITLE: *"Karma Chameleons"*
AWARD: *Merit*

440

PUBLICATION: *Science '85*
ART DIRECTOR: *Wayne Fitzpatrick*
DESIGNER: *Wayne Fitzpatrick*
ILLUSTRATOR: *Brad Holland*
PUBLISHER: *Science '85/American Association for the Advancement of Science*
CATEGORY: *Story Presentation— Illustration*
TITLE: *"Technology for Peace"*
AWARD: *Merit*

441

PUBLICATION:	*Newsweek*
ART DIRECTOR:	*Robert Priest*
DESIGNER:	*Margret Joskow*
PHOTOGRAPHERS:	*Various*
PUBLISHER:	*Washington Post Co.*
CATEGORY:	*Story Presentation—Design*
TITLE:	*"Moscow's New Generation"*
AWARD:	*Merit*

442

PUBLICATION:	*Pro Review*
ART DIRECTOR:	*David Brier*
DESIGNER:	*David Brier*
PHOTOGRAPHER:	*Steve Krongard*
AGENCY:	*David Brier Design*
CLIENT:	*Dynamic Publications*
CATEGORY:	*Story Presentation—Design*
AWARD:	*Merit*

MERIT

CHIAT'S DAY

Will one bad Apple ad spoil the whole lunch?

By Ron Rosenbaum

YOU'RE IN A BAR. GUY COMES in, sits down. Hip urban beer-drinker type. Picks up a bottle on the bar, glances at the label. Frowns and says: "I hate California."

Doesn't stop there. Proceeds to launch into stream of anti-California invective: *"Have a nice day,"* he mimics, mockingly, in a cretinous simper. *"Surf's up,"* he says with a brain-fried smile.

"I mean their idea of culture is yogurt," he snickers.

"Formal dinner parties mean you wear socks. Blondes everywhere, pink tofu! Excuse me? Soy burgers? I really hate it," he concludes with a heartfelt sneer.

"I even hate what they drink," he adds, picking up the bottle, which—we now see for the first time—is labeled "California Cooler."

"What'll you have buddy?" the bartender asks him.

The guy nods sheepishly at the bottle. "One of those," he says.

The camera pulls back and the announcer delivers the voice-over punch line, which also appears on the screen: CALIFORNIA COOLER. ONE MORE THING TO HATE ABOUT CALIFORNIA.

It's a memorable commercial, one of those that makes watching network TV

marginally worthwhile (it's scheduled to break nationally this spring). It's smart, it's funny. You have to admire the marketing cleverness with which it addresses a difficult problem: how to sell a flavored-wine drink to beer drinkers. You have to appreciate the way it captures that elusive grail of all beer-drinker ads: Authentic Attitude. What the Löwenbräu "here's to good friends" guys missed because they were a little too creepily self-conscious about their precious camaraderie. What the Stroh's guys are striving for but don't quite attain because their humor is just a little too complacently cutesy.

But more than that, it's one of those commercials that captures something evanescent but real going on in contemporary culture, captures the bicoastal split in our national consciousness, the continuing dialogue between the pleasure principle (California permissiveness, the suggestion of the polymorphous perverse embodied in "pink tofu") and the reality principle (East Coast urban wise guys, work-ethic "realism"). Captures it authentically, and then cleverly, sneakily, seductively figures out a way to reach out and touch the secret, sheepish California impulse hidden within the urban beer-drinker's soul.

"One more thing to hate about Califor-

nia" is the kind of line that has made Chiat/Day Inc., the bicoastal, California-based ad agency that created it, the hottest "creative" agency on both coasts. It's the kind of campaign that—along with those for Apple and Nike and Pizza Hut—has got the ad trade papers doing big features on a California-led "creative revival." It's the kind of thing that—in the minds of many on Madison Avenue—has made agency head Jay Chiat one more thing to hate about California.

The day before my lunch with Chiat (pronounced Shy-at), I'd gotten some coincidental confirmation that he really was on the mind of Madison Avenue. In the lobby of the Pan Am Building, I ran into a guy I knew at Yale, who's since become vice-president/creative director at a major Madison Avenue agency. This is a very charming, very preppy guy—heir to the John O'Hara-era adman tradition. Not one, in other words, to fall for every new ad fad.

But he took Chiat quite seriously. "He's making the rest of us look bad," he declared. "Absolutely. It's going to take us a while to get up to speed with the kind of work they've been doing."

What's interesting about the kind of work they've been doing is how often a Chiat/Day ad campaign has turned out to be not just a headliner in the ad trades but

Big risk: Chiat/Day's "Lemmings" ad for Apple was the first to depict the mass suicide of middle managers.

a mainstream media event in its own right.

First there was the spectacular "1984" TV spot for Apple. The one that ran only once nationally (during the Super Bowl), but which instantly became the most talked-about TV commercial in years (okay, until "Where's the Beef?"). If you didn't catch it when it ran, you probably saw clips of it on the "Today" show or "Entertainment Tonight." Once you've seen it, you can't forget director Ridley

Scott's *Clurn's* haunting, heart-stirring 60-second epic about regimentation and freedom. It's set in an evil, blue-tinted Orwellian society in which mindless, zomboid, blue-tinted worker drones worship a fearsome, blue-tinted Big Brother haranguing them from a huge screen about the beauty of oneness and the creation of a "garden of ideological purity." We cut from close-ups of the mindless, robotic, chanting faces to quick glimpses of the only non-blue-

tinted figure: a full-colored, full-blooded, California golden-girl Olympian striding to the rescue in running shorts, bearing some kind of sledgehammer, radiating *intensely* healthy vibes, releasing the sledgehammer with a wild, deep, sensual primal cry, and succeeding in blowing up Big Brother's giant television screen with one sustained face.

Truly an amazing ad. It was another one that worked by stirring up the tension between repression and release

PHOTOGRAPHS BY DEBORAH FEINGOLD

Way it a triumph or a fiasco? Chiat still feels good about the campaign. Jobs still has serious doubts.

But Jobs has an idea for Chiat: Apple could run a full-page "retraction" of "Lemmings" in The Wall Street Journal.

And Chiat has an idea for Jobs: Chiat/Day could buy the adjoining page and retract the retraction. "We disagree."

THE ORTHODOX APPROACH

One guiding principle at
47th Street Photo comes from the
book of Goldstein: sell, sell, sell

BY DAVID ROSENTHAL

444

PUBLICATION:	*Manhattan, inc.*
ART DIRECTOR:	*Nancy Butkus*
DESIGNER:	*Nancy Butkus*
PHOTOGRAPHER:	*William Coupon*
PUBLISHER:	*Metrocorp*
CATEGORY:	*Story Presentation—*
	Photography
TITLE:	*"The Orthodox Approach"*
AWARD:	*Merit*

The Team

*Some are leaving, others are
changing jobs, but they still
proudly call themselves Reaganauts*

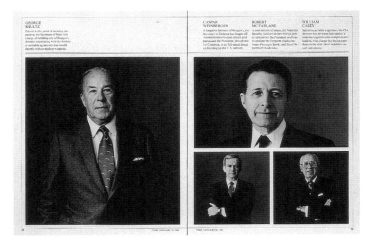

445

PUBLICATION:	*Time*
ART DIRECTOR:	*Rudy Hoglund*
DESIGNER:	*Tom Bentkowski*
PHOTOGRAPHER:	*Michael Evans*
PUBLISHER:	*Time Inc.*
CATEGORY:	*Story Presentation—Design*
TITLE:	*"The Team"*
AWARD:	*Merit*

446

PUBLICATION: *Tables*
ART DIRECTOR: *Shelley Williams*
DESIGNER: *Mike Marcum*
ILLUSTRATOR: *Philip Garner*
PUBLISHER: *Tim Street-Porter*
CATEGORY: *13-30 Corporation*
CATEGORY: *Story Presentation—Design*
TITLE: *"Serv-o-World"*
AWARD: *Merit*

447

PUBLICATION: *Vintage*
ART DIRECTOR: *Robin Rappaport*
DESIGNER: *Robin Rappaport*
PHOTOGRAPHER: *Marty Jacobs*
PUBLISHER: *Vintage Magazine, Inc.*
CATEGORY: *Story Presentation—Design*
TITLE: *"Exotic Cornucopia"*
AWARD: *Merit*

448

PUBLICATION: *Enterprise*
ART DIRECTOR: *Douglas Wolfe*
DESIGNER: *Douglas Wolfe*
ILLUSTRATOR: *José Cruz*
AGENCY: *Hawthorne/Wolfe Design*
CLIENT: *Southwestern Bell Corporation*
CATEGORY: *Story Presentation—Design*
TITLE: *"Food Fabulous Food"*
AWARD: *Merit*

449

PUBLICATION:	*Enterprise*
ART DIRECTOR:	*Douglas Wolfe*
DESIGNER:	*John Howze*
ILLUSTRATOR:	*Seymour Chwast*
AGENCY:	*Hawthorne/Wolfe Design*
CLIENT:	*Southwestern Bell Corporation*
CATEGORY:	*Story Presentation—Design*
TITLE:	*"Lessons from the School of Entrepreneurs"*
AWARD:	*Merit*

450

PUBLICATION:	*American Photographer*
ART DIRECTOR:	*Howard Klein*
DESIGNER:	*Howard Klein*
PHOTOGRAPHER:	*W. Eugene Smith*
PUBLISHER:	*CBS Magazines, Inc.*
CATEGORY:	*Story Presentation—Design*
TITLE:	*"The Passion of St. Eugene"*
AWARD:	*Merit*

451

PUBLICATION:	*National Geographic*
ART DIRECTOR:	*J. Robert Teringo*
SR. ART EDITOR:	*Howard Paine*
ILLUSTRATOR:	*Jay Matternes*
PUBLISHER:	*National Geographic Society*
CATEGORY:	*Story Presentation— Illustration*
TITLE:	*"4,000,000 Years of Bipedalism"*
AWARD:	*Merit*

GQ/JULY 1985

Fall Suits With Dash

San Francisco, 1929. It is well past midnight. The fog has settled in. The uncomfortable and honky tonks of the Tenderloin District are silent. Nearby, in his furnished apartment on Post Street, a tall, lean, graying man lights yet another cigarette and rolls a fresh sheet of paper into the typewriter. The city of this time is wide open, left-reeling. The gentleman at the typewriter is no stranger to its nightlife. But now he is contemplating on what he does better than anyone: the craft of mystery writing. He is in the midst of a ghostly, wise creation board that will produce four novels, a novella and several short stories, in only thirty-six months. At the moment he is writing his masterpiece, The Maltese Falcon. Samuel Dashiell Hammett, 34, is at the peak of his waning powers.

A few readers were shocked, but most were amazed and delighted by the tough-talking sophistication of Hammett's heroes and the amoral guile of his villains. Critics praised his work not so much for the complexity of his styles as for the richness of his dialogue. Today we can sample a body of writing that is a legacy of style and substance, a wealth of living, breathing characters. One has only to think of the dogged, determined Continental Op, the conniving Brigid O'Shaughnessy, or Joel Cairo and Caspar Gutman. Better still, think of Hammett's alter ego, Sam Spade, tall and lean, his mouth a tough, complacent V as he narrowly eyes his quarry. He inhales the cigarette smoke and blows it out in a long, pain cloud. On the following pages, GQ turns to the beauty and hidden joys of Dashiell Hammett's San Francisco.

No mystery about it. From pattern to fit, this season's tailored clothing evokes the style and sophistication of Sam Spade, Nick Charles and their dashing creator, Dashiell Hammett.

452

PUBLICATION:	*GQ*
ART DIRECTOR:	*Mary Shanahan*
DESIGNER:	*Mary Shanahan*
PHOTOGRAPHER:	*Max Vadukal*
PUBLISHER:	*Condé Nast*
CATEGORY:	*Story Presentation—Design*
TITLE:	*"Fall Suits with Dash"*
AWARD:	*Merit*

STRAIGHT ARROW WENNER, AFTER BOTERO
by Jack Huberman

JANN WENNER IS (GULP!) 40

Forget what you've heard about Rolling Stone's erstwhile enfant terrible. Can a man who goes home to lunch with his infant son be so bad!

By E. Graydon Carter

He walks head up, elbows out, with an athletic, jaunty swagger—Lou Costello in a Giorgio Armani suit.

453

PUBLICATION:	*GQ*
ART DIRECTOR:	*Mary Shanahan*
DESIGNER:	*Robert Raines*
ILLUSTRATOR:	*Jack Huberman*
PHOTOGRAPHER:	*Richard Avedon*
PUBLISHER:	*Condé Nast*
CATEGORY:	*Story Presentation—Design*
TITLE:	*"Jann Wenner Profile"*
AWARD:	*Merit*

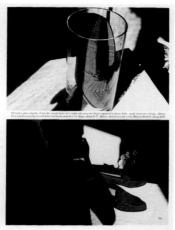

454

PUBLICATION:	*GQ*
ART DIRECTOR:	*Mary Shanahan*
DESIGNER:	*Margot Frankel*
PHOTOGRAPHER:	*François Deconinck*
PUBLISHER:	*Condé Nast*
CATEGORY:	*Story Presentation—Design*
TITLE:	*"Suede Shoes"*
AWARD:	*Merit*

455

PUBLICATION:	*GQ*
ART DIRECTOR:	*Mary Shanahan*
DESIGNER:	*Mary Shanahan*
PHOTOGRAPHER:	*Pamela Hansen*
PUBLISHER:	*Condé Nast*
CATEGORY:	*Story Presentation—Design*
TITLE:	*"Fall Weekend"*
AWARD:	*Merit*

456

PUBLICATION:	*US*
ART DIRECTOR:	*Robert Priest*
DESIGNER:	*Janet Waegel*
PHOTOGRAPHER:	*Michael Comte*
PUBLISHER:	*Straight Arrow Publications*
CATEGORY:	*Story Presentation—Design*
TITLE:	*"Dustin Does TV"*
AWARD:	*Merit*

457

PUBLICATION:	*US*
ART DIRECTOR:	*Robert Priest*
DESIGNER:	*Janet Waegel*
PHOTOGRAPHER:	*Mark Hanauer*
PUBLISHER:	*Straight Arrow Publications*
CATEGORY:	*Story Presentation—Design*
TITLE:	*"The New Short Kid Hits It Big"*
AWARD:	*Merit*

458

PUBLICATION:	*US*
ART DIRECTOR:	*Robert Priest*
DESIGNER:	*Janet Waegel*
ILLUSTRATOR:	*Karin Silverstein*
PHOTOGRAPHER:	*Richard Avedon*
PUBLISHER:	*Straight Arrow Publications*
CATEGORY:	*Story Presentation— Photography*
TITLE:	*"Cyndi Lauper's Dress to Excess"*
AWARD:	*Merit*

459

PUBLICATION:	*US*
ART DIRECTOR:	*Robert Priest*
DESIGNER:	*Janet Waegel*
PHOTOGRAPHER:	*Richard Avedon*
PUBLISHER:	*Straight Arrow Publications*
CATEGORY:	*Story Presentation—Design*
TITLE:	*"Cyndi Lauper's Dress to Excess"*
AWARD:	*Merit*

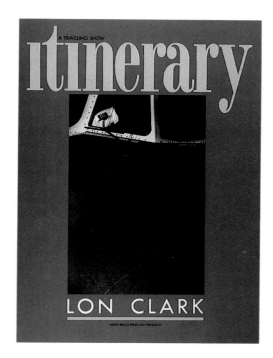

460

PUBLICATION:	*Itinerary*
ART DIRECTOR:	*Lon Clark*
PHOTOGRAPHER:	*Lon Clark*
PUBLISHER:	*North Beach Press*
CATEGORY:	*Story Presentation—Photography*
AWARD:	*Merit*

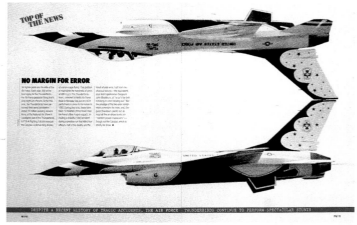

461

PUBLICATION:	*Picture Week*
ART DIRECTOR:	*Mary K. Baumann*
DESIGNERS:	*Mary K. Baumann, Linda Nussbaum, Sandra Di Pasqua*
ILLUSTRATOR:	*Murray Greenfield*
PHOTOGRAPHERS:	*Various*
PUBLISHER:	*Time Inc.*
CATEGORY:	*Story Presentation—Photography*
TITLE:	*"Top of the News"*
AWARD:	*Merit*

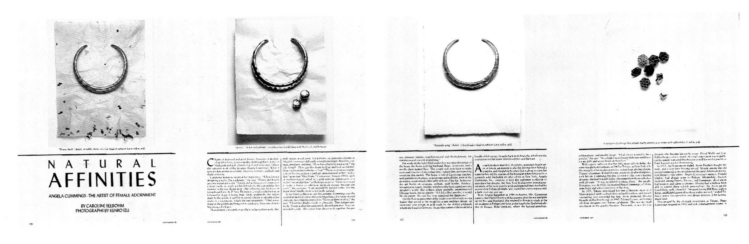

462

PUBLICATION:	*Connoisseur*
ART DIRECTOR:	*Carla Barr*
DESIGNER:	*Carla Barr*
PHOTOGRAPHER:	*Kenro Uzo*
PUBLISHER:	*Hearst Corporation*
CATEGORY:	*Story Presentation—Design*
TITLE:	*"Natural Affinities"*
AWARD:	*Merit*

463

PUBLICATION:	*Connoisseur*
ART DIRECTOR:	*Carla Barr*
DESIGNER:	*Albert Chiang*
PHOTOGRAPHER:	*William Wegman*
PUBLISHER:	*Hearst Corporation*
CATEGORY:	*Story Presentation—Design*
TITLE:	*"Breaking Out"*
AWARD:	*Merit*

BY DIDI MOORE PHOTOGRAPHS BY KENRO IZU PRODUCED BY KATHLEEN B. HEARST

THE WORLD
IN A GRAIN OF GOLD

GRANULATION, A JEWELER'S TECHNIQUE LOST FOR 2,500 YEARS,
IS ENJOYING A SPIRITED REVIVAL

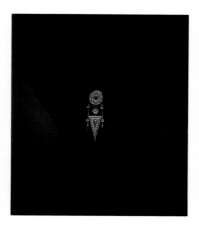

464

PUBLICATION:	*Connoisseur*
ART DIRECTOR:	*Carla Barr*
DESIGNER:	*Carla Barr*
PHOTOGRAPHER:	*Kenro Uzo*
PUBLISHER:	*Hearst Corporation*
CATEGORY:	*Story Presentation—Design*
TITLE:	*"The World in a Grain of Gold"*
AWARD:	*Merit*

WHAT MAKES KARL LAGERFELD TICK

BAROQUE
TO HIS BONES

BY G. Y. DRYANSKY   PHOTOGRAPHS BY JAN MICHAEL
PRODUCED BY KATHLEEN B. HEARST

"I HAVE MANY LINES AND, I HOPE,
NO WRINKLES"

465

PUBLICATION:	*Connoisseur*
ART DIRECTOR:	*Carla Barr*
DESIGNER:	*Carla Barr*
PHOTOGRAPHER:	*Jan Michael*
PUBLISHER:	*Hearst Corporation*
CATEGORY:	*Story Presentation—Design*
TITLE:	*"Baroque to His Bones"*
AWARD:	*Merit*

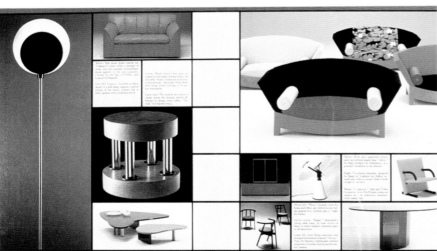

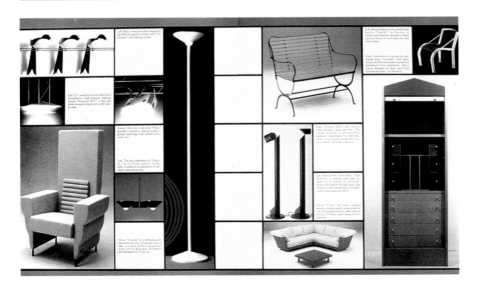

466

PUBLICATION:	*Connoisseur*
ART DIRECTOR:	*Carla Barr*
DESIGNER:	*Carla Barr*
PHOTOGRAPHER:	*Various*
PUBLISHER:	*Hearst Corporation*
CATEGORY:	*Story Presentation—Design*
TITLE:	*"Con Molto Brio"*
AWARD:	*Merit*

MOTHER JONES

MATT MAHURIN

M.M.

PORTRAIT OF AN ARTIST AS A YOUNG MAN

Matt Mahurin's work is described as dark, grotesque, mysterious, and serious. These are not buzzwords usually associated with commercial success. Yet, at only 25, Mahurin has had a meteoric career. He has been published in more than 25 national publications, including *Time*, for which he did a cover on family violence.

Mahurin says that after the *Time* cover, he spoke personally to numerous women who had responded so deeply to his vision of their pain that they contacted him. "After talking to 20 or 30 or them, it really didn't matter to me what anybody else said about the illustrations."

Since then, his work has been in constant demand. Yet, only a few years ago, he was considered just another student with a "bad attitude" at the Art Center College of Design in Los Angeles. Teachers there suggested that his images—soldiers in Beirut, the persecution of Jews, and anorexia nervosa victims—were not what was moving in the commercial illustration market.

However, what is considered commercial is not what inspires Mahurin. He speaks directly to the important issues of our times. He does that with an intense sensitivity to light and dark, and a subtle sense of almost Renaissance colors and shadows. The result is a powerful piece of art that appeals to both the intellect and the emotions. In our October issue, when he dealt with the threat of nuclear war, the image was so strong that we turned the illustration into a limited edition poster (see inside back cover).

When we first talked about doing this portrait, I made a selection of his best work to date. Mahurin then offered to do this series of original pieces for us. It's that kind of energy that distinguishes him.

As in several of these paintings, he starts with a photo and builds on its image with paint, producing a final piece in only a few hours. "I think my work happens quickly because I'm very impatient. My approach is very physical and very quick—if I start spending too much time on anything, I hate it and I destroy it."

Mahurin has experienced success so quickly and at such an early age that he's wary of stagnating. To avoid that danger, he is now spending more time experimenting with photography. We're fortunate to be in on the beginning of a career that is just starting to evolve.

—*Louise Kollenbaum*

467

PUBLICATION:	*Mother Jones*
ART DIRECTOR:	*Louise Kollenbaum*
DESIGNER:	*Dian-Aziza Ooka*
ILLUSTRATOR:	*Matt Mahurin*
PUBLISHER:	*Foundation for National Progress*
CATEGORY:	*Story Presentation—Design*
TITLE:	*"Portrait of an Artist as a Young Man"*
AWARD:	*Merit*

APARTHEID

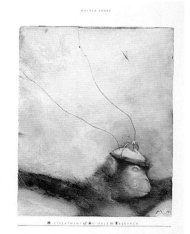

MISTREATMENT OF ANIMALS IN RESEARCH

468

PUBLICATION: *New York*
ART DIRECTOR: *Robert Best*
DESIGNER: *Robert Best*
PUBLISHER: *Murdoch Magazines*
CATEGORY: *Single Special Issue—Design*
TITLE: *"The Best of New York"*
AWARD: *Gold*

GALA SPECIAL ISSUE

$1.75 SEPTEMBER 16, 1985

New York

FALL PREVIEW

THEATER

MOVIES

TELEVISION

ART

PHOTOGRAPHY

MUSIC

DANCE

BOOKS

ARCHITECTURE

NIGHTLIFE

SPORTS

FASHION

SHOPPING

RESTAURANTS

JASON ROBARDS IN
THE ICEMAN COMETH.

MOVIES

REDFORD HUNTS STREEP
IN 'OUT OF AFRICA'

469

PUBLICATION:	*New York*
ART DIRECTOR:	*Robert Best*
DESIGNER:	*Robert Best*
PUBLISHER:	*Murdoch Magazines*
CATEGORY:	*Single Special Issue—Design*
TITLE:	*"Fall Preview"*
AWARD:	*Silver*

TELEVISION

SPIELBERG UNREELS HIS
'AMAZING STORIES'

JOHN LEONARD

FASHION

SILVER

470

PUBLICATION: *Mercedes*
ART DIRECTOR: *John Tom Cohoe*
DESIGNER: *John Tom Cohoe*
PUBLISHER: *Mercedes-Benz*
of North America
CATEGORY: *Single Special Issue—Design*
TITLE: *"Centennial Issue"*
AWARD: *Silver*

471

PUBLICATION:	*New York*
ART DIRECTOR:	*Robert Best*
DESIGNER:	*Robert Best*
PUBLISHER:	*Murdoch Magazines*
CATEGORY:	*Single Special Issue—Design*
TITLE:	*"What's Really Going On?"*
AWARD:	*Merit*

472

PUBLICATION:	*New York*
ART DIRECTOR:	*Robert Best*
DESIGNERS:	*David Walters,*
	Rhonda Rubinstein
PUBLISHER:	*Murdoch Magazines*
CATEGORY:	*Single Special Issue—Design*
TITLE:	*"Summer Pleasures"*
AWARD:	*Merit*

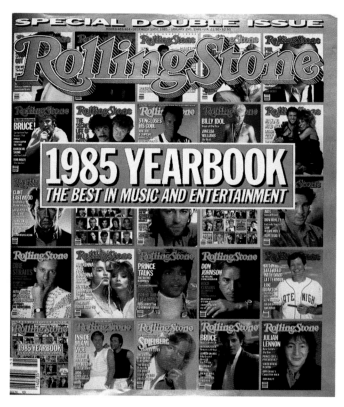

473

PUBLICATION:	*Rolling Stone*
ART DIRECTOR:	*Derek W. Ungless*
DESIGNERS:	*Raul Martinez,*
	Angelo Savaides
PUBLISHER:	*Straight Arrow Publications, Inc.*
CATEGORY:	*Single Special Issue—Design*
TITLE:	*"1985 Yearbook—The Best in*
	Music and Entertainment"
AWARD:	*Merit*

474

PUBLICATION: *Picture Week*
ART DIRECTOR: *Mary K. Baumann*
DESIGNERS: *Mary K. Baumann, Linda Nussbaum, Sandra DiPasqua, Murray Greenfield, Joseph Paschke, Silvia Chalawick, John Shacut, Darby Holmes*
PUBLISHER: *Time Inc.*
CATEGORY: *Single Special Issue—Design*
TITLE: *"The Best Pictures of '85"*
AWARD: *Merit*

MERIT

475

PUBLICATION:	*Newsweek*
ART DIRECTOR:	*Robert Priest*
DESIGNER:	*Robert Priest*
PUBLISHER:	*Washington Post Co.*
CATEGORY:	*Single Special Issue—Design*
TITLE:	*"The Legacy of Vietnam"*
AWARD:	*Merit*

476

PUBLICATION:	*The Boston Globe*
ART DIRECTOR:	*Lucy Bartholomay*
DESIGNER:	*Lucy Bartholomay*
PUBLISHER:	*The Boston Globe*
CATEGORY:	*Single Special Issue—Design*
TITLE:	*"Changing Tides"*
AWARD:	*Merit*

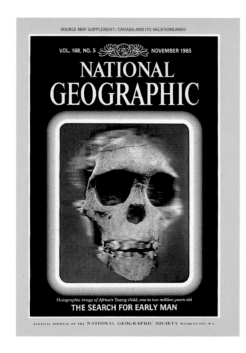

Canada's Icy
Wilderness Park **KLUANE**

Poised for a fall, ice at the Lowell Glacier's toe menaces kayakers on the Alsek River. Unsurpassed among Canada's national parks for wildness and beauty on a stunning scale, Kluane is a realm of big ice, bigger mountains, large challenges, and great rewards.

By DOUGLAS LEE

Photographs by
GEORGE F. MOBLEY

477

PUBLICATION: *National Geographic*
ART DIRECTOR: *Howard Paine*
DESIGNERS: *Robert W. Madden, Gerard A.*
                 Valerio, Constance H. Phelps,
                 J. Robert Teringo
PUBLISHER: *National Geographic Society*
CATEGORY: *Single Special Issue—Design*
TITLE: *November 1985 Issue*
AWARD: *Merit*

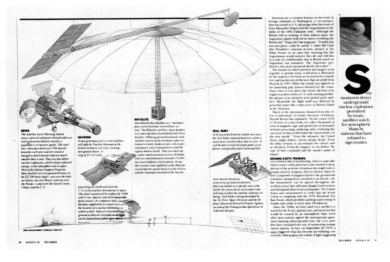

478

PUBLICATION: *Science '85*
ART DIRECTOR: *Wayne Fitzpatrick*
DESIGNERS: *Wayne Fitzpatrick, John Isley*
PUBLISHER: *American Association for the*
                 Advancement of Science, Inc.
CATEGORY: *Single Special Issue—Design*
TITLE: *"Technology for Peace"*
AWARD: *Merit*

479

PUBLICATION:	*The New York Times Magazine*
ART DIRECTOR:	*Tom Bodkin*
DESIGNER:	*Tom Bodkin*
PUBLISHER:	*The New York Times*
CATEGORY:	*Single Special Issue—Design*
TITLE:	*"World of New York/*
	101 Reasons"
AWARD:	*Merit*

480

PUBLICATION:	*The New York Times Magazine*
ART DIRECTOR:	*Ellen Burnie*
PHOTOGRAPHER:	*Peter Lindberg*
PUBLISHER:	*The New York Times*
CATEGORY:	*Single Special Issue*
TITLE:	*"Fashions of the Times"*
AWARD:	*Merit*

MERIT

481

PUBLICATION: *The New York Times Magazine*
ART DIRECTOR: *Nancy Kent*
DESIGNER: *Nancy Kent*
PHOTOGRAPHER: *Jeanne Giovanni*
PUBLISHER: *The New York Times*
CATEGORY: *Single Special Issue—Design*
TITLE: *"Home Design"*
AWARD: *Merit*

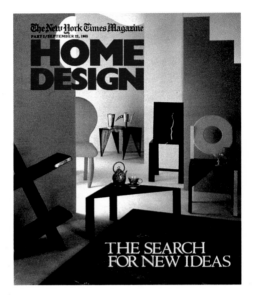

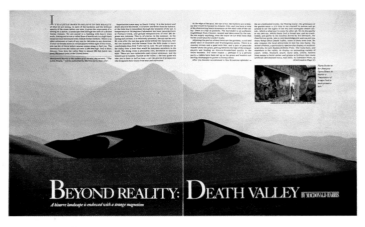

482

PUBLICATION:	*The New York Times Magazine*
ART DIRECTOR:	*Tom Bodkin*
DESIGNER:	*Tom Bodkin*
ILLUSTRATOR:	*Barry Root*
PUBLISHER:	*The New York Times*
CATEGORY:	*Single Special Issue—Design*
TITLE:	*"Sophisticated Traveler"*
AWARD:	*Merit*

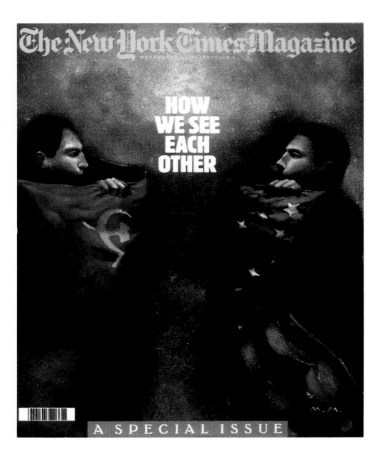

483

PUBLICATION: *The New York Times Magazine*
ART DIRECTOR: *Ken Kendrick*
DESIGNER: *Diana LaGuardia*
ILLUSTRATOR: *Matt Mahurin*
PUBLISHER: *The New York Times*
CATEGORY: *Single Special Issue—Design*
TITLE: *"How We See Each Other"*
AWARD: *Merit*

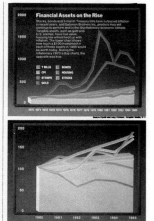

484

PUBLICATION: *The New York Times Book Review*
ART DIRECTOR: *Steve Heller*
DESIGNER: *Steve Heller*
ILLUSTRATOR: *Mark D. Summers*
PUBLISHER: *The New York Times*
CATEGORY: *Single Special Issue—Design*
TITLE: *"Christmas '85"*
AWARD: *Merit*

485

PUBLICATION: *The New York Times*
ART DIRECTOR: *Richard Aloiso*
DESIGNER: *Richard Aloiso*
ILLUSTRATOR: *Richard Osaka*
CATEGORY: *Single Special Issue—Design*
TITLE: *"Personal Investing '86"*
AWARD: *Merit*

MERIT

ILLUSTRATION PORTFOLIO № 6

SCHOOL OF VISUAL ARTS

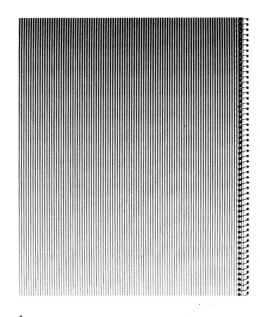

GENEVIEVE BONFIELD

INTRODUCTION

486

PUBLICATION:	*Illustration Portfolio 6*
ART DIRECTOR:	*William Kobasz*
DESIGNER:	*William Kobasz*
PUBLISHER:	*School Of Visual Arts Press*
CATEGORY:	*Single Special Issue—Design*
AWARD:	*Merit*

KAM MAK

487

PUBLICATION:	*Illustration Portfolio 5*
ART DIRECTOR:	*William Kobasz*
DESIGNER:	*William Kobasz*
PUBLISHER:	*School Of Visual Arts Press*
CATEGORY:	*Single Special Issue—Design*
AWARD:	*Merit*

MERIT

488

PUBLICATION:	*American Ceramics*
ART DIRECTOR:	*Douglas Freuh*
DESIGNER:	*Massimo Vignelli*
PHOTOGRAPHER:	*Brad Guice*
PUBLISHER:	*American Ceramics*
CATEGORY:	*Single Special Issue—Design*
TITLE:	*"American Ceramics 4/3"*
AWARD:	*Merit*

489

PUBLICATION:	*Mead Annual Report*
ART DIRECTOR:	*Bennett Robinson*
DESIGNER:	*Bennett Robinson*
AGENCY:	*Corporate Graphics, Inc.*
CLIENT:	*Mead Paper Corporation*
CATEGORY:	*Single Special Issue—Design*
TITLE:	*"Wild Johnson on Mead Black and White"*
AWARD:	*Merit*

490

PUBLICATION:	*IDC New York 16*
ART DIRECTOR:	*Massimo Vignelli*
DESIGNERS:	*Michael Bierut,*
	Lucy Cossentino
AGENCY:	*Vignelli Associates*
CLIENT:	*International Design Center*
CATEGORY:	*Single Special Issue—Design*
AWARD:	*Merit*

491

PUBLICATION:	*IDC New York 15*
ART DIRECTOR:	*Massimo Vignelli*
DESIGNERS:	*Michael Bierut,*
	Lucy Cossentino
AGENCY:	*Vignelli Associates*
CLIENT:	*International Design Center*
CATEGORY:	*Single Special Issue—Design*
AWARD:	*Merit*

MERIT

re:cap

Volume 7, Number 1   MOBIL CORPORATION CIVIC ACTION PROGRAM NEWSLETTER   February 1985

Reagan goes after the budget deficit — *his way*

Trim the federal fat

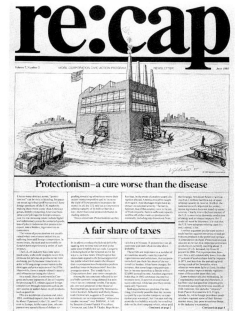

re:cap

Volume 7, Number 2   MOBIL CORPORATION CIVIC ACTION PROGRAM   NEWSLETTER   June 1985

Protectionism–a cure worse than the disease

A fair share of taxes

Renewing, not gimmicking, Superfund

Should mega-mergers be viewed with alarm?

Gains made in right to know

Tax proposals threaten many employee benefits

A fair share of taxes

Oil mergers — clue to industry future?

TAX CODE

A simpler tax code could be a *worse* tax code

Treasury 'reform' plan hits workers' benefits

The list of options for income tax reform

Make the Superfund more fair

492

PUBLICATION:	*Re:Cap*
ART DIRECTOR:	*Jerry Demoney*
DESIGNER:	*Jerry Demoney*
ILLUSTRATOR:	*Victor Juhasz*
CLIENT:	*Mobil Oil Corporation*
CATEGORY:	*Single Special Issue—Design*
AWARD:	*Merit*

493

PUBLICATION:	*Re:Cap*
ART DIRECTOR:	*Jerry Demoney*
DESIGNER:	*Jerry Demoney*
ILLUSTRATOR:	*Victor Juhasz*
CLIENT:	*Mobil Oil Corporation*
CATEGORY:	*Single Special Issue—Design*
AWARD:	*Merit*

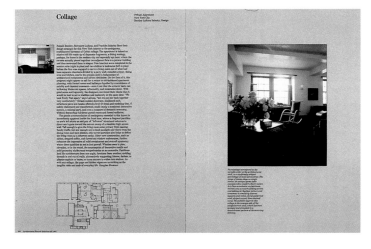

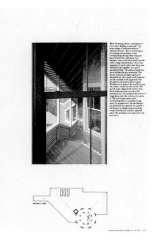

494

PUBLICATION:	*Architectural Record*
ART DIRECTOR:	*Alex H. Stillano*
DESIGNERS:	*Alex H. Stillano,*
	Alberto Bucchianeri,
	Anna Egger-Schlesinger
PUBLISHER:	*McGraw-Hill*
CATEGORY:	*Single Special Issue—Design*
TITLE:	*"Record Interiors"*
AWARD:	*Merit*

495

PUBLICATION:	*Architectural Record*
ART DIRECTOR:	*Alex H. Stillano*
DESIGNERS:	*Alex H. Stillano,*
	Alberto Bucchianeri,
	Anna Egger-Schlesinger
PUBLISHER:	*McGraw-Hill*
CATEGORY:	*Single Special Issue—Design*
TITLE:	*"Record Houses"*
AWARD:	*Merit*

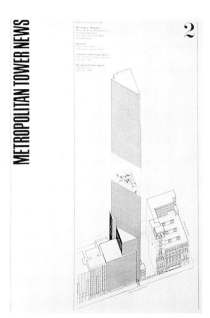

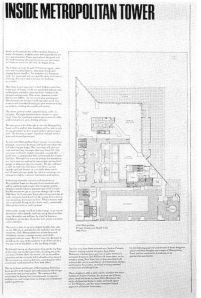

496

PUBLICATION:	*Metropolitan Tower News*
ART DIRECTOR:	*Michael Bierut*
DESIGNER:	*Constance Ross*
AGENCY:	*Vignelli Associates*
CLIENT:	*Harry Macklowe Real Estate Company*
CATEGORY:	*Single Special Issue—Design*
AWARD:	*Merit*

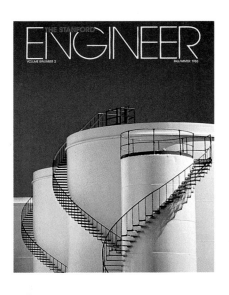

497

PUBLICATION:	*Stanford Engineer*
ART DIRECTOR:	*Alexander Atkins*
DESIGNER:	*Alexander Atkins*
AGENCY:	*Alexander Atkins, Inc.*
CLIENT:	*Stanford University*
CATEGORY:	*Single Special Issue—Design*
AWARD:	*Merit*

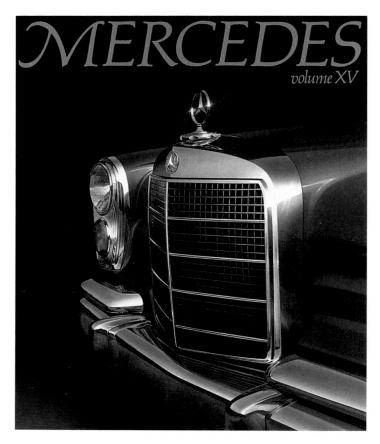

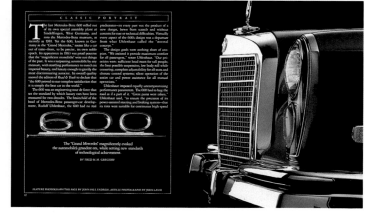

498

PUBLICATION:	*Mercedes*
ART DIRECTOR:	*Peter Morance*
DESIGNER:	*Peter Morance*
AGENCY:	*McCaffrey, McCall, Inc.*
CLIENT:	*Mercedes-Benz of North America*
CATEGORY:	*Single Special Issue—Design*
TITLE:	*Mercedes Volume XV*
AWARD:	*Merit*

499

PUBLICATION:	*Mercedes*
ART DIRECTOR:	*Peter Morance*
DESIGNERS:	*Peter Morance, James Dustin*
PHOTOGRAPHERS:	*Brad Miller, John Paul Endre*
AGENCY:	*McCaffrey, McCall, Inc.*
CLIENT:	*Mercedes-Benz of North America*
CATEGORY:	*Single Special Issue—Design*
TITLE:	*Mercedes XVII*
AWARD:	*Merit*

MERIT

500

PUBLICATION:	*Nautical Quarterly*
ART DIRECTOR:	*Clare Cunningham*
DESIGNER:	*Clare Cunningham*
PUBLISHER:	*Nautical Quarterly Co.*
CATEGORY:	*Single Special Issue—Design*
TITLE:	*Winter 1985 Issue*
AWARD:	*Merit*

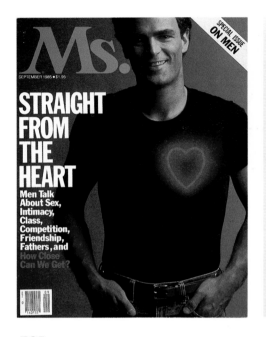

501

PUBLICATION:	*Ms.*
ART DIRECTOR:	*Phyllis Schefer*
DESIGNER:	*Phyllis Schefer*
PUBLISHER:	*Ms. Foundation for Education and Communication, Inc.*
CATEGORY:	*Single Special Issue—Design*
TITLE:	*"Straight from the Heart"*
AWARD:	*Merit*

502

PUBLICATION:	*J.C., The Magazine of the Jockey Club*
ART DIRECTOR:	*Massimo Vignelli*
DESIGNER:	*Michael Bierut*
AGENCY:	*Vignelli Associates*
CLIENT:	*John B. Coleman*
CATEGORY:	*Single Special Issue—Design*
AWARD:	*Merit*

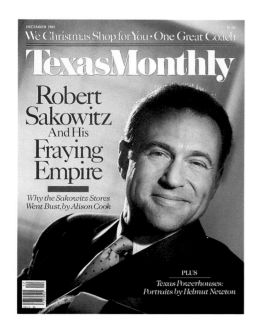

503

PUBLICATION:	*Texas Monthly*
ART DIRECTOR:	*Fred Woodward*
DESIGNERS:	*Fred Woodward, David Kampa*
PUBLISHER:	*Texas Monthly, Inc.*
CATEGORY:	*Single Special Issue—Design*
TITLE:	*December 1985 Issue*
AWARD:	*Merit*

504

PUBLICATION:	*A Working Guide to Letterhead Production*
ART DIRECTOR:	*Dean Pingrey*
DESIGNER:	*Dean Pringrey*
PHOTOGRAPHER:	*Dan Patterson*
AGENCY:	*Willis Case, Harwood Advertising*
CLIENT:	*Gilbert Paper Co.*
CATEGORY:	*Single Special Issue—Design*
AWARD:	*Merit*

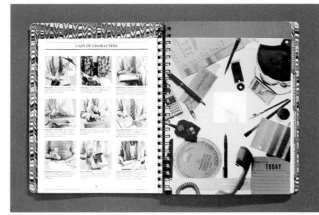

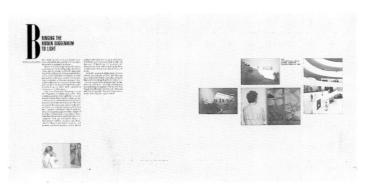

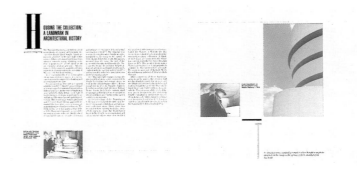

505

PUBLICATION:	*The Hidden Guggenheim*
ART DIRECTOR:	*Fausto Pellegrini*
DESIGNER:	*Fausto Pellegrini*
AGENCY:	*Jan Krukowski Associates*
CLIENT:	*Guggenheim Museum*
CATEGORY:	*Single Special Issue—Design*
TITLE:	*"The Hidden Guggenheim"*
AWARD:	*Merit*

506

PUBLICATION:	*Quest #3*
ART DIRECTOR:	*Howard Ronder*
DESIGNER:	*Scott Blair*
AGENCY:	*Ronder Design Group*
CLIENT:	*AT&T Communications*
CATEGORY:	*Single Special Issue—Design*
AWARD:	*Merit*

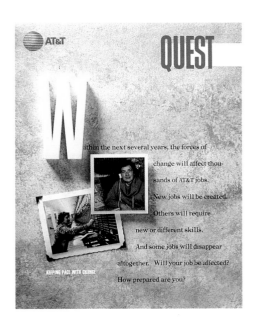

507

PUBLICATION:	*Image*
ART DIRECTORS:	*Robert Meyers, Julia Wyant*
DESIGNER:	*Carla Tedeschi*
AGENCY:	*Robert Meyers Design, Inc.*
CLIENT:	*International Museum of Photography*
CATEGORY:	*Single Special Issue—Design*
AWARD:	*Merit*

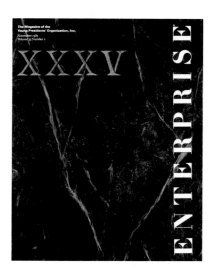

508

PUBLICATION:	*Enterprise*
ART DIRECTOR:	*Diana DeLucia*
DESIGNER:	*Diana DeLucia*
CLIENT:	*Young President's Organization*
CATEGORY:	*Single Special Issue—Design*
AWARD:	*Merit*

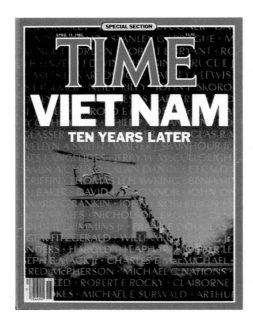

509

PUBLICATION:	*Time*
ART DIRECTOR:	*Rudy Hoglund*
DESIGNER:	*Tom Bentkowski*
PUBLISHER:	*Time Inc.*
CATEGORY:	*Single Special Issue—Design*
TITLE:	*"Vietnam—Special Section"*
AWARD:	*Merit*

510

PUBLICATION:	*Time*
ART DIRECTOR:	*Rudy Hoglund*
DESIGNER:	*Tom Bentkowski*
PUBLISHER:	*Time Inc.*
CATEGORY:	*Single Special Issue—Design*
TITLE:	*"Man of the Year"*
AWARD:	*Merit*

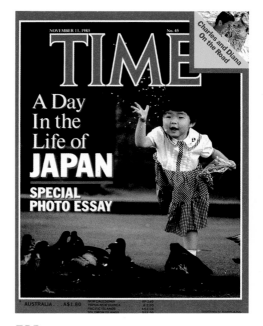

511

PUBLICATION:	*Time*
ART DIRECTOR:	*Rudy Hoglund*
DESIGNER:	*Arthur Hochstein*
PUBLISHER:	*Time Inc.*
CATEGORY:	*Single Special Issue—Design*
TITLE:	*"A Day in the Life of Japan"*
AWARD:	*Merit*

512

PUBLICATION:	*Time*
ART DIRECTOR:	*Rudy Hoglund*
DESIGNER:	*Tom Bentkowski*
PUBLISHER:	*Time Inc.*
CATEGORY:	*Single Special Issue—Design*
TITLE:	*"Immigrants—Special Issue"*
AWARD:	*Merit*

ENTIRE ISSUES

(continued on page 46)

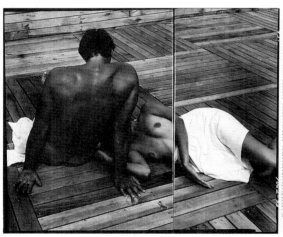

513

PUBLICATION:	*GQ*
ART DIRECTOR:	*Mary Shanahan*
DESIGNER:	*Mary Shanahan*
PUBLISHER:	*Condé Nast*
CATEGORY:	*Entire Issue—Overall Design*
AWARD:	*Silver*

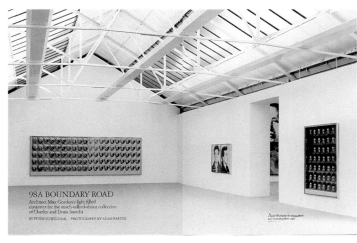

514

PUBLICATION: *House & Garden*
ART DIRECTOR: *Karen Lee Grant*
DESIGNER: *Lloyd Ziff*
PUBLISHER: *Condé Nast*
CATEGORY: *Entire Issue—Overall Design*
AWARD: *Silver*

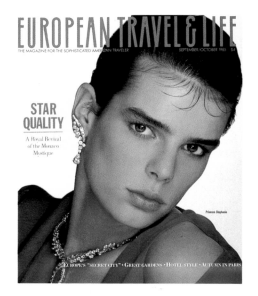

515

PUBLICATION:	*European Travel & Life*
ART DIRECTOR:	*Terry Koppel*
DESIGNERS:	*Terry Koppel, April Garston*
PUBLISHER:	*Inabnit Communications, Inc.*
CATEGORY:	*Entire Issue—Overall Design*
AWARD:	*Silver*

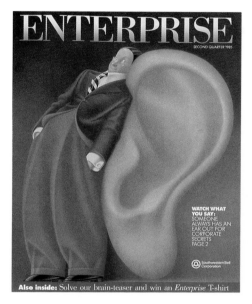

SHHH!
You never know who might be listening

In our new, competitive environment, it's more important than ever to be tight-lipped about corporate secrets

Unlock your mind, and a batch of new ideas will pour forth

If you get in touch with your playful side, you'll find a wealth of resourcefulness

FABULOUS FOOD!

516

PUBLICATION:	*Enterprise*
ART DIRECTOR:	*Douglas Wolfe*
DESIGNER:	*Douglas Wolfe*
AGENCY:	*Hawthorne/Wolfe Design, Inc.*
CLIENT:	*Southwestern Bell Corporation*
CATEGORY:	*Entire Issue—Overall Design*
AWARD:	*Silver*

517

PUBLICATION:	*American Photographer*
ART DIRECTOR:	*Howard Klein*
DESIGNER:	*Howard Klein*
PUBLISHER:	*CBS Magazines*
CATEGORY:	*Entire Issue—Overall Design*
AWARD:	*Merit*

518

PUBLICATION:	*Mercedes*
ART DIRECTOR:	*Peter Morance*
DESIGNER:	*Peter Morance*
AGENCY:	*McCaffrey, McCall, Inc.*
CLIENT:	*Mercedes-Benz of North America*
CATEGORY:	*Entire Issue—Overall Design*
TITLE:	*Mercedes XV, XVI, XVII*
AWARD:	*Merit*

DOUGLAS HOPKINS

Using a new film, the photographer crafts a perfect beauty.

The first photograph Douglas Hopkins took suggests a motive behind his choice of a profession. At age 14, during a prolonged childhood with a father in military-female systems design, Hopkins recalls, "I had built a model of a defense rocket, with a puff of cotton for the smoke, and took a picture of it really close up. I printed it myself, and when I took it to school, I told everyone it was a close-up of a defense rocket." Well amused by the memory 20 years later, he adds with a chuckle, "They believed me."

Although Hopkins's present specialty—beauty photography—may at first seem far afield from that early quest for deceptive effect, the same fascination with the power of a fabricated image remains with him.

"My taste," says Hopkins, "is for perfection in lighting, which is the means you to in submissive of it, you just see a beautiful face." Or, more correctly, an exquisite lie, since we the model melted, the perfect face is a crea-tion of the photographer. Having improved his tech-nical and considerably since

After receiving a new composite from 12-year-old Ford model Melissa Arnold at right, Hopkins was struck by how much she resembled his friend Barbara Blackburn, a 28-model Hopkins paired the two models for these triptychs in white.

ISLAM'S FORGOTTEN WAR

After five years and countless casualties, ancient enemies Iran and Iraq are still mired in a crippling conflict. by Drew Middleton

Not since the medieval cru-sades have followers of the Is-lamic faith played so prominent and fractious a role on the world stage. In the years between the seizure of American hostages by Iranian Shiite radicals in 1979 and the kidnapping last June of 39 American hostages by Shiite fundamentalists in Le-banon, hundreds of thousands of Moslems—Shiite and Sunni—have slain one another in the war between Iran and Iraq. Iranian native Manoocher of

519

PUBLICATION:	*ESD News*
ART DIRECTOR:	*Alan G. Urban*
DESIGNER:	*Alan G. Urban*
AGENCY:	*Urban Taylor Associates*
CLIENT:	*IBM Corporation*
CATEGORY:	*Entire Issue—Overall Design*
AWARD:	*Merit*

520

PUBLICATION:	*The Reporter*
ART DIRECTOR:	*Siobhan Nehin*
DESIGNER:	*Sheila Wilson-Morrison*
PHOTOGRAPHER:	*George Kamper*
AGENCY:	*Levy, King & White, Inc.*
CLIENT:	*Millard Fillmore Hospitals*
CATEGORY:	*Entire Issue—Overall Design*
AWARD:	*Merit*

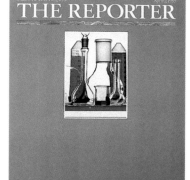

521

PUBLICATION: *The Berkeley Monthly*
ART DIRECTOR: *Laura Cirolia*
DESIGNER: *Michael Grossman*
PUBLISHER: *The Berkeley Monthly*
CATEGORY: *Entire Issue—Overall Design*
AWARD: *Merit*

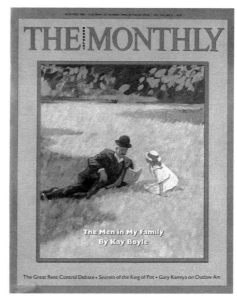

522

PUBLICATION: *Creative Marketing*
ART DIRECTOR: *Varsha Mehta*
DESIGNERS: *Varsha Mehta, Rachel Bokota*
ILLUSTRATOR: *Michael David Brown*
CLIENT: *Ciba-Geigy, Inc.*
CATEGORY: *Entire Issue—Overall Design*
AWARD: *Merit*

MERIT

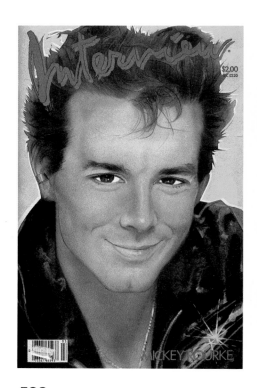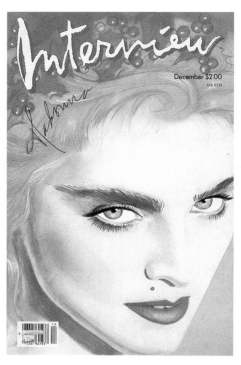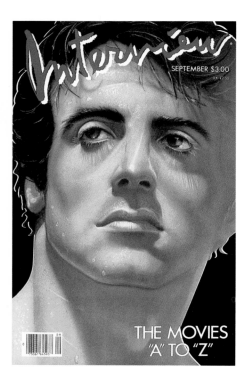

523

PUBLICATION:	*Interview*
ART DIRECTOR:	*Marc Balet*
PUBLISHER:	*Interview Enterprises, Inc.*
CATEGORY:	*Entire Issue—Overall Design*
AWARD:	*Merit*

524

PUBLICATION:	*Campus Voice Biweekly*
ART DIRECTOR:	*Sally Ham*
DESIGNER:	*Sally Ham*
ILLUSTRATORS:	*Mark Alan Stamaty, Randall Enos, Henrik Drescher, Ron Hauge, Gary Zamchick, Lynda Barry, Richard McNeel, George Kocar, Steven Guarnaccia*
PUBLISHER:	*13-30 Corporation*
CATEGORY:	*Entire Issue—Overall Design*
AWARD:	*Merit*

525

PUBLICATION: *Saturday Review*
ART DIRECTOR: *Brian Noyes*
DESIGNER: *Brian Noyes*
PUBLISHER: *Saturday Review Magazine*
CATEGORY: *Entire Issue—Overall Design*
AWARD: *Merit*

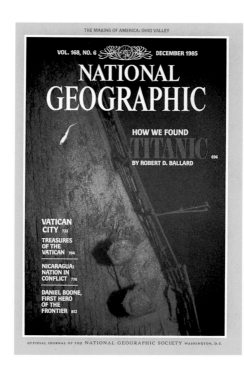

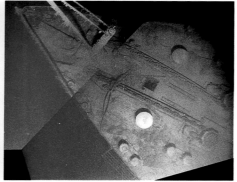

526

PUBLICATION:	*National Geographic*
ART DIRECTOR:	*Howard Paine*
DESIGNER:	*Howard Paine*
PUBLISHER:	*National Geographic Society*
CATEGORY:	*Entire Issue—Overall Design*
AWARD:	*Merit*

527

PUBLICATION: *The Sciences*
ART DIRECTOR: *Daniel J. McClain*
DESIGNER: *Daniel J. McClain*
PUBLISHER: *New York Academy of Sciences*
CATEGORY: *Entire Issue: Overall Design*
AWARD: *Merit*

528

PUBLICATION:	*Squibbline*
ART DIRECTOR:	*Anthony Russell*
DESIGNER:	*Barbara Nieminen*
ILLUSTRATORS:	*Mary Lynn Blasutta, Mark Ulrich, Yvonne Buchanan, Shirley Kaneda*
AGENCY:	*Anthony Russell, Inc.*
CLIENT:	*Squibb Corporation*
CATEGORY:	*Entire Issue—Overall Design*
AWARD:	*Merit*

529

PUBLICATION:	*The Real Times*
ART DIRECTOR:	*Sam Savage*
DESIGNER:	*Douglas Eymer*
CLIENT:	*McCormack & Dodge, A Company of Dun & Bradstreet*
CATEGORY:	*Entire Issue—Overall Design*
AWARD:	*Merit*

530

PUBLICATION:	*Audubon*
ART DIRECTOR:	*Daniel J. McClain*
DESIGNER:	*Daniel J. McClain*
PUBLISHER:	*National Audubon Society*
CATEGORY:	*Entire Issue—Overall Design*
AWARD:	*Merit*

531

PUBLICATION:	*Texas Monthly*
ART DIRECTOR:	*Fred Woodward*
DESIGNERS:	*Fred Woodward, David Kampa*
PUBLISHER:	*Texas Monthly, Inc.*
CATEGORY:	*Entire Issue—Overall Design*
AWARD:	*Merit*

MERIT

FORMATS

532

PUBLICATION:	*European Travel & Life*
ART DIRECTOR:	*Terry Koppel*
DESIGNER:	*Terry Koppel*
PUBLISHER:	*Inabnit Communications*
CATEGORY:	*Format—Design*
TITLE:	*"Contents Page"*
AWARD:	*Merit*

E U R O P E A N

JOURNAL

Letter

From

LONDON

NOTES FROM THE UNDERGROUND: WHO'S REALLY WHO

Who's Who has several thousand entries, mostly members of the Underground, Britain's secret establishment. Richard Compton Miller's *Who's REALLY Who*, on the other hand, restricts itself to 450 personalities most of us will have heard of from the gossip pages. I'm not going to review it for you, though anyone interested in the highly peculiar British social scene may be a little surprised at finding a certain duchess described as "tall and imperious." Certainly she is imperious, but she must be one of the shortest women in London. Members of the Underground ("Undies") may remember another entry, Mary Quant. She changed their clothes. She did not originate the mini-skirt as the book says, but she did invent, in the late fifties, day fashion for the Underground—casual, mainly colourless dresses that deceived the uninitiated into believing they had been bought, for a fifth of their actual price, at a chain store.

When socialism hit Britain in 1945, the to-b-established ment either left the country or went underground and pretended to be poor. Neat sack dresses began to replace the grim twin-sets and tweed skirts the Undies wore in the mundane hours between silk nightdresses and low-cut taffeta ball gowns. Undies thought they looked inconspicuous in these plain shifts, and though very, very rich, they hoped to avoid the attention of jumped-up Labour politicians.

Undies generally live in the shires, though they used to have the odd apartment in Belgravia or Chelsea. The men keep their clothes and Land Rovers and the trendier Range Rovers bottom.

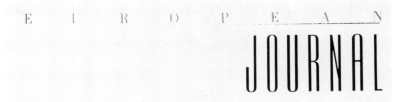

For the Undies who can shoot straight, the only acceptable weapon is a handmade Purdey shotgun.

ever, while the women buy lots of expensive underwear from Night Owls in the Fulham Road and then scent from Floris in Jermyn Street—where, ironically, change is returned on miniature, plush-covered stools to avoid nail breakage, a rather pointless courtesy since most Undies have lost their nails under the collars of their retrievers. Labradors are now "out" because of a TV advertisement showing a cute Labrador puppy cavorting with loo paper, and although Undies watch a lot of television to prove they are ordinary, they do not wish to be regarded as too ordinary.

Male Undies are the opposite of Foodies and will eat almost anything, particularly overcooked lamb chops, which they order "well done" at their London clubs—perhaps Brook's or White's. In mixed company, they eat more lamb chops at Claridge's or the Connaught, where they also enjoy the bread-and-butter pudding—soft and comforting, because Undies worry about their teeth rotting after too many cheap cakes at the race meetings.

Female Undies hate minimalism and anything tarts like "style." They have accounts at Fortnum & Mason, where they buy peaches in brandy for one another—and tinned ham for themselves. Here they also buy very expensive large black evening dresses, which they crush into Fortnum & Mason supermarket-style plastic bags.

There are hardly any dukes in *Who's REALLY Who*, but the Undies' exception is the Duke of Westminster, who really can't stay underground, since together with the Church and the Crown Commissioners he owns most of London, and the leaseholds he sells have a happy habit of expiring—although only every fifty years or so.

"They only keep them up for Americans to rent," Noel Coward's line from his song "The Stately Homes of England," is becoming truer by the day. Except (to be accurate) they are selling the leaseholds, and at a price that would scare other Englishmen out of the midday sun.

Undies believe London is becoming science fiction: policemen insist on locking round yellow clamps to the front tires of the Undies' discreet foreign cars and plaster the windscreens with rude notices about nonpayment of parking fines; theaters sell "drink kits" enveloped in plastic, which the Undies break their teeth trying to open; and, worst of all, in Chelsea corner shops, Indians with no respect for the memory of the Raj correct the Undies' mathematics while counting out their change.

EUROPEAN TRAVEL & LIFE, MAY/JUNE 1986

E U R O P E A N

JOURNAL

Letter

From

PARIS

EXCUSE ME, PARLEZ-VOUS FRANGLAIS?

C'est trop much? The French fascination with *American Way of Life* is apparently out of hand, and the Mitterrand government intends to do something about it. A new law proposed by Socialist Deputy Georges Sarre to put a stop to "the invasion of Anglo-American jargon," also known as franglais, is now in debate in the National Assembly.

The issue of long standing (the term *franglais* cropped up back in 1959 and was popularized in 1964 by René Étiemble's book *Parlez-vous Franglais*, in which such...

Le fast food or restaurant rapide? For President it's a matter of national honor.

EUROPEAN TRAVEL & LIFE, JULY/AUGUST 1986

E U R O P E A N

JOURNAL

Letter

From

NEW

YORK

ADJUSTING TO LIFE IN THE STATES

You have a renowned name, a sizeable fortune, and an important position in Europe. You and your wife make an attractive and elegant couple. You have decided to make America your home—specifically New York. Here are the same diverse and complex reasons that lead so many other Europeans to do the same. Allow me to give you some pointers based on experience.

Everything has its price. For a serious New Yorker, this usually means a contribution to charity.

EUROPEAN TRAVEL & LIFE, SEPTEMBER/OCTOBER 1986

533

PUBLICATION:	*European Travel & Life*
ART DIRECTOR:	*Terry Koppel*
DESIGNER:	*Terry Koppel*
PUBLISHER:	*Inabnit Communications*
CATEGORY:	*Format—Design*
TITLE:	*"European Journal"*
AWARD:	*Merit*

FOREIGN AFFAIRS

BY JENIFER HARVEY LANG

The Fine Points of Pub Etiquette

> AN OUTSIDER CAN HAVE A GOOD TIME AT A "LOCAL" IF HE KNOWS THE RIGHT MOVES.

NOTHING IS MORE DAUNTING THAN WALKING into a dimly lit barroom and having conversation stop, dart players freeze in mid-throw, all eyes turn toward you as you stand in the doorway, framed by the clear light of the street. An outsider can have a good time in a "local," an everyday English pub, but, like a stranger sauntering down the main street in Dodge City, he or she has to know the right moves.

A pub is not a bar with a foreign name; it is a British institution, frequently, but rarely successfully, copied around the world. The best and most traditional are those that could be called "talking pubs," places where new and old friends get together to exchange conversation and take the edge off the day. These pubs are like extended living rooms; they serve the local citizens who

Publicans are cordial to first-time customers but partial to regulars, the lifeblood of their pubs.

most likely have known one another all their lives. The living room analogy is a literal one, because pubs got started hundreds of years ago in the houses of people who brewed beer at home. Theirs became *public houses*, where people came to buy beer and talk to friends. During the Industrial Revolution, breweries grew to enormous sizes, and many bought up hundreds of pubs in their areas. These became known as *tied houses*.

Today, 85 percent of the pubs in England are tied houses, selling only the products of their parent companies. The remaining 15 percent, or about 10,000 pubs, are *free houses*, and can sell any brand of beer. Tied house signs invariably name their parent brewery, while free house signs advertise no brands. In either case, the word "pub" never appears on the sign outside, if indeed there is a sign. Usually a painting depicts the name of the pub: Ye Old Cheshire Cheese or The Hoop and Grapes.

Visiting a pub requires a few decisions, the first of which is determining what entrance to use. Some old-fashioned pubs have three rooms with three separate doors. This is a remnant of the eighteenth and nineteenth centuries, when pubs reflected the English preoccupation with class distinctions. One room, the *public bar*, serves working-class men still in their work clothes; sawdust usually covers the floor, and a cuspidor sits in the corner. The *saloon bar* (sometimes called the *lounge* or *buffet* bar), with upgraded decor and prices, caters to professionals, men and women. The most expensive and elegant section of a pub is called the *snug* or the *private bar*, and it is here that old ladies who drink port and lemon are welcome and most comfortable. Sometimes glass dividers called *snob screens* separate the sections. Pubs whose signs read *Off-Licence* or *Jug and Bottle* sell bottles to go.

In the saloon bar and the private bar, a waitress may serve drinks, but in the public bar customers go to the bar to get service for themselves. Patrons stay at the bar with their drink if there is room, or they return to a bar shelf or even stand in the middle of the room. Those at the bar are polite about giving way to another customer who wishes to squeeze in, get a drink, and retreat.

A visitor trying to catch the attention of the bartender always has the problem of how to address him. In a large hotel it is safe to say "barman," but in a smaller pub the bartender is probably the proprietor, and that would be an insult. Since the technical terms landlord and publican sound a bit pompous, and since

FOREIGN AFFAIRS

BY JENIFER HARVEY LANG

Understanding the Subtle Customs of Coffee

FOREIGN AFFAIRS

BY JENIFER HARVEY LANG

Deciphering the Details of Toasting

534

PUBLICATION: *European Travel & Life*
ART DIRECTOR: *Terry Koppel*
DESIGNER: *Terry Koppel*
PUBLISHER: *Inabnit Communications*
CATEGORY: *Format—Design*
TITLE: *"Foreign Affairs"*
AWARD: *Merit*

MERIT

535

PUBLICATION:	*Texas Monthly*
ART DIRECTORS:	*Fred Woodward, Kathy Marcos*
DESIGNERS:	*Fred Woodward, David Kampa*
ILLUSTRATOR:	*Marcia Stieger*
PHOTOGRAPHERS:	*Steven Pumphrey,*
	Robert Maxham
PUBLISHER:	*Texas Monthly, Inc.*
CATEGORY:	*Format—Design*
TITLE:	*"Around the State"*
AWARD:	*Merit*

536

PUBLICATION:	*Texas Monthly*
ART DIRECTOR:	*Fred Woodward*
DESIGNERS:	*Fred Woodward, David Kampa*
ILLUSTRATORS:	*Lou Beach, Etienne Delessert,*
	Ray-Mel Cornelius
PUBLISHER:	*Texas Monthly, Inc.*
CATEGORY:	*Format—Design*
TITLE:	*"Western Art"*
AWARD:	*Merit*

537

PUBLICATION: *L.A. Style*
ART DIRECTOR: *Rip Georges*
DESIGNER: *Rip Georges*
PHOTOGRAPHER: *Jim McHugh*
PUBLISHER: *L.A. Style, Inc.*
CATEGORY: *Format—Design*
TITLE: *"Interior Motives"*
AWARD: *Merit*

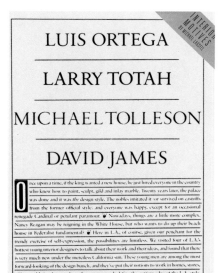

LUIS ORTEGA

LARRY TOTAH

MICHAEL TOLLESON

DAVID JAMES

Once upon a time, if the king wanted a new house, he just hired everyone in the country who knew how to paint, sculpt, gild and inlay marble. Twenty years later, the palace was done and it was *the* design style. The nobles imitated it or survived on castoffs from the former official style; and everyone was happy, except for an occasional renegade Cardinal or petulant paramour. ❧ Nowadays, things are a little more complex. Nancy Reagan may be reigning in the White House, but who wants to do up their beach house in Federalist fundamental? ❧ Here in L.A., of course, given our penchant for the trendy exercise of self-expression, the possibilities are limitless. We visited four of L.A.'s hottest young interior designers to talk about their work and their ideas, and found that there is very much new under the merciless California sun. These young men are among the most forward-looking of the design bunch, and they've put their notions to work in homes, stores, offices and lofts. Among them they pretty much define the cutting edge of the L.A. style.

LUIS ORTEGA

LARRY TOTAH

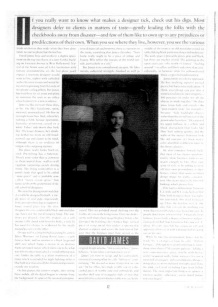

DAVID JAMES

MICHAEL TOLLESON

MERIT

WINNERS

SHORT FICTION BY HAL ACKERMAN

538

PUBLICATION:	*L.A. Style*
ART DIRECTOR:	*Rip Georges*
DESIGNER:	*Rip Georges*
PHOTOGRAPHER:	*Steve Rothfeld*
PUBLISHER:	*L.A. Style, Inc.*
CATEGORY:	*Format—Design*
TITLE:	*"Winners"*
AWARD:	*Merit*

Heathcliff Goes To High School

SUN CHILD

539

PUBLICATION:	*Saturday Review*
ART DIRECTOR:	*Brian Noyes*
DESIGNER:	*Brian Noyes*
PUBLISHER:	*Saturday Review Magazine*
CATEGORY:	*Format—Design*
TITLE:	*"Briefings: Masks"*
AWARD:	*Merit*

540

PUBLICATION:	*The Village Voice*
ART DIRECTOR:	*Michael Grossman*
DESIGNERS:	*George Delmerico,*
	Barbara Glauber
PHOTOGRAPHERS:	*Sylvia Plachy, Adam Nastoonp*
PUBLISHER:	*VV Publishing Corp.*
CATEGORY:	*Format—Design*
TITLE:	*"Contents Page"*
AWARD:	*Merit*

541

PUBLICATION:	*Buy*
ART DIRECTORS:	*Bett McLean, Lawrence Arnet*
DESIGNERS:	*Lawrence Arnet, Deb Hardison*
PHOTOGRAPHER:	*Charles Brook, E. Silva*
PUBLISHER:	*13-30 Corporation*
CATEGORY:	*Format—Design*
TITLE:	*"Trends"*
AWARD:	*Merit*

2 TRENDS 3

Teenagers Influence Family Purchases
The MTV generation is a major target group in and of itself. What's more, teens exert significant influence on products that older people buy.

By Susanne Pelletier

Aluminum Cookware Reconsidered
Recent scientific reports have linked aluminum to Alzheimer's disease, creating an unresolved dilemma for the housewares buyer.

NOVEMBER 1985

BUY

2 TRENDS 3

How to Use Economic Forecasts
Economists' predictions are among the tools retailers use to formulate their buying plans. But can you depend on the forecasts?

Americans Return To Traditional Food

High-Tech Furnishings Are "In"
Industrial furniture and materials are not only practical and economical—now they're fashionable.

JANUARY 1985

BUY

2 TRENDS 3

Economists Predict Moderate Growth
The outlook for the rest of the year is fairly optimistic, with the possibility of a slowdown late in the year due to high federal deficits.

By Katherine Hall

Country Is Here to Stay

Finishing Off the Kitchen
Kitchens are in a state of transition. One indication of the trend is a change in the color and design of finishing materials.

APRIL 1985

BUY

REDESIGNS

542

PUBLICATION:	*US*
ART DIRECTOR:	*Robert Priest*
DESIGNER:	*Janet Waegel*
PHOTOGRAPHER:	*David Baily*
PUBLISHER:	*Straight Arrow Publications*
CATEGORY:	*Redesign*
AWARD:	*Silver*

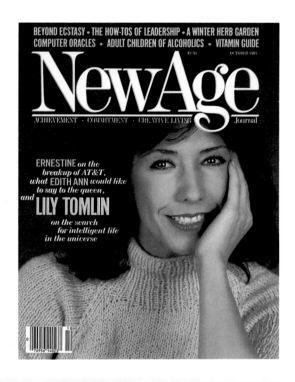

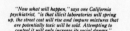

Lily Tomlin and friends are back with a new Broadway show and more insights about how things really are.

543

PUBLICATION: *New Age Journal*
ART DIRECTOR: *Greg Paul*
DESIGNERS: *Greg Paul, Chris Frame,*
                 Jill Winitzer
PUBLISHER: *New Age Journal*
CATEGORY: *Redesign*
AWARD: *Merit*

THE LIVE AID SPECTACULAR
HOW COKE BLUNDERED

Newsweek

July 22, 1985 / $1.95

REAGAN'S PROGNOSIS
The Cancer Scare · How Swift a Recovery?

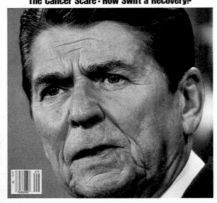

UNDER THE VOLCANO: BURIED ALIVE

Newsweek

November 28, 1988 · $1.95

THE SUMMIT

How to Deal With Moscow

INTERNATIONAL

'Buried Alive'

A volcanic cascade of mud and lava devastates a
town in Colombia and kills thousands

A futile rescue effort: Dying woman

A savage onslaught that uprooted trees, washed away cars and ripped apart houses:

Rescuer pulling a survivor out of the debris

In the path of destruction: Trying to extract a young woman caught in the mud

52 NEWSWEEK NOVEMBER 25, 1985

NEWSWEEK NOVEMBER 25, 1985 53

544

PUBLICATION: *Newsweek*
ART DIRECTOR: *Roger Black*
DESIGNER: *Roger Black*
PUBLISHER: *Washington Post Co.*
CATEGORY: *Redesign*
AWARD: *Merit*

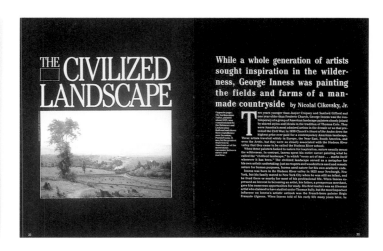

545

PUBLICATION:	*American Heritage*
ART DIRECTOR:	*Beth Whitaker*
DESIGNER:	*Beth Whitaker*
ILLUSTRATOR:	*J.C. Leyendecker*
PUBLISHER:	*American Heritage, Inc.*
CATEGORY:	*Redesign*
AWARD:	*Merit*

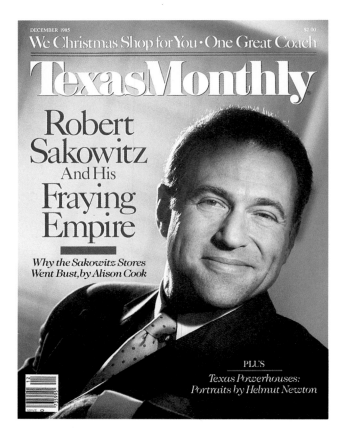

*Cover photography by Charles Ford
Styling by Heidi Schulzi*

TEXAS MONTHLY (ISSN 0148-7736) is published every month by TEXAS MONTHLY, Inc. Michael R. Levy, President, P.O. Box 1569, Austin, Texas 78767 under all phases. 1600 LavacaStreet, Austin, Texas 78701, 512-476-7085. For subscription service call 1-800-247-5470. Copyright 1985 by TEXAS MONTHLY, Inc. All rights reserved. The following are registered trademarks of TEXAS MONTHLY and no other: TEXAS MONTHLY, Around the State, The Roar of the Crowd, Reporter, and Touts. Behind the Lines is a federally registered trademark. Reproduction of any part or in whole or in part of the contents without written permission of the Publisher is prohibited. The Publisher assumes no responsibility for the care and return of unsolicited materials. Return postage must accompany material if it is to be returned. In no event shall such material subject this magazine to any claim for holding over or similar charges. Subscription in Texas, one year $18, two years $34. In the United States of America, one year $18, two years $34, other countries add. Elsewhere, $30 a year. Payable in U.S. currency. Single-copy price $2. Back issues $3.50. Payment must accompany all single-copy orders. For subscription and single-copy orders, address changes, renewals, and adjustments, write to TEXAS MONTHLY, Subscription Department, P.O. Box 1569, Austin, Texas 78767. Six weeks are required for entry of order and change of address. Send old and new address and mailing label (for speedier service) when writing about your subscription. Address all other correspondence to TEXAS MONTHLY, P.O. Box 1569, Austin, Texas 78767. POSTMASTER: Send TEXAS MONTHLY is a member of the Audit Bureau of Circulations, the Magazine Publishers Association, and the City and Regional Magazine Association. The Known Office of Publication, as defined under section 562.1J of the United States Postal Service Domestic Mail Manual, is located at 1600 West Oak Place, Suite 306, Houston, Texas 77027. POSTMASTER: Send Form 3579 to TEXAS MONTHLY, Subscription Department, P.O. Box 1569, Austin, Texas 78767. Second-class postage paid at Houston, Texas, and at additional mailing offices.

546

PUBLICATION:	*Texas Monthly*
ART DIRECTOR:	*Fred Woodward*
DESIGNERS:	*Fred Woodward, David Kampa*
PUBLISHER:	*Texas Monthly, Inc.*
CATEGORY:	*Redesign*
AWARD:	*Merit*

AROUND THE STATE

A SELECTIVE GUIDE TO AMUSEMENTS AND EVENTS

Edited by Patricia Sharpe and Helen Thompson

For a chilling summertime mystery, try the Natural Bridge Caverns outside New Braunfels, where it stays a cool seventy degrees on even the hottest day. As you wander down long passageways, through secret chambers, and into rooms the size of football fields, you can admire age-old formations of shimmering translucent rock that are still growing—an inch every hundred years. Except for the lights and walkways, this subterranean realm looks much the same as it did when it was discovered in 1960. Owners Clara and Harry Heidemann (pictured in the Castle of the White Giants) say that after a heavy rain, you can hear the rushing underground rivers that began carving out the caverns 140 million years ago. Now a U.S. landmark, the caverns open daily at 10 with tours every thirty minutes. Tour time is one hour and fifteen minutes. Take I-35 north from San Antonio about thirteen miles to exit 175 (512-651-6101). Adults $5.75; children three to twelve $4.75.

PHOTOGRAPH BY STEVEN PUMPHREY

Movies

QUEEN OF THE RODEO

In Sweet Dreams *Jessica Lange restores the thrilling hellcat growl to the legend of Patsy Cline.*

In Sweet Dreams Jessica Lange is Patsy Cline, and Ed Harris is her husband, Charlie, a tightly packed bundle of love and trouble.

After worrying herself to a limp frazzle in *Country,* Jessica Lange swings around in *Sweet Dreams,* the Patsy Cline story, and gives a joyous, cut-loose performance. Dressed in cowgirl fringe, she's the queen of the rodeo. Patsy Cline was a country singer famous for her yips and growls, who, as she became comfortable in the recording studio, smoothed her tone until it was as pure and fleecy as a trail of vapor in a clear blue sky, yet her voice was never merely a brush of angel feathers. There was too much hard-knocking life in Patsy Cline for her to sound dainty and chaste. Firmly grounded, she knew how to attract lightning. After a string of country and crossover hits, Cline's career was cut tragically short in 1963, when her prop plane crashed, killing all aboard (retrieved from the wreckage was Cline's Confederate cigarette lighter, now on display at the Country Music Hall of Fame). Written by Robert Getchell and directed by Karel Reisz, *Sweet Dreams* concentrates on the success years of Cline's too-short career—the touring, the studio sessions, the move from a cramped cubbyhole of an apartment into a big white house on a hill. It passes with a glance over her first marriage to emphasize her second, to a tightly packed bundle of love and trouble named Charlie Dick (Ed Harris). This biographical stuff *Sweet Dreams* handles dutifully, tearing off the months on the calendar with a dull, even rip. The excitement comes from Jessica Lange—it's her show. To the legend of Patsy Cline she restores the thrilling hellcat growl.

When Natalia Makarova won a Tony award for her performance in *On Your Toes,* she thanked her husband in *On Your Toes,* she thanked her husband at the rostrum, adding with dipsy charm, "He didn't actually help, but he didn't get in the way either." That's how I feel about Karel Reisz's direction in *Sweet Dreams;* he has

BY JAMES WOLCOTT

547

PUBLICATION:	*Success*
ART DIRECTOR:	*Louis Cruz*
DESIGNER:	*Louis Cruz*
ILLUSTRATOR:	*Robert Vannutt*
PHOTOGRAPHER:	*Carl Fisher*
PUBLISHER:	*Hal Publications*
CATEGORY:	*Redesign*
AWARD:	*Merit*

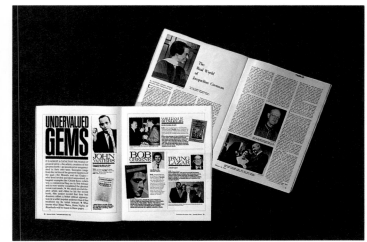

548

PUBLICATION: *Saturday Review*
ART DIRECTOR: *Brian Noyes*
DESIGNER: *Brian Noyes*
PUBLISHER: *Saturday Review*
CATEGORY: *Redesign*
AWARD: *Merit*

549

PUBLICATION:	*Michigan*
ART DIRECTOR:	*Michael Walsh*
DESIGNER:	*Michael Walsh*
PUBLISHER:	*Detroit News*
CATEGORY:	*Redesign*
AWARD:	*Merit*

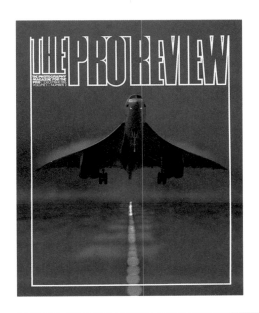

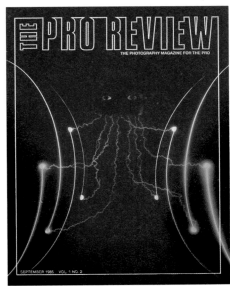

550

PUBLICATION: *The Pro Review*
ART DIRECTOR: *David Brier*
DESIGNER: *David Brier*
AGENCY: *David Brier, Inc.*
PUBLISHER: *Dynamic Publications*
CATEGORY: *Redesign*
AWARD: *Merit*

ANNUAL REPORTS

Metropolitan Life
and Affiliated Companies
Annual Report

1984

551

PUBLICATION:	*Metropolitan Life*
ART DIRECTOR:	*Bennett Robinson*
DESIGNER:	*Bennett Robinson*
ILLUSTRATOR:	*Guy Billout*
PHOTOGRAPHER:	*Bruce Davidson*
AGENCY:	*Corporate Graphics*
CLIENT:	*Metropolitan Life*
CATEGORY:	*Annual Report*
AWARD:	*Silver*

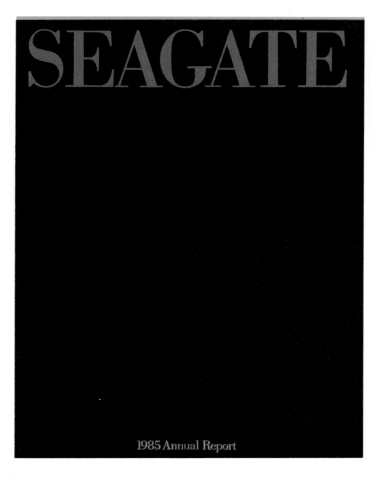

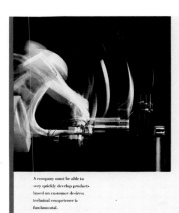

552

PUBLICATION:	*Seagate 1985*
ART DIRECTOR:	*Ted Williams*
DESIGNER:	*Ted Williams*
PHOTOGRAPHER:	*Nickolay Zurek*
AGENCY:	*Ted Williams and Partners*
CLIENT:	*Seagate Technology*
CATEGORY:	*Annual Report*
AWARD:	*Silver*

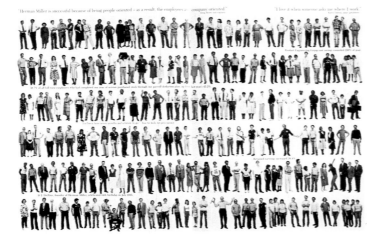

553

PUBLICATION:	*Herman Miller*
ART DIRECTORS:	*Stephen Frykholm,*
	Sara Giovanitti
DESIGNER:	*Stephen Frykholm*
PHOTOGRAPHER:	*Bill Lindhout*
CLIENT:	*Herman Miller, Inc.*
CATEGORY:	*Annual Report*
TITLE:	*"Say Hello to the Owner"*
AWARD:	*Merit*

554

PUBLICATION:	*Charles Stark Draper Lab*
ART DIRECTOR:	*Bennett Robinson*
DESIGNER:	*Bennett Robinson*
ILLUSTRATOR:	*Tom Christopher*
AGENCY:	*Corporate Graphics, Inc.*
CLIENT:	*Charles Stark Draper Lab, Inc.*
CATEGORY:	*Annual Report*
AWARD:	*Merit*

MERIT

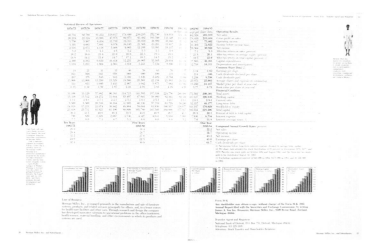

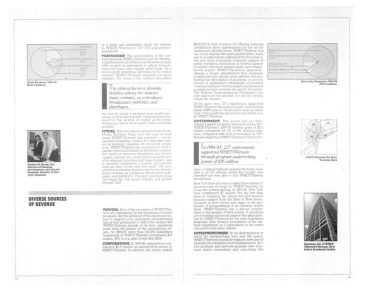

555

PUBLICATION:	*WNET/13*
ART DIRECTOR:	*Fausto Pellegrini*
DESIGNER:	*Fausto Pellegrini*
AGENCY:	*Jan Krukowski Associates*
CLIENT:	*WNET/Channel Thirteen/PBS*
CATEGORY:	*Annual Report*
TITLE:	*"And the Best is Yet to Come"*
AWARD:	*Merit*

556

PUBLICATION:	*New World Bank 1985*
ART DIRECTOR:	*Paul V. Ciavarra*
DESIGNER:	*Paul V. Ciavarra*
PHOTOGRAPHER:	*Jim Thomas*
AGENCY:	*Ingalls Design Group*
CLIENT:	*New World Bank for Savings*
CATEGORY:	*Annual Report*
AWARD:	*Merit*

557

PUBLICATION:	*MHC Today*
ART DIRECTOR:	*Anthony Russell*
DESIGNER:	*Mark Ulrich*
AGENCY:	*Anthony Russell, Inc.*
CLIENT:	*Manufacturers Hanover Trust*
CATEGORY:	*Annual Report*
AWARD:	*Merit*

558

PUBLICATION:	*Curtis Burns 1985*
ART DIRECTORS:	*Robert Meyer, Jean Page*
DESIGNER:	*Jean Page*
PHOTOGRAPHERS:	*Ron Wu, Michael Molkenthin*
AGENCY:	*Robert Meyer Design*
CLIENT:	*Curtis Burns, Inc.*
CATEGORY:	*Annual Report*
AWARD:	*Merit*

The

Art Directors

Club of

Los Angeles

1983/1984

Annual Report

559

PUBLICATION:	*Art Directors Club of Los Angeles*
ART DIRECTOR:	*Jerry Rosentswieg*
DESIGNER:	*James Marrin*
PHOTOGRAPHER:	*Todd Gray*
AGENCY:	*Marrin Design*
CLIENT:	*Art Directors Club of Los Angeles*
CATEGORY:	*Annual Report*
AWARD:	*Merit*

MERIT

560

PUBLICATION:	*Datacopy*
ART DIRECTOR:	*Anthony Milner*
DESIGNER:	*Earl Glee*
PHOTOGRAPHER:	*Henrik Kam*
AGENCY:	*Marl Anderson Design*
CLIENT:	*Data Corporation*
CATEGORY:	*Annual Report*
TITLE:	*"Datacopy"*
AWARD:	*Merit*

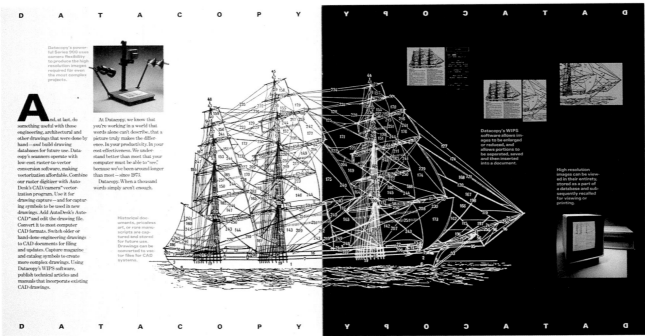

Art Directors

Designers

Illustrators

Photographers

Publications

ADVERTISEMENTS

Your eye for color knows it's Brown.

The subtle colors are subtle. The vivid colors are vivid. The image is so lifelike, it practically leaps off the page. The printer? Your eye for color knows.

Waseca. MN. Company Headquarters (507) 835-2410 ▪ Minneapolis. MN (612) 854-7095
▪ New York. NY (212) 765-4831 ▪ Chicago. IL (312) 332-4199 ▪ Dallas.TX (214) 248-3354
▪ Newport Beach. CA (714) 644-4030 ▪ Redwood City. CA (415) 364-1110

BROWN
Printing Company

"Today, creating the best in design requires exploring and exceeding the limits of your imagination."

Understanding today's
tools and discovering their
possibilities distinguishes the
best from the crowd.

PPI's leadership and commitment to
quality in electronic publishing systems
and prepress services presents new
opportunities for innovation in creative design.

PPI

PEOPLE
PURSUING
INNOVATION

Publishers Phototype International, Inc. • 463 Barell Avenue • Carlstadt, New Jersey 07072 • 201/935-3200

Low-cost, high-quality composite originals in minutes . . .
Here's the proof!

The CPR 403®
Digital Image Recorder

The CPR 403 Digital Image Recorder from Hell Graphic Systems offers you a more efficient and cost effective way of obtaining high-quality, first generation composite originals or full color prints.

Integrated into Hell's state-of-the-art Chromacom® digital retouching and page composition systems, the CPR 403 operates automatically with short exposure and processing times to provide finished continuous tone color prints or transparencies of exceptional quality on low-cost photographic color print material.

The CPR 403 can expose the image data base in the Chromacom system and within minutes yield a hard copy of the makeup and

retouching operations performed at the Combiskop® work station. Up to fifty 21'' x 29'' proofs can be made and automatically processed in a continuous operation.

With this innovative technology, your graphics house can conveniently utilize color proofs for:
■ Archival prints
■ A new scanning original
■ Job approval before film is made
■ Making corrections

Proofing via the CPR 403 is the cost-saving alternative to dye transferring, retouching, and prepress proofs.

Specify a graphics trade shop that utilizes a Chromacom system with the CPR 403 and see the proof for yourself. For further information or a CPR 403 color proof of the photo below, contact:

Hell Graphic Systems, Inc.
25 Harbor Park Drive
Port Washington, NY 11050
(516) 484-3000

WE SEPARATE BEAUTY FROM A BEAST.

Underexposed, scratched and grainy, this was an endangered chrome. But as an example of bad art, it makes a very good point.

Which is, that it takes rare expertise to separate beastly artwork.

Weak originals won't stand up to multiple generations if the film has to be overworked to "get it right." So Kordet stalks trouble spots predatorially. And unlike others, Kordet's first shot achieves deadly accuracy.

Many fall prey to the great proof ploy, unaware that there are tricks of the trade to make them look convincing. But if the film doesn't meet SWOP standards, it'll never print well.

Anyone can make beautiful separations from a beautiful chrome. Kordet's touch can tame a beast.

THE KORDET GROUP

50 West 23rd Street, New York, N.Y. 10010
(212) 627-4111

New York, NY
Oceanside, NY
Carlstadt, NJ
Los Angeles, CA

- Competitive cost
- Flexibility in production time
- Knowledge of sales reps
- Service and fine quality
- Financial stability

Can you expect all of these from your printer ?

 DAI NIPPON is ready to serve you. You can get on the spot consultation from professional salesman.

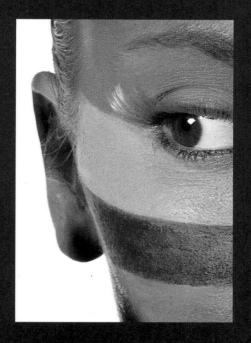

LET YOUR COLORS COME THROUGH.

Let your colors come through on new CELESTA Litho Gloss.

What words would you use to describe the colors of a rare bird? Beautiful. Lush. Splendorous. Occasionally, even spectacular.

You could use the same words to describe the colors that can be achieved with this new CELESTA® Litho Gloss paper.

Examine the reproduction of the magnificent peacock, for example. Can't you almost hear the rustle of the luxurious plumage, feel the subtle variations in the feathery textures?

Stays true to your colors.

That's because this new paper has been engineered to give an incredibly smooth surface, a brilliant printed gloss. With a pure, untinted whiteness that lets CELESTA stay true to your colors no matter how challenging the assignment.

New CELESTA Litho Gloss. A most extraordinary paper, for your most demanding jobs.

CELESTA
Stays true to your colors.

Up against a tight deadline? Use Westvaco's fast PressDate® Service. Order 1,200 to 40,000 pounds of CELESTA® Litho Gloss or CELESTA® Litho Dull (70, 80 or 100 lb., 25 x 38-500 basis) finished to your specified size, and we'll ship your order in five days or less. PressDate Service is just as fast for our matching CELESTA® Cover Gloss (80 or 100 lb., 20 x 26-500 basis). Order 1,200 to 40,000 lbs., packed in standard sizes on mini-skids.

For complete sales information, call your nearest Westvaco representative, listed below. For technical information, dummies, white sheets or printed samples, call 1-800-CELESTA.

This advertisement was lithographed, 5-up, on a 35 x 59 sheet of CELESTA Litho Gloss paper, 80#, 25 x 38-500 basis. A matched ink with matte varnish was used on Page 2. Precision-sheeted by Westvaco's AccuTrim™ machines.

Westvaco Corporation, Fine Papers Division, 299 Park Avenue, New York, NY 10171.

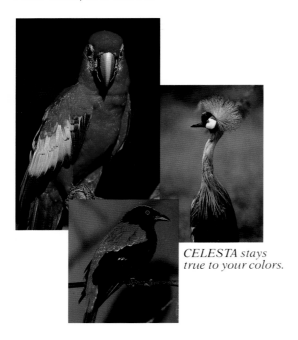

CELESTA stays true to your colors.

Westvaco

Fine Papers Division